Golf For Dummies, 3rd Edition

by Gary McCord

Foreword by David Feherty

Wiley Publishing, Inc.

Golf For Dummies®, 3rd Edition

Published by
Wiley Publishing, Inc.
111 River St.
Hoboken, NJ 07030-5774
www.wiley.com

For general information on our other products and services, please contact our Customer Care Department within the U.S. at 800-762-2974, outside the U.S. at 317-572-3993, or fax 317-572-4002.

For technical support, please visit www.wiley.com/techsupport.

Wiley also publishes its books in a variety of electronic formats. Some content that appears in print may not be available in electronic books.

Library of Congress Control Number: 2005936643

ISBN-13: 978-0-471-76871-5

ISBN-10: 0-471-76871-5

Manufactured in the United States of America

10 9 8 7 6 5 4 3 2 1

3B/QZ/QR/QW/IN

About the Author

"Life is full of ups and downs, good and bad, but it wouldn't be fun any other way." Living by this optimistic philosophy, **Gary McCord** persisted through years of mediocrity before finding success. An outstanding player, television announcer, instructor, author, speaker, and even movie actor, he has become a golf celebrity.

McCord is well known for enduring 23 years and 422 tournaments on the PGA Tour without nabbing a single victory. A man of good humor, he sported a "NO WINS" license plate for years to poke fun at his less-than-glamorous work as a professional golfer.

"Trapped in the headlights of bankruptcy," as he liked to put it, McCord pursued other avenues in golf, and found himself launching a broadcasting career. He scored big when a CBS Sports executive tossed him a headset and asked him to do golf commentary — giving him only 15 minutes to prepare. A friend of failure, McCord jumped in with no fear and impressed CBS with his performance. Twenty years later, he is still providing color commentary for CBS golf events. Fans and critics alike praise him for his knowledgeable perspective, refreshing humor, and sometimes irreverent wit toward a game known for taking itself too seriously.

Broadcasting changed his perspective on golf. Realizing that a better understanding of the golf swing would help his TV work, McCord studied under Mac O'Grady, a legendary guru of the game. After two years of study he emerged with knowledge, confidence, and an improved golf game.

Gary's own golf really came together just as he began his career on the Champions Tour after his 50th birthday. In 1999, his first full season on that tour, he won two events — the Toshiba Senior Classic and the Ingersoll-Rand Senior Tour Championship — to finish 17th on the official money list with nearly $1,000,000 in prize money. Since then, he has continued to play well, usually finishing in the top 30 on the money list while playing a limited schedule of 10 to15 events per year.

When he isn't broadcasting or playing golf, McCord keeps busy with myriad other projects. He portrayed himself in and served as technical director for the golf movie *Tin Cup,* starring Kevin Costner, Rene Russo, and Don Johnson. He is also a writer. In addition to writing *Golf For Dummies,* he is the author of a collection of essays about his life on tour, *Just a Range Ball in a Box of Titleists.* His bestselling *Golf For Dummies* was released in DVD form in 2004.

McCord and his friend and CBS Sports colleague David Feherty are known to millions of golf fans and gamers as the voices of EA Sports' Tiger Woods PGA Tour video games. McCord also instructs and consults with more than 20 PGA Tour players. Along with another friend and fellow CBS commentator, Peter Kostis, he co-founded the Kostis/McCord Learning Center at Grayhawk Golf Club in Scottsdale, Arizona.

Gary brings a sense of fun to everything he does and never takes himself too seriously. He and his wife, Diane, share the "ups and downs" of a busy life together at their homes in Scottsdale and Denver.

Dedication

I dedicate this book to my mom, Ruth, and to David Feherty's make-believe best friend, Flossy — his pet goat. They light up our lives.

Author's Acknowledgments

It is a smart dummy who surrounds himself with good people. This book was taken to the next level by Kevin Cook. Very good people. Here's hoping we'll keep up with our readers' ascent to the top of golf's food chain. Grip it and read it!

My wife, Diane, is simply the best. Her patience with my work and understanding with my schedule I am unable to comprehend. She is my life's caddie, and a better one I could not have. To my mom, Ruth, my daughter, Krista, and my four granddaughters, Breanne, Kayla, Jenae, and Terra: You will all get still more free books. Thanks for thinking about me when I've been away my whole life.

Many thanks to the Wiley team: Acquisitions Editor Stacy Kennedy, Project Editor Elizabeth Kuball, Technical Editor John Brott, Photographer Daniel Mainzer, Project Coordinator Kathryn Shanks, Editorial/Acquisitions Intern Jenny Baylor, Associate Graphics Processor Lauren Goddard, and Supervisor of Graphics Shelley Lea. They worked hard to get this book just right!

Publisher's Acknowledgments

We're proud of this book; please send us your comments through our Dummies online registration form located at www.dummies.com/register/.

Some of the people who helped bring this book to market include the following:

Acquisitions, Editorial, and Media Development

Project Editor: Elizabeth Kuball

(Previous Editions: Pamela Mourouzis and Colleen Totz)

Acquisitions Editor: Stacy Kennedy

Consultant: Kevin Cook

Technical Editor: John Brott

Editorial Manager: Michelle Hacker

Editorial Supervisor and Reprint Editor: Carmen Krikorian

Editorial Assistants: Hanna Scott, Nadine Bell, David Lutton

Cover Photos: © Steve Belkowitz/Taxi/Getty

Cartoons: Rich Tennant (www.the5thwave.com)

Composition Services

Project Coordinator: Kathryn Shanks

Layout and Graphics: Andrea Dahl, Denny Hager, Stephanie D. Jumper, Clint Lahnen, Barbara Moore, Lynsey Osborn, Heather Ryan

Special Art: Pam Tanzey

Photography: Paul Lester, Scott Baxter Photography, Daniel Mainzer Photography

Proofreaders: Laura Albert, Leeann Harney, Joe Niesen, TECHBOOKS Production Services

Indexer: TECHBOOKS Production Services

Special Help

Jenny Baylor, Lauren Goddard, Shelley Lea

Publishing and Editorial for Consumer Dummies

Diane Graves Steele, Vice President and Publisher, Consumer Dummies

Joyce Pepple, Acquisitions Director, Consumer Dummies

Kristin A. Cocks, Product Development Director, Consumer Dummies

Michael Spring, Vice President and Publisher, Travel

Kelly Regan, Editorial Director, Travel

Publishing for Technology Dummies

Andy Cummings, Vice President and Publisher, Dummies Technology/General User

Composition Services

Gerry Fahey, Vice President of Production Services

Debbie Stailey, Director of Composition Services

Contents at a Glance

Table of Contents

Foreword

Possibly the only saving grace for this publication is the fact that I'm writing the foreword, and I'm only doing it because the nimrod who wrote it has threatened to publish pictures of Peter Kostis shaving my back in the shower. Bearing in mind that this book was written by a man whose advice helped me off the PGA Tour in both Europe and the United States and into a TV booth, if I were you I wouldn't set my hopes too high. To be honest, I'd trust an Octoberfest-addled polka fiend with my beer before trusting McCord with any kind of instructional manual, but this thing is a *For Dummies* book, so it might just work.

To be serious for a nanosecond, I must say this book is the best guide for new golfers that the world has ever known. I hope reading the following pages will at least help you correct the most common error in golf, which is taking the game — and more importantly yourself — too seriously. Just remember, you are *meant* to suck at golf. Anyone who doesn't is a freak of nature.

Yours with deep reluctance,

David Feherty

Introduction

Welcome to *Golf For Dummies,* 3rd Edition. If this is the first golf book you've ever read, don't worry. I've read more of them than I can count. Plus, I've had a chance to go back over everything I wrote in the first two editions and make it even clearer and funnier.

My first thoughts about writing *Golf For Dummies* were no doubt similar to your present feelings about golf. I knew that I wanted to do it, but I also knew that it would take a lot of my time and attention. Did I want to devote most of my spare time to an endeavor that was so *hard?* Why not? I haven't given anything back to society in a while!

Besides, the whole thing sounded like fun. So is golf.

About This Book

I want this book to appeal to players at every level. Although my buddies on the PGA Tour will probably read it just to see if I can construct a sentence, I like to think that I have something to offer even the best golfers. The guys I grew up with at San Luis Rey golf course in Southern California will check out *Golf For Dummies* to see whether I've used any of their funniest lines. And I hope that the title will pique the interest of many people who have never played the game.

In any case, you have in your hands a sometimes-funny, instruction-packed, wide-eyed look at a game full of fascination that will serve you for the rest of your days on the links.

This, then, is no ordinary golf-instruction book. Most of the volumes you can find in your local bookstore are written by professional players or teachers. As such, these books focus solely on the golf swing. *Golf For Dummies* covers a lot more than the swing. This book ought to be the only book you need before you develop a golf dependency. (Please contact a physician when you feel the first symptoms coming on — frustration, talking to yourself after missing a shot, that kind of thing. These are the warning signs. ***Remember:*** From a medical standpoint, this book is cheaper than a visit to the doctor.)

Having said all that, I'm assuming that you have dabbled with golf, have found that you like it, and would like to get better. In my experience, most people give golf a try before they pick up the instructions. It must be an ego thing, kind of like those people who don't like to ask for directions when they get lost because they feel that it's an admission of failure. Most people want to see what they can achieve on their own before they call in the cavalry. Then if they still can't find their way, they get frustrated.

My aim is to get you beyond whatever stage your golf game is at without your having to resort to other texts. *Golf For Dummies* will build for you the solid foundation needed to become not just someone who can hit a golf ball, but a real golfer. There's a big difference between the two, as you'll soon discover.

Conventions Used in This Book

When this book was printed, some Web addresses may have needed to break across two lines of text. If that happened, rest assured that I haven't put in any extra characters (like hyphens) to indicate the break. When using one of these Web addresses, just type in exactly what you see in this book, pretending that the line break doesn't exist.

What You're Not to Read

The publishers and I have put this book together with your convenience in mind. Nice, huh? What that means is simple:

- When you see the Technical Stuff icon (shown later in this Introduction), you can skip that text if you want. It's not essential to understanding the rest of the book.
- The same goes for sidebars, which are scattered through the book, printed on gray backgrounds. Sidebars are extra added attractions. I've tried to make them fun and informative, but they aren't crucial to the rest of the book. Feel free to skip over them — you won't hurt my feelings.

Foolish Assumptions

Because you picked up this book, I assume that you're interested in golf. I also assume that you're not already a great golfer, or else you'd be out there making millions on the PGA Tour. Beyond that, I'm going to figure that you're a little like I was when I became a professional golfer.

When I started out on the PGA Tour in 1974, I was full of fight and enthusiasm but lacked a basic knowledge of golf-swing mechanics. A warm panic would start to rise in me about ten minutes before I was due to tee off. Doubt and dread would accompany me to the first tee. My brain would be racing, trying to figure out what *swing thought* (that one aspect of the swing that you meditate on to keep focused) to use that day. Most of the time, I'd be left with a thought like, "Keep the left elbow toward magnetic north on the downswing." Usually, that action resulted in a silly-looking slice into a parking lot. I swung the club that way for most of my career. So I know what it's like to play without knowledge or a solid foundation. Believe me, I'm a lot happier — and having a lot more fun — now that I know what I'm doing.

The reason I'm qualified to help you now is that I have made a serious effort to become a student of the game. When I started working on golf telecasts for CBS, I didn't know much about the inner workings of the swing. But my new job forced me to learn. My odyssey led me to seek advice from some of the world's greatest teachers.

One of them was Mac O'Grady, a golfer I grew up with in Southern California. He has developed a knowledge of the golf swing that, in my opinion, is unequaled. O'Grady has researched his method with passion since 1983. The result is a swing model that has been tested and never found wanting. I have been lucky to study under O'Grady, and I can't thank him enough. But I do not cover Mac's model in this book; his knowledge is for advanced golfers. No one has ever called me advanced, so I'm gonna stick to basics in this book.

How This Book Is Organized

Golf For Dummies will lead you through the process of becoming a golfer. Beginners need many questions answered as they take on the game. I've organized this book so that you take those steps one at a time and can return anytime for a quick reference. May this walk be a pleasant one!

Part I: Getting Started: No, You Can't Hit the Ball Yet

Where do I play, and what's the course record? Wait a minute! First you need to know what this game is about. You need clubs. You need to know how to swing the clubs. You may want to take a lesson to see whether you like the game, and then find golf clubs that fit you. In this part, I show you where to shop for clubs and give you some tips on the questions to ask before you make your purchase. Then I give you some ideas about what kind of golf courses to play. Picking up golf is a never-ending process of discovery, and it starts right here.

Part II: You Ain't Got a Thing If You Ain't Got That Swing

This part gets right to the point. I give you a close look at the workings of the golf swing and help with your mental preparation. You also get a good look at the short game, where most scoring takes place. I show you how to blast your way out of bunkers and make those 4-foot putts.

Part III: Common Faults and Easy Fixes

In this part, I tackle the tough shots and help you deal with bad luck and bad weather. You'll develop many faults during your golfing life, and this part addresses a majority of them. (You bought this book, so I won't fault you for that.)

Part IV: Taking Your Game Public

In this part, you get the final touches of your education as a golfer. You see how the rules were established, how to conduct yourself on the golf course, and the fine art of betting. You even get the do's and don'ts of golf-course etiquette. After you read this part, you'll be able to walk onto any golf course and look like you know what you're doing.

Part V: Golf: It's Electric!

A sad fact of life is that you can't always be out on the course. In this part, I show you how to tap into the best of golf on television and online. Turn on the TV to see tournaments to fantasize about and, of course, my smiling face. Boot up your computer, and I'll introduce you to a world of information, golf forums, and more.

Part VI: The Part of Tens

This part contains the best of, the worst of — and some things that don't mean anything to anybody except me. I just thought you might enjoy knowing about them.

Part VII: Appendixes

Golfers have a language all their own. Appendix A lists all the terms you'll need to add to your vocabulary. Appendix B lists some of the more popular golf organizations, products, and resources, along with a select list of schools around the country.

Icons Used in This Book

I guide you through this maze of golf wit and wisdom with some handy road signs. Look for these friendly icons; they point you toward valuable advice and hazards to watch out for.

Duck! This is an awareness alert. Pay attention.

This icon marks golf hazards to avoid. Be careful!

This icon flags information that shows you easy ways to improve your game.

Do this or I will never speak to you again.

Talk like this, and golfers will understand you.

This might make your head spin; take two aspirin and get plenty of rest.

This icon flags information that's important enough to repeat.

Where to Go from Here

Go ahead, pick your spots. This book isn't designed to be read like a novel from cover to cover. If you're a complete novice, read Appendix A first — get comfortable with the language. If you're a little more advanced and need help with some specific aspect of your game or swing, you can find that information in Chapters 6 through 10. The rest of the book will help you make that vital jump from "golf novice" to "real golfer."

As my former boss at CBS, Frank Chirkinian, said, "Golf is not a game; it's a way of life. If it was a game, someone would have figured it out by now."

I hope this book helps you "figure it out."

Part I

Getting Started: No, You Can't Hit the Ball Yet

"I like this course – I just wish the fairways weren't so long."

In this part . . .

This part explores the Zenlike qualities of golf: Why is golf here? Who in the world would think of something this hard to do for fun? This game must have been invented by someone who guards the netherworld!

In this part of the book, I describe a typical golf course. I also show you how to buy clubs and accessories that will make you look like a pro. I show you how to learn this game. I discuss where to take lessons and how best to survive the lesson tee. In this part, you get a whirlwind tour, from the driving range all the way up to a full 18-hole course — including the penthouse of golf, the private country club.

Get ready; it's time to play golf!

Chapter 1

What Is This Thing Called Golf?

In This Chapter

- Knowing the goals of the game
- Answering the question: Why play golf?
- Looking at a typical course
- Becoming a "real" golfer

Golf is a simple game. You've got clubs and a ball. You have to hit the ball into a series of holes laid out in the middle of a large, grassy field. After you reach the 18th hole, you may want to go to a bar and tell lies about your on-course feats to anyone you didn't play with that day. If you're like most people, you play golf for relaxation and a chance to see the great outdoors. If you're like Arnold Palmer, Jack Nicklaus, Greg Norman, and Tiger Woods, you make a bazillion dollars on top of seeing the great outdoors.

Of course, there are some obstacles. To paraphrase Winston Churchill, who called golf "a silly game played with implements ill-suited for the purpose," the game isn't always straightforward.

The Goals of the Game

Simply stated, the goal of golf is to get the ball into each of 18 holes in succession with the fewest number of shots, using no more 14 clubs. After you hit the ball into all the holes, you add up your scores from all the holes. The lower your total score, the better. That is golf. That is the goal.

The game lies in the journey. As you play, you devise ways to get the ball into the hole in as few strokes as possible. Many outside stimuli — and many more inside you — make this endeavor very interesting.

The best advice I can give you is to take the game slowly, make prudent decisions, and never hit a shot while contemplating other matters. Golf should be played with total concentration and a complete disregard for your ego. Try a monastic existence, at least for the duration of the round. Golf tempts you to try feats of derring-do. You must judge your talents and abilities. You alone determine your success or failure: Should you try to make it over the water and go for the green that's 240 yards away?

Figure 1-1 shows how to plan your course of action. You start at the tee and move to Position A. If the ball goes 240 yards and a watery grave is lurking to the left, don't try the improbable and go for it. Lay up to Position B, and go from there to the green via C. Take the talents that you have and explore this ever-fascinating game of maneuvering a ball through the hazards of your mind. Welcome to my nightmare.

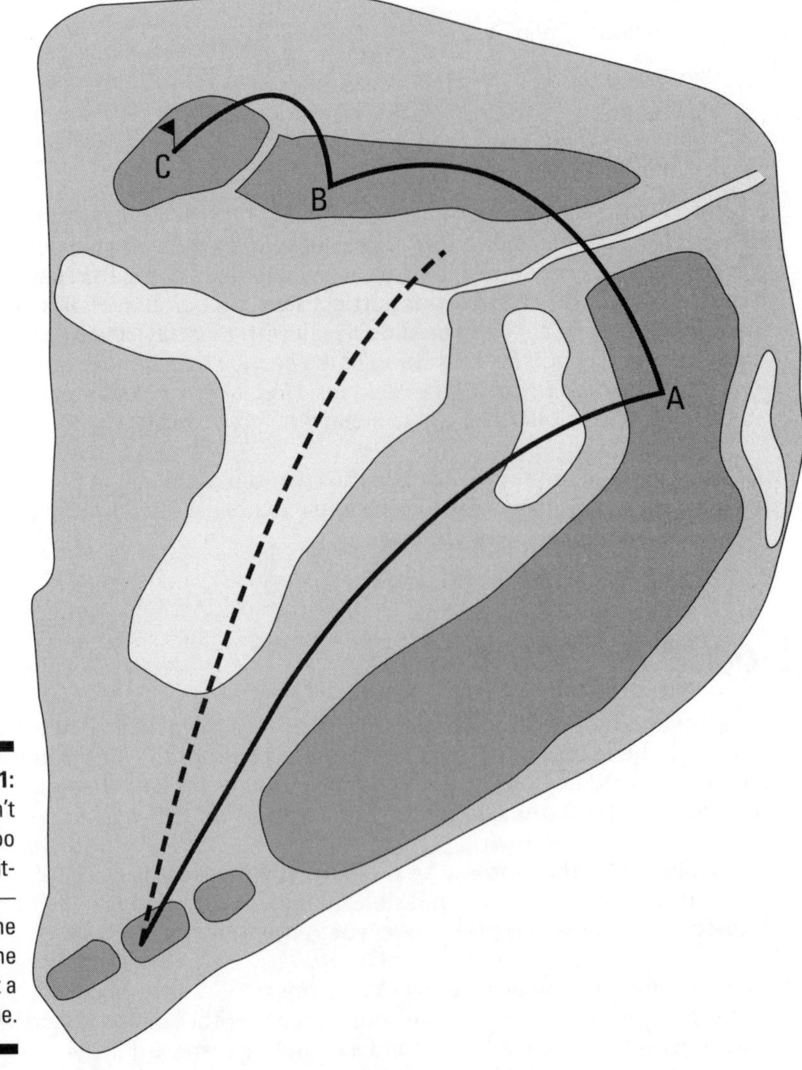

Figure 1-1: Don't get too ambitious — play the game one step at a time.

Why it's the hardest game of all

As I see it, golf is the world's hardest game for two reasons:

- The ball doesn't move on its own.
- You have, on average, about three minutes between shots.

In other words, you don't react to the ball as you do in most sports. A baseball is thrown, hit, and spit on. A football is passed, tossed, kicked, and run up and down the field. A basketball is shot, rebounded, and dribbled all over the place. A golf ball just sits there and defies you not to lose it.

In most sports, you have but an instant to react to the action. Your natural athleticism takes over, and you play to the whim of the ball. In golf, you get to think about what you're doing for much too long. Thinking too much strangles the soul and suffocates the mind.

Golf would be easier if the ball moved a little and you were on skates.

Score is everything. As you see in Chapters 8, 9, and 10, most scoring occurs within 100 yards of the hole. If you can save strokes here, your score will be lower than that of the player whose sole purpose in life is to crush the ball as far as possible. So practice your putting, sand play, and short shots twice as much as your driving. Your hard work will pay off, and your friends will be the ones dipping into their wallets.

Why Play Golf?

You've probably heard that business leaders are constantly making huge deals on the course, advancing their careers. Well, "constantly" may be an overstatement — business leaders, like other players, spend much of their time on the course looking for wayward golf balls. But it's true that golf may help you climb the corporate ladder. That's one reason to play.

And it's about the 167th-most-important reason. More-important reasons include spending time with friends, staying in shape, and enjoying some of the most beautiful scenery you'll ever see. (All tennis courts are pretty much the same, but each golf course is different from every other, and many are designed to show off their gorgeous settings.) Golf is a physical *and* mental challenge — it tests your skill and your will.

It's also a game for a lifetime. Your friends may play football and basketball in high school, but how many are still returning kickoffs or grabbing rebounds when they're 30 or 40 or 60 years old?

The most important reason to play, though, is that golf is magic. It's maddening, frustrating, crazy — and totally addictive. When it becomes part of your life, you can barely imagine life without it.

What You'll Find on a Typical Course

Most golf courses have 18 holes, although a few, usually because of a lack of money or land, have only 9. Courses beside the sea are called *links,* in honor of the parts of Scotland where the game began. (They were the link between beach and farmland.) The *19th hole* is golfspeak for the clubhouse bar — the place where you can reflect on your game over a refreshing beverage of your choice. (See Appendix A for the lowdown on golf jargon.)

How long is a typical golf course? Most are between 5,500 and 7,000 yards. A few monsters are longer, but leave those courses to the pros you see on TV. Start at the low end of that scale and work your way up.

Every hole you play will be a par-3, a par-4, or a par-5. (Par-2s are for minigolf courses; the exceedingly rare par-6s tend to be gimmicks.) *Par* is the number of strokes a reasonably competent player should take to play a particular hole. For example, on a par-5 hole, a regulation par might consist of a drive, two more full swings, and two putts. Two putts is the standard on every green.

Three putts isn't good. One putt is a bonus. The bottom line is that in a perfect round of par golf, half the allocated strokes should be taken on the greens. That premise makes putting important. (I talk about how to putt in Chapter 8.)

Obviously, a par-5 is longer than a par-4 (two full swings, two putts), which in turn is longer than a par-3 (one full swing, two putts). With rare exceptions, par-3s are from 100 to 250 yards in length; par-4s are between 251 and 475 yards long, barring severe topography; and par-5s are anything longer than that.

Many courses in the United States have a total par of 72, consisting of ten par-4s (40), four par-3s (12), and four par-5s (20). But you can find golf courses with total pars of anywhere from 62 to 74. Almost anything goes. Table 1-1 lists the yardages that determine par on a hole, for men and women. It's worth noting that these guidelines don't always refer to precise yardages, but to what the United States Golf Association calls a hole's "effective playing length." A 460-yard hole that went straight uphill, for example, could be a par-5 for men.

Table 1-1 Regulation Yardages

	Women	*Men*
Par-3	210 yards or less	250 yards or less
Par-4	211 to 400 yards	251 to 470 yards
Par-5	401 to 575 yards	471 to 690 yards
Par-6	More than 575 yards	More than 690 yards

Source: United States Golf Association.

That's the big picture. You often find several different teeing areas on each hole so that you can play the hole from different lengths. The vast majority of holes have more than one teeing area — usually four. I've seen courses with as many as six different tees on one hole. Deciding which tee area to use can make you silly. So the tee areas are marked with color-coded tees that indicate ability:

- The **gold tees** are invariably the back tees and are for blessed strikers only.
- The **blue tees** are usually slightly ahead of the gold and make the holes shorter, but still plenty hard. Club competitions are played from these tees.
- The **white tees** are for everyday, casual play, and are the right choice for beginning golfers. Stray from the white tees at your peril.
- The **red tees** are traditionally used by women, although many women I play with use the same tees I play.

How You Can Become a "Real" Golfer

What's a "real" golfer? There are three essentials:

- You understand the game.
- You can play it a little.
- You never dishonor its spirit.

Anyone can smack a ball aimlessly around a course. (I can already hear my fellow professionals saying, "Yeah — like you, McCord!") But that doesn't make you a real golfer. There's much more to this game than hitting a ball with a stick.

How can you start becoming a "real" golfer? It's easy: Read this book. You'll find everything you need to get started, from equipment to instruction to common problems, etiquette, betting, and more. I tell you about the pitfalls that beginners face (and I'm not just talking bunkers), and how to avoid them.

You need to start by buying golf clubs and balls. You don't have to shell out thousands of dollars to get started. You can start simple — use cheap equipment at first, and spend more if you enjoy the game. (Check out Chapter 2 for tips on what you need to get started.)

After you have golf clubs, you need to know how to grip the club: The *V* between the thumb and forefinger of your top hand should point to your right shoulder. That seems simple, but you wouldn't believe how many beginners get it wrong — and complicate their voyage to the promised land of "real" golfers. (Chapter 6 has more information on this gripping — pardon the pun — topic.)

When you've got the grip down pat, you're ready to swing. Believe me, the swing is not as easy as it looks. That's why I devote an entire chapter — Chapter 7 — to developing your own swing. That's where you can determine what type of golfer you are. You can also find out about swing plane, various checkpoints during the swing, and what amateurs can glean from the swings of such great players as Arnold Palmer, Jack Nicklaus, Annika Sorenstam, and Tiger Woods.

You've probably heard about golf etiquette, handicaps, and one- and two-stroke penalties — and maybe even such goofy-sounding things as nassaus, skins, and barkies. If not, don't worry. You'll soon be tossing such terms around like a pro. (Chapters 13, 14, and 15 give you the fine points of playing with experienced golfers on public and private courses.) Knowing when to hit (and when *not* to), how to keep score, and how to bet are integral parts of the game.

Living the Golf Life

As any true golf nut will tell you, there's more to the game than playing it. There's the fun of feeding your addiction by watching the sport on TV, following it on the Internet, and playing golf video games when there's a foot of snow outside. (See Chapters 16, 17, and 18 for my guide to televised golf, the game's best Web sites, and other outlets.)

If the golf bug bites you, as it has bitten millions of others, that little sucker will have you living and breathing birdies, bogeys, barkies, and digital dimples — all the stuff that keeps golf nuts going when they're not actually out on the course, slapping balls who knows where.

Cool historical things to know about golf

- The first reference to golf dates back to the reign of King James II of Scotland. In 1457, King James decreed that "futeball" and "gowf" were forbidden so that Scottish men could concentrate on their archery practice — the better to beat their enemies, the English, on the battlefield. Golf remained outlawed until 1501.
- Dutch historians including Steven von Hengel have argued that golf originated in Holland around 1297. A form of the game, called *spel metten kolve* and also called *colf* (which means *club*), was popular in the late 13th century. Colf, it is believed, was played mostly on ice.
- The first instruction book, written by Thomas Kincaid, appeared in 1687. Among his tips: "Maintain the same posture of the body throughout (the swing) . . . and the ball must be straight before your breast, a little towards the left foot." How did he know?
- In 1743, a shipment of 96 golf clubs and 432 golf balls made its way from Scotland to Charleston, South Carolina. Such a big order suggests it was intended for a group of golfers. Another golf club or society may have been organized in Savannah, Georgia, in 1796, only to be disbanded later. It would be another century before American golf got going for good.
- America's first permanent golf club was formed in 1888 in Yonkers, New York. The St. Andrews golf club played on a three-hole layout that ended near a large apple tree. The club's golfers became known as the Apple Tree Gang. They hung their coats on the tree before they teed off. According to legend, they finished play one day to find their coats stolen by a rival gang known for its disdain of fruit.
- In 1890, the term *bogey* was coined by Hugh Rotherham — only back then it referred to playing a hole in the perfect number of strokes, or a *ground score,* which we today call *par.* Shortly after the invention of the Haskell ball, which made reaching a hole in fewer strokes possible, bogey came to represent a score of one over par for a hole.
- The term *birdie* wasn't coined until 1898, emanating from Atlantic Country Club out of the phrase "a bird of a hole." This gap in terminology is no doubt attributed to the difficulty in attaining a bird, a fact that endures to this day.
- A match-play exhibition was held in 1926, pitting Professional Golfers Association members from Britain and America. Played in England, the home team dominated 13½ to 1½. The next year, at Worcester Country Club, the teams met again, only this time possession of a solid gold trophy was at stake, donated by a wealthy British seed merchant named Samuel A. Ryder. Thus were born the Ryder Cup Matches.
- The Hershey Chocolate Company, in sponsoring the 1933 Hershey Open, became the first corporate title sponsor of a professional tournament. So blame the cocoa guys.
- A local telecast of the 1947 U.S. Open in St. Louis marked the advent of televised golf, a red-letter day in golf history if ever there was one. Now I could finally have a job.

Chapter 2

Gearing Up

In This Chapter

- Choosing a golf ball
- Buying golf clubs
- Knowing which club to use
- Dressing like a pro
- Buying accessories

In the last 100 years, golf has changed enormously, but the most noticeable difference is in equipment. The game may be inherently the same, but the implements used to get from tee to green and into the hole are unrecognizable compared to the rather primitive implements used by Young Tom Morris (one of the great, early pioneers of golf) and his Scottish buddies in the late 19th century. Okay, so early golf equipment had more romantic names: Niblick, brassie, spoon, driving-iron, mashie, and mashie-niblick are more fun than 9-iron, 3-wood, 1-iron, 5-iron, and 7-iron. But golf equipment today is much better.

The old Scottish *worthies* (a great name for players) used clubs whose shafts were wooden — hickory, to be exact. Individually, these clubs may have been fine, but what were the chances of finding a dozen or so identical pieces of wood? Slim to none.

Nowadays, you have no excuse for playing with equipment ill suited to your swing, body, and game. There's too much information out there to help you. And that's the purpose of this chapter — to help you find your way through what can be a confusing maze of statistics and terminology.

Golf Balls: The Dimple Derby

Many technological advances have occurred in the game of golf over the years, but perhaps nothing has changed more than the golf ball. It's no coincidence that the United States Golf Association (USGA) and Royal and Ancient Golf Club (R&A) keep a tight rein on just how far a ball can go nowadays. If the associations didn't provide regulations, almost every golf course on the planet would be reduced to a pitch and putt. We'd all be putting through windmills just to keep the scores up in the 50s.

For the record, here are the specifications the USGA imposes on Titleist, Maxfli, and the rest of the ball manufacturers:

- **Size:** A golf ball may not be smaller than 1.68 inches in diameter. The ball can be as big as you want, however. Just don't expect a bigger ball to go farther — it won't. I've never seen anyone use a ball bigger than 1.68 inches in diameter.
- **Weight:** The golf ball may not be heavier than 1.62 ounces.
- **Velocity:** The USGA has a machine for measuring how fast a ball comes off the face of a club. That's not easy, because impact lasts only 450 millionths of a second, and a good ball can zoom off at more than 170 miles an hour.

  No legal ball may exceed an initial velocity of 250 feet per second at a temperature between 73 and 77 degrees. A tolerance of no more than 2 percent is allowed, which means an absolute max of 255 feet per second. This rule ensures that golf balls don't go too far. (In addition to balls, the USGA now tests bouncy-faced drivers to keep a lid on distance.)
- **Distance:** Distance is the most important factor. For years the standard was the USGA's "Iron Byron" robot (named for sweet-swingin' Byron Nelson). No ball struck by Iron Byron could go farther than 280 yards. A tolerance of 6 percent was allowed, making 296.8 yards the absolute farthest the ball could go. Today the robot has some help from high-tech ball launchers in the USGA labs, and the upper limit has risen to 317 yards.

  Yeah, right. Iron Byron, meet the PGA Tour! Guys like Tiger Woods, Ernie Els, and their buddies just aren't normal — they regularly blast drives way past 350 yards!
- **Shape:** A golf ball must be round. An anti-slice ball on the market a few years ago was weighted on one side and failed this test. Nice try, though!

Even with these regulations, take a look around any golf professional's shop and you'll see many different brands. And upon closer inspection, you'll find that every type of ball falls into one of two categories: Either the manufacturer is claiming that this ball goes farther and straighter than any other ball in the cosmos, or it's telling you that this ball gives you more control.

Try not to get overwhelmed. Keep in mind that golf balls come in only three basic types: one-piece, two-piece, and three-piece. You can forget one-piece balls — they tend to be cheap and nasty and found only on driving ranges. So that leaves two-piece and three-piece balls.

When golf was a (lopsided) ball

Early golf was played with a feathery golf ball — a stitched leather ball stuffed with boiled goose feathers. A feather ball cost three times as much as a club, and because feathery balls were delicate, players had to carry three to six balls at a time. The balls flew poorly in wet weather (a problem in Scotland), and were hard to putt, because they weren't round. They were closer to egg shaped, in fact.

Although the feathery ball was a vast improvement over the wooden balls that preceded it, the gutta percha was an extraordinary breakthrough. In 1848, the Reverend Adam Paterson of St. Andrews introduced the gutta percha ball, or *gutty,* which was made from the sap of the gutta tree found in the tropics. When heated, the rubberlike sap could easily be fashioned into a golf ball. This invention, not to mention the spread of the railways, contributed to the expansion of golf. The gutty was considerably more durable than the feathery and much more affordable. After golfers discovered that bramble patterns and other markings on the gutty enhanced its aerodynamics, this ball swiftly achieved dominance in the marketplace.

After 1900, the Haskell rubber-cored ball quickly replaced the gutta percha as the ball of choice. Invented two years earlier by Cleveland resident Coburn Haskell and manufactured by the B. F. Goodrich Rubber Company of Akron, Ohio, the Haskell ball, featuring a gutty cover and a wound rubber core, traveled farther (up to 20 yards more on average) and delivered greater durability.

It didn't take much time for this new ball to gain acceptance, especially after Alexander "Sandy" Herd defeated renowned Harry Vardon and James Braid in the 1902 British Open at Hoylake, England, using the same Haskell ball for 72 holes. Most golfers today, on the other hand, use six to eight golf balls during a single round of a tour event.

The rest of the 20th century was spent refining the Haskell. In 1905, William Taylor invented the first dimpled ball, improving flight because the dimple pattern maximized lift and minimized drag. Around the time Taylor was playing with his dimples, Elazer Kempshall of the United States and Frank Mingay of Scotland were independently experimenting with liquid-core balls. In 1920, gutta percha began to fade entirely from use, replaced by a soft rubber called *balata.* It was another 50 years before a popular alternative to the Haskell came along. In 1972, Spalding introduced the first two-piece ball, the Executive.

Today, two-, three-, and even four-piece balls dominate the market. (A three-piece ball has a thin extra layer between the cover and the core; a four-piece ball has a core within a core.) Many pros use three- or four-piece balls whose cover hardness, launch angle, and spin rate are perfectly tuned to their games.

Don't worry; deciding on a type of ball is still easy. You don't even have to know what a two-piece or three-piece ball contains or why it has that many "pieces." Leave all that to the scientists. And don't worry too much about launch angle or spin rate, either. Today's balls are technological marvels, designed to take off high and spin just enough to go as straight as possible.

Go with a two-piece ball. I wouldn't recommend a three-piece ball to a beginning golfer. Tour pros and expert players use such balls to maximize control. For many years, the best players used balls with covers made of *balata,* a soft, rubbery substance. Today, many high-performance three-piece balls have covers of something even better — high-performance urethane elastomer, which is a fancy way of saying "expensive superplastic." But you don't need that stuff. As a beginner, you need a reliable, durable ball. Unless you have very deep pockets and more cash than Bill Gates, go the surlyn, two-piece route. (*Surlyn* is a type of plastic first developed by the Dupont Corporation.) Most amateurs with double-digit handicaps use this type of ball. A surlyn-covered ball's harder cover and lower spin rate give you less feel — which is why better players tend not to use them — but, assuming that you don't whack them off the premises, they last longer. They just might roll farther, too.

Golf balls used to come in three compressions: 80, 90, or 100. The 80-compression ball was the softest, and the 100 the hardest. When I was growing up, I thought that the harder the ball (100 compression), the farther it would go. Not the case. All balls go far when hit properly, but each one feels a little different. How hard or soft you want the ball to feel has to do with your personal preference. These days, you needn't worry about compression. It's no longer such a big deal. Just determine whether you like a harder or softer feel, and swing away.

Take all the commercial hype with a grain of salt. Make that a handful. The most important things you need to know when buying golf balls are your own game, your own tendencies, and your own needs. Your local PGA professional can help you choose the golf ball best suited to you.

How to Choose Your Weapons

Deciding on a set of clubs to use can be as simple or as complicated as you want to make it. You can go to any store that doesn't have a golf pro, pick a set of clubs off the shelf, and then take them to the tee. You can go to garage sales. You can check with the pro at your local municipal course. Any or all of these methods can work. But your chances of choosing a set with the correct loft, lie, size of grip, and all the other stuff involved in club fitting are worse than my chances of winning on *American Idol.*

Having said that, I must add that it wasn't so long ago that *unsophisticated* was a fair description of every golf-club buyer. Yeah, the better player might waggle a new club a few times and "know" that it wasn't for him — hardly the most scientific approach!

If you're just beginning to play golf, keep in mind that you may discover that this game is not for you. So you should start out with rental clubs at a driving range. Most driving ranges have rental clubs. Go out and hit balls with these clubs. If you still want to play golf after hitting a few balls, then buy your own clubs.

Find an interim set of clubs

If you're just starting out (and you've played with rental clubs for a while), find cheap clubs to use as an interim set during your adjustment period. You're learning the game, so you don't want to make big decisions on what type of clubs to buy yet. If you keep your ears open around the golf course or driving range, you may hear of someone who has a set that he or she is willing to sell. You can also ask whether the person has any information on clubs that could be sold cheaply. Go take a look at garage sales that have golf clubs for sale, or try the classified ads of your weekend newspaper. And, of course, you can check the Internet — the fastest-growing marketplace in golf. (In Chapter 17, I describe some of my favorite Internet golf sites.) You can become your own private investigator and hunt down the best buy you can find. Buy cheap for now — you've got plenty of time for the big purchase.

Try all sorts of clubs — ones with steel shafts, graphite shafts (which are lighter and, therefore, easier to swing), big-headed clubs, *investment-cast clubs* (made by pouring hot metal into a mold), *forged clubs* (made from a single piece of metal), *cavity-backed clubs* (ones that are hollowed out in the back of the iron). You have more choices than your neighborhood Baskin-Robbins. ***Remember:*** You're in your experimental stage.

Don't be afraid to ask your friends if you can try their clubs on the range. I do this all the time on the tour when a new product comes out. Try out these clubs, and you can judge for yourself whether they feel good. But if you don't like the club that you just tried, don't tell the person who loaned it to you that the club stinks — that's not good golf etiquette. Simply hand the club back and say thanks.

Try this on for size

Today, club fitting is big business. Tour pros and average amateur golfers have access to the same club fitting technology and information. It's important for all golfers — male and female — to use the right equipment for their body types and physical conditions. For instance, many manufacturers of golf clubs specialize in creating clubs for women that have softer shafts, which are lighter and more flexible.

Here are some factors every golfer should consider:

- **The grip:** Determine how thick the grip on your clubs should be. Grips that are too thin encourage too much hand action in your swing; grips that are too thick restrict your hands too much. Generally, the proper-sized grip should allow the middle and ring fingers on your left hand to barely touch the pad of your thumb when you hold the club. If your fingers don't touch your thumb, the grip is too big; if your fingers dig into the pad, the grip is too thin.

- **The shaft:** Consider your height, build, and strength when you choose a club. If you're really tall, you need longer (and probably stiffer) shafts.

  What does your swing sound like? If your swing makes a loud *swish* noise and the shaft is bending like a long cast from a fly-fishing rod at the top of your swing, you need a very strong shaft. If your swing makes no noise and you could hang laundry on your shaft at the top of your swing, you need a regular shaft. Anybody in between needs a medium-stiff to stiff shaft.

- **Loft:** Then there's your typical ball flight. If you slice, for example, you can get clubs with less loft — or perhaps offset heads — to help alleviate that common problem. For more information about slicing, see Chapter 11.
- **The clubhead:** Consider the size of the clubhead. Today, you can get standard, midsize, and oversize heads on your clubs. I recommend you use bigger clubheads for your early days of playing golf. Bigger clubheads are more forgiving and can help psychologically, too. With some of today's jumbo clubheads, your swing thought may well be, "With this thing, how could I miss?"
- **The iron:** Advanced players choose irons that are perfectly suited to their swings. Forged, muscle-backed irons are for good players who hit the ball on the clubface precisely. Cavity-backed irons are for players who hit the ball all over the clubface.

  The bigger the clubface, the more room for error — hence the bigger-headed metal woods that are popular today for all you wild swingers out there.

Because of all the technology that is available, purchasing golf clubs nowadays is like buying a computer: Whatever you buy may be outdated in six months. So be frugal and shop for your best buy. When you get a set that fits you and you're hitting the ball with consistency, stick with that set. Finding a whole set of clubs that matches the temperament of your golf swing is hard. Find the ones that have your fingerprints on them and stick with 'em.

Ten questions to ask before you buy

- **Do you have a club fitting program?** Check with your local PGA golf professional and see whether he has a club fitting program. If he doesn't, he'll be able to direct you to someone in the area who does. After you've started this game and found you like it enough to continue playing, choosing the right equipment is the biggest decision you'll have to make. So talk to a PGA golf professional.
- **What's the price of club fitting?** Don't be too shy to ask this question. Club fitting can be expensive. You should be the judge of how much you can afford.

- **What shaft length do I need for my clubs?** Golfers come in different heights and builds. Some people are tall with short arms, and some are short with long arms. People have different postures when they bend over to address the golf ball, and they need different shaft lengths to match that posture. This is where PGA golf professionals can really help; they're trained to answer questions like these and can make club fitting very easy.
- **What lie-angle do I need on my clubs?** Here's the general rule: The closer you stand to the ball, the more *upright* your club needs to be. As you get farther away from the ball, the lie-angle of your clubs should be *flatter.*
- **What grip size do I need?** The bigger your hands are, the bigger grip you need. If you have a tendency to slice the ball, you can try smaller grips that help your hands work faster. If you have a tendency to hook the ball, you can use bigger grips that will slow down your hands and help you beat that hook.
- **What material — leather, cord, all-rubber, half-rubber — do you recommend for my grips?** Many different materials can make up a golf grip. Leather is the most expensive and the hardest to maintain. It's for accomplished players; I don't recommend leather for beginners. Stick to an all-rubber grip — and change your grips every year if you play at least once a week. I use a combination of rubber and cord — and it has nothing to do with my name. These grips help me hold on to the club in hot weather. My hands are callused, though, so they don't hurt from the rubbing of the cord.
- **What kind of irons should I buy — investment-cast, forged, oversized, or cavity-back?** The best advice I can give is to look for an investment-cast, cavity-backed, oversized golf club. For beginners, this is the best choice. Just take my word for it — I haven't got enough paper to explain all the reasons.
- **Should I use space-age materials like boron, titanium, or graphite in my shafts? Or should I go with steel?** Steel shafts are the cheapest; all the others are quite a bit more expensive, so keep your budget in mind. See if you can test some of these other shafts to see how they compare with steel, which is still very good and used by most of the players on tour.
- **What type of putter should I use: center-shafted or end-shafted? Do I want a mallet putter, a belly putter, or a long putter?** There's been an explosion of putter technology in the past few years. You can try out the result at the golf course where you play. Just ask the pro if you can test one of the putters on the rack. If you have a friend or playing partner who has a putter you think you may like, ask to try it. For more on putters and putting, see Chapter 8.
- **If you're going to buy new clubs, ask the pro if you can test them for a day.** Most of the time, someone who's trying to make a sale will give you every opportunity to try the clubs. Golf pros are just like car dealers; they'll let you test-drive before you buy.

Build your own clubs

You can get quite sophisticated when choosing a club. Club-component companies specialize in selling clubs piece by piece. You can literally build your own set of clubs to your own specifications; you just have to do some research first. A lot of people are building their own clubs, judging by the success of firms like Golfsmith. For one thing, these clubs are cheaper than the clubs you can buy off the shelf.

Although building your clubs does require time and effort, the end result is the same. Component companies can sell you everything you need. You can get catalogs, call their toll-free numbers, or visit their Web sites (see Appendix B). Component companies offer grip tape, solvents, clamps, epoxy, shaft-cutting tools, shaft extensions, grip knives, and every kind of shaft, head, and grip imaginable. You name it, they've got it. You just have to know what you want. If you're not sure, order a club-making video or book first. You never know — you may end up an expert in the field.

When You Know Your Game

Before 1938, the Rules of Golf allowed players to carry as many clubs as they wanted. Since then, however, golfers have been restricted to a maximum of 14 clubs in their bags at any one time. But no rule tells you which 14 clubs to use, so you have leeway. You can match the composition of your set to your strengths and weaknesses.

I'm assuming that you're going to carry a driver, a 3-wood, a putter, and irons 4 through 9. Nearly everyone does. So you have five clubs left to select. The first thing you need to know, of course, is how far you're likely to hit each club. (That's golfspeak for hitting the ball with the club. Don't go smashing your equipment!) After you know that, you can look into plugging the gaps. Those gaps are most important at the short end of your set.

I recommend that you carry three wedges, each with a different loft. I do. I use a 48-degree pitching wedge, a 54-degree sand wedge, and a 59-degree lob wedge. I hit them 125 yards (pitching wedge), 105 yards (sand wedge), and 85 yards (lob wedge). That way, the yardage gap between them is not significant. If I carried only the 125-yard wedge and the 85-yard wedge, that would leave a gap of 40 yards — too much. If I leave myself with a shot of about 105 yards, right in the middle of my gap, I've got problems. Carrying the 105-yard wedge plugs that gap. If I didn't have it, I'd be forced to manufacture a shot with a less-than-full swing. And that's too hard, especially under pressure. Full swings, please!

Okay, that's 12 clubs taken care of. You have two left. I recommend carrying at least one lofted wood. Make that two. Low-numbered irons are too unforgiving. So give yourself a break. Carry a 5-wood and even a 7-wood. These clubs are designed to make it easy for you to get the ball up in the air. They certainly achieve that more quickly than a 2-iron.

Another option is the hybrid club. Sometimes called a *utility club,* the hybrid is sort of an iron, and sort of a fairway wood. It's a fairly recent entry — a forgiving club that gets the ball airborne in a hurry. You can even use it for chipping, as Todd Hamilton did on a shot that clinched the 2004 British Open. Hybrid clubs, which come in different lofts, are getting more and more popular. You should swing a few, and consider carrying a hybrid instead of that 7-wood, 5-wood, or maybe even your 4-iron.

Figure 2-1 shows the clubs that I have in my bag.

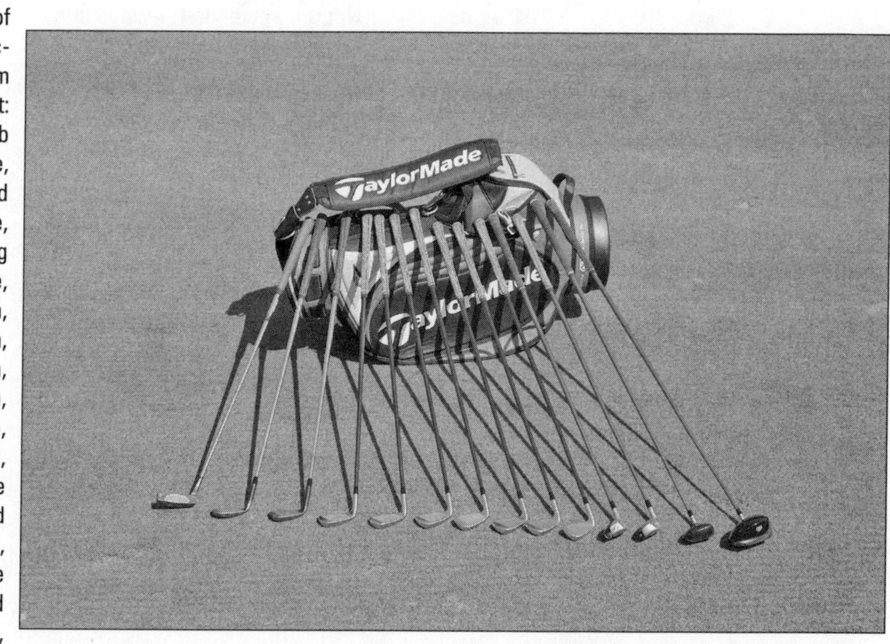

Figure 2-1: My implements of destruction — from left to right: putter, lob wedge, sand wedge, pitching wedge, 9-iron, 8-iron, 7-iron, 6-iron, 5-iron, 4-iron, 21-degree Hybrid Rescue, 18-degree Hybrid Rescue, 3-wood, driver.

When to Use Each Club

Table 2-1 shows how far the average golfer generally hits with each club when he makes solid contact. When you start to play this game, you probably won't attain these yardages. As you practice, you'll get closer to these numbers.

You should know your average. The best way to find out is to hit, oh, 50 balls with each club. Eliminate the longest five and the shortest five and then pace off to the middle of the remaining group. That's your average yardage. Use your average yardage to help you gauge which club to use on each shot.

Table 2-1 Which Club Should You Use?

Club	*Men's Average Distance*	*Women's Average Distance*
Driver	230 yards	200 yards
3-wood	210 yards	180 yards
2-iron	190 yards	Not recommended; 4-wood or hybrid = 170 yards
3-iron	180 yards	Not recommended; 5-wood or hybrid = 160 yards
4-iron	170 yards	150 yards (Consider a hybrid instead)
5-iron	160 yards	140 yards
6-iron	150 yards	130 yards
7-iron	140 yards	120 yards
8-iron	130 yards	110 yards
9-iron	120 yards	100 yards
Pitching wedge	110 yards	90 yards
Sand wedge	90 yards	80 yards
Lob wedge	65 yards	6 yards

Tradition versus Technology: Keep Tinkering with Success

Technology is the guiding light of fundamental change that is inherent to a capitalistic society in search of a more expensive way to hit the #$&!?*@ ball farther.*

—Quote on the bathroom wall of the Wayward Soul Driving Range in Temecula, California

Technology and all its implications is a conversation topic that PGA Tour players visit quite often. Is the ball too hot? Are the big-headed titanium drivers giving the golf ball too much rebound? Is Tiger getting rich? I think that most players would answer these questions in the affirmative. Should golfers take a stance on the tenuous line between the balance of tradition and technology? "Probably not" would be the answer if all were polled.

To see where golf is today, you have to examine its past; then you can try to predict golf's future. This section helps you gaze into the crystal ball to focus on what the future has to offer.

Whoever said that golf is played with weapons ill suited for their intended purpose probably hadn't played with clubs made of titanium and other composite metals. These clubs allegedly act like a spring that segments of the golfing populace believe propels the golf ball — also enhanced by state-of-the-art materials and designs — distances it was not meant to travel. This phenomenon is called the *trampoline effect,* which some folks may mistake for a post-round activity for reducing stress. In fact, this effect is the product of modern, thin-faced metal clubs.

This phenomenon has fueled a debate pitting the forces of technology (the evil swine) against those of tradition (those languorous leeches who never see special-effects movies). Equipment that makes the game easier for the masses helps the game grow, the techno-wizards say. Traditionalists fret that classic courses are becoming obsolete, the need for new super-long courses may make the game cost more in both time and money, and golf may become too easy for elite players. Regardless of which side you agree with (you may, indeed, back both camps), one fact is undeniable: Improving golf equipment has been an unceasing process throughout the game's history.

People have been developing the golf ball and clubs for many years. In the last 100 years, however, science has played an increasing role in golf-club development, with a strong influence coming from research into new metals, synthetic materials, and composites. Other developments worth noting:

- The introduction of the casting method of manufacturing clubheads in 1963.
- The introduction of graphite for use in shafts in 1973.
- The manufacture of metal woods in 1979 (first undertaken by TaylorMade). This last creation rendered persimmon woods obsolete, although a small number are still crafted.

The application of titanium to clubheads raised the bar in technological development (yet again) just a few years ago. Lighter than previous materials yet stronger than steel, titanium allows club makers to create larger clubheads with bigger sweet spots that push the legal limit of 470 cubic centimeters. Such clubs provide high-handicap golfers a huge margin for error — there's nothing quite like the feel of a mishit ball traveling 200 yards! But it's golf balls flying in excess of 300 yards that raise suspicions that these new clubs are making the ball too "excitable."

Golf balls have been under scrutiny for much longer, probably because each new generation of ball has had an ever greater impact on the game. Ball development makes golf easier and more enjoyable for the average person and, thus, cultivates more interest.

Modern balls tout varied dimple patterns, multiple layers, and other features that attempt to impart a certain trajectory, spin, greater accuracy, and better feel, as well as the ever-popular maximum distance allowed under the Rules of Golf established by the USGA. A recent change in the Rules added more than 20 yards to the old maximum of 296.8 yards. But even way back in 1998, John Daly averaged 299.4 yards on his measured drives on the PGA Tour. By 2004 the leader, Hank Kuehne, averaged 314, and the trend is upward. Uh-oh.

In the coming years, golf stands to become increasingly popular, and if history tells us anything, it's that technology is apt to contribute to the game's popularity. However, advances in golf equipment may occur at a relatively glacial pace. The early 21st century likely won't come close to rivaling the first ten years of the 20th for technological impact or dramatic innovation.

Why? For one thing, scientists are running out of new stuff they can use to make clubheads — at least stuff that isn't edible. An expedition to Saturn may yield possibilities. Metallurgists are going to be challenged, although so far they're staying ahead of the game. New entries in the substance category include beta titanium, maraging steel, graphite (yes, in clubheads), and liquid metal, all purportedly better than current club materials.

Dick Rugge, Senior Technical Director for the USGA, is one of the prominent folks standing in the way of radical equipment enhancement. His job is to regulate the distance a golf ball should travel, yet he doesn't want to stifle technology altogether. The goal is to give the average golfer an advantage (whether it comes from the equipment itself or the joy of having better equipment) while keeping the game a challenge for the top players.

But someone is always trying to build a better mousetrap. And although everyone wants more distance, most performance-enhancing innovations are likely to come in putter designs. On average, the USGA approves more than one new putter every day, and many of the new ones look like something out of *Star Wars.* Still, no one has yet invented a yip-proof blade. When somebody does, that genius is going to make a fortune.

We may also see more changes in the ball — although, again, dramatic alterations in ball design are unlikely. Customizing may become more commonplace. You may also see more layering of golf-ball materials to help performance.

Weapons of our fore! fathers

The earliest players carved their own clubs and balls from wood. Later, skilled craftsmen assumed the task. Long-nosed wooden clubs are the oldest-known designed clubs — and the most enduring equipment ever conceived, remaining in use from the 15th century until the late 19th century. Long-noses were made from pear, apple, beech, or holly trees and were used to help achieve maximum distance with the feathery golf ball, which dates all the way back to 1618.

Later, other parts of the golf set developed: *play clubs,* which included a range of spoons with varying lofts; *niblicks,* a kin of the modern 9-iron or wedge that was ideal for short shots; and a *putting cleek* — a club that has undergone (and is still undergoing) perhaps the most rigorous experimentation. I know that my putters have undergone severe tests of stamina and stress. You're probably familiar with the I'm-going-to-throw-this-thing-into-orbit-and-let-Zeus-see-if-he-can-putt-with-it test, as well as the ever-popular break-it-over-my-knee-so-it-can't-harm-anyone-again test. These tests should be conducted only by professionals.

The development of the gutta percha ball, much harder than a feathery, forced club makers to become truly revolutionary. Some club makers tried using leather, among other materials, in their clubs in an attempt to increase compression and, therefore, distance (obviously, a recurring theme throughout the ages). Others implanted metal and bone fragments in the clubface. In 1826, Scottish club makers began using hickory imported from the United States to manufacture shafts, and hickory was quickly adopted as the wood of choice.

It's probably a good thing that the fore! fathers never saw what may have been the goofiest innovation of all: the orange ball Jerry Pate used to win the 1982 Players Championship.

Not to be discounted are improvements in turf technology — an overlooked area boasting significant breakthroughs in the last 20 years. For example, in 1977, the average Stimpmeter reading for greens around the country (the Stimpmeter measures the speed of a putting surface — or any surface on a course) was 6.6. This means that a ball rolled from a set slope traveled 6½ feet. Today, the average is closer to 9 feet. The biggest future breakthroughs will probably come from humans. Physiological improvement and psychological refinement may be the surest paths to more distance and lower scoring.

So hit the gym, take up Pilates, hit your psychologist's couch, get in touch with your inner self, eat bran and all the protein bars you can stand, drink 20 glasses of water a day, and take a stab at self-hypnotism if you have to. And if all that fails to add 10 yards off the tee, then you can try a different ball. Ain't innovation grand?

Clothes: How to Dress Like a Pro

The easiest way to date an old picture of a golfer, at least approximately, is by the clothes he or she is wearing. Sartorially, the game has changed enormously since the Scots tottered 'round the old links wearing a jacket, shirt, and tie.

Back at St. Andrews, the restraint of the clothing affected the golf swing. Those jackets were tight! In fact, I believe that was the single biggest influence on the early golf swings. A golfer had to sway off the ball and then let his left arm bend on the backswing to get full motion. Also, he had to let go with the last three fingers of his left hand at the top of the swing. It was the only way a golfer could get the shaft behind his head. Put on a tweed jacket that's a little too small and try to swing. You'll see what the early golfers had to go through.

Fabrics have changed from those days of heavy wool and restricted swings. Light cotton is what the splendidly smart golfer wears today — if he or she hasn't switched to one of the new, high-tech fabrics that wick perspiration away from the body. (I always said golf was no sweat.) Styles have changed, too. When I came on tour in the early 1970s, polyester was the fabric of choice. Bell-bottoms and bright plaids filled golf courses with ghastly ridicule. We've evolved to better fabrics — and a softer, more humane existence on the course. Some guys on tour now wear expensive pants with more-expensive belts. And a few, like Jesper Parnevik, are known for the retro look — plaids and pastels like we wore back in the '70s! But most players wear off-the-rack clothes provided by clothing manufacturers.

Women have undergone an enormous fashion transformation on the course, too. Years ago, they played in full-length skirts, hats, and blouses buttoned up to the neck. All very restricting, I imagine. Now, of course, they're out there in shorts and pants.

First of all, dress within your budget. This game can get expensive enough; there's no need to outdress your playing partners. My general rule is to aim to dress better than the starter at the course. (The *starter* is the person in charge of getting everyone off the first tee.) The starter's style is usually a reflection of the dress standards at that particular golf course. If you're unsure about the style at a particular course, give the pro shop a call to find out the dress code.

The bottom line is to dress comfortably and look good. If you dress well, you may appear as if you can actually play this game with a certain amount of distinction. People can be fooled. You never know!

Golf shoes are the final aspect of a golfer's ensemble. Shoes can be a fashion statement — alligator or ostrich. They can be comfortable — tennis shoes or sandals with spikes. They can take on the lore of the Wild West in the form of cowboy boots with spikes or, as my mentor Fairway Louie used to highlight his golfing attire, they can even be military combat boots.

What's on the bottom of the shoe is all the rage now. The traditional metal spikes have been replaced with all sorts of *soft spikes.* Soft spikes reduce spike marks and wear and tear on the greens. They're also easier on the feet. If the style of shoes is worthy, you can even go directly from the golf course to the nearest restaurant without having to change shoes. The golf world is becoming a simpler place to live.

Accessories: The Stuff You Need

When it comes to accessories, there's a whole golfing subculture out there. By accessories, I mean things like

- Covers for your irons
- Plastic tubes that you put in your bag to keep your shafts from clanging together
- Tripod tees to use when the ground is hard
- Golf watches that keep your score
- Rubber suction cups that allow you to lift your ball from the hole without bending down

I've even seen a plastic clip that fits to the side of your bag so that you can "find" your putter quickly. You know the sort of things. Most accessories appear to be good ideas, but then you often use them only once.

The place to find all this sort of stuff is in the classified advertising sections of golf magazines. But take my advice: Don't bother. Real golfers — and you want to look and behave like one — don't go in for that stuff. Accessories are very uncool. The best golf bags are spartan affairs and contain only the bare essentials:

- About six balls
- A few wooden tees
- A couple of gloves
- A rain suit
- A pitch-mark repair tool
- A few small coins (preferably foreign) for markers
- Two or three pencils
- A little bag (leather is cool) for your wallet, money clip, loose change, car keys, rings, and so on

Your bag should also have a towel (a real, full-size one) hanging from the strap. Use your towel to dry off and clean your clubheads. Keep a spare towel in your bag. If it rains, you can't have too many towels.

I mentioned headcovers. Keep them only on your woods or metal woods. Golfers have a wide range to choose from. You have your cuddly animal devotees. Other players like to be identified with a particular golf club, university, or sports team. Some players are content merely to advertise the manufacturer of the club they're using.

Bottom line? I recommend that you get headcovers with which you readily identify. Create your own persona. For example, tour player Craig "The Walrus" Stadler has walrus headcovers. Esteban Toledo, a former boxer, uses little boxing gloves. Australian Steve Elkington doesn't use headcovers.

As for your golf bag, you don't need a large tour-sized monstrosity with your name on the side. I've got one because I play professionally and someone pays me to use their equipment. But you should go the understated route. Especially if you're going to be carrying your bag, go small and get the kind with legs that fold down automatically to support the bag. First, you don't want to be loaded down on a hot day. And second, the last thing you want to do is draw attention to yourself. Blend in. Be one with the environment.

Chapter 3

Do I Need Lessons?

In This Chapter

- Keeping a record of how you've played
- Knowing where to go for lessons
- Getting the most for your golf-lesson money
- Finding information from other sources

Suppose you just started to play golf by hitting some balls at the driving range. Your friends took you over to the range at lunch, and you launched a couple of balls into the sunshine and thought you might want to learn the game. Where do you go?

- **You can learn from friends.** Most of us start out this way, which is why we develop so many swing faults. Friends' intentions are good, but their teaching abilities may not be.
- **You can learn by hitting balls.** I learned to play the game this way. The flight of the ball told me everything. I would go to the driving range and hit balls day and night. The pure act of swinging a golf club in a certain way made the ball fly in different trajectories and curves. This learning process is a very slow one because you have to learn through experimentation.
- **You can learn from books.** There are many books written on golf instruction that can lead you through the fundamentals of the game. But you can go only so far by teaching yourself from a book.
- **You can take lessons from a PGA professional.** This is the most expensive and most efficient way to learn the game. Lessons can cost as little as $8 an hour and as much as $300 or more. The expensive guys are the ones you read about in *Golf Digest* and *Golf Magazine* and the ones you watch on TV. All golf professionals can help you with the basics of the game.

Ten things a good instructor should have

- Lots of golf balls
- Patience
- A sense of humor
- Enthusiasm
- An ability to teach players at all levels
- An ability to explain the same thing in ten different ways
- An encouraging manner
- A method that he or she believes in
- An ability to adapt that method to your needs
- More golf balls

Finding Out What You Need to Work On

Keeping a record of how you've played for a few weeks before taking a lesson is a good idea. This information is invaluable for your pro. And don't track just your scores. Keep track of

- How many fairways you hit
- How many greens you hit
- How many putts you average
- How many strokes it usually takes you to get the ball into the hole from a greenside bunker

Tracking all these things may seem like overkill, but doing so helps the pro quickly detect tendencies or weaknesses in your game. Then the pro knows where to look for your problems. If nothing else, tracking your play saves time — time you're paying for! Figure 3-1 shows how to keep track of all those numbers on your score card.

Men's Course Rating/Slope
Blue 73.1/137
White 71.0/130

Women's Course Rating/Slope
Red 73.7/128

Blue Tees	White Tees	Par	Hcp	JOHN				HOLE	HIT FAIRWAY	HIT GREEN		No. PUTTS	Hcp	Par	Red Tees
377	361	4	11	4				1	✓	✓		2	13	4	310
514	467	5	13	8				2	✓	0		3	3	5	428
446	423	4	1	7				3	0	0		2	1	4	389
376	356	4	5	6				4	0	0		2	11	4	325
362	344	4	7	5				5	0	✓		3	7	4	316
376	360	4	9	6				6	✓	0		2	9	4	335
166	130	3	17	4				7	0	✓		3	17	3	108
429	407	4	3	5				8	✓	✓		3	5	4	368
161	145	3	15	5				9	0	0		2	15	3	122
3207	2993	35		50				Out	4	4		22		35	2701
			Initial										Initial		
366	348	4	18	5				10	0	0		2	14	4	320
570	537	5	10	7				11	✓	0		3	2	5	504
438	420	4	2	5				12	✓	0		2	6	4	389
197	182	3	12	4				13	0	0		2	16	3	145
507	475	5	14	5				14	✓	✓		2	4	5	425
398	380	4	4	5				15	0	✓		3	8	4	350
380	366	4	6	5				16	✓	0		2	10	4	339
165	151	3	16	4				17	0	0		2	18	3	133
397	375	4	8	5				18	0	0		2	12	4	341
3418	3234	36		45				In	3	2		20		36	2946
6625	6227	71		95				Tot	7	6		42		71	5647
Handicap													Handicap		
Net Score													Net Score		
Adjust													Adjust		

Scorer Attested Date

Figure 3-1: Keep a record of how many fairways and greens you hit and how many putts you hit. Your teacher can then identify any problem areas.

Where to Go for Lessons

Golf lessons are usually available wherever balls are hit and golf is played: driving ranges, public courses, resorts, private clubs. The price usually increases in that same order — driving-range pros usually charge the least. As for quality, if the pro is PGA-qualified — look for the term *PGA professional* posted in the pro shop or on his or her business card — you can be reasonably sure you'll get top-notch instruction.

A qualified PGA teaching professional may charge between $25 and $50 per session, which can range from 30 minutes to an hour. A professional has a good sense of how much to tell you and at what rate of speed; not all lessons require a specific amount of time.

When checking out places that offer golf lessons, ask whether they have video-analysis capabilities. When you're able to watch yourself on video, you and your instructor can pinpoint problem areas for improvement. If nothing else, a video record is a great way to track and monitor your progress as you build your fundamental skills.

Golf schools

No matter where you live in the United States, a golf school should be fairly close by. Golf schools are set up for all levels of players — and many of them are aimed at those just learning the game. (Appendix B contains a list of recommended golf schools.)

Golf schools are great for beginners. You'll find yourself in a group — anything from 3 to 20 strong, which is perfect for you. There's safety in numbers, and it's reassuring. You'll find that you're not the only beginner. And you never know: Watching others struggle with their own problems may help you with *your* game.

Most of the better golf schools advertise in golf magazines. Be warned, though. These schools tend to be relatively expensive. They did very well in the 1980s when the economy was perceived to be strong and people had more disposable income. Since then, however, golf schools haven't been so successful. Golf-school lessons are big-ticket items, which makes them among the first things people omit from their yearly budgets.

Having said that, many people are still going to golf schools. Why? Because they work. You get, on average, three days of intensive coaching on all aspects of the game from a good teacher. Because the groups are usually small, you get lots of one-on-one attention, too. Then you have the experiences of others. You can learn a lot by paying attention to what your fellow students are being told.

Don't feel that you have to be hitting shots all the time. Take regular breaks — especially if you're not used to hitting a lot of balls — and use the time to learn. Soak up all the information you can. Besides, regular breaks are the best way I know to avoid those blisters you see on the hands of golf-school students!

Driving ranges

I used to work at a driving range in Riverside, California. I spent hours picking up golf balls on the range and hitting those same balls when I was off work. The range was bare dirt, the balls were old, and the floodlights had lost their luminescence. But it was a great spot to learn the travails of the game.

Driving ranges have changed a lot since then. Many are very sophisticated, with two or three tiers and putting greens, and some have miniature golf courses attached to them. Some very good (and some not-so-good) instructors work at these facilities. Most of them can show you the basic mechanics of the swing and get you off on the right foot.

Be sure to ask whether the pro at your local driving range is a PGA golf professional. If so, you can be assured that he or she is fully qualified to guide you through golf's lesson book. If not, the person still may know a lot about the game, but proceed with caution.

Local clubs

Even if you're not a member, getting a lesson from the local club pro is usually possible. He or she will probably charge a little more than a driving-range pro, but the facilities will likely be a lot better. Certainly, the golf balls will be. And chances are, you'll have access to a putting green and a practice bunker, so you can get short-game help, too.

What's a playing lesson?

A *playing lesson* is just what it sounds like. You hire a professional to play any number of holes with you. This theme has three main variations, all of which can help you become a better golfer:

- **You can do all the playing.** The professional walks with you, observing your strategy, swing, and style, and makes suggestions as you go. I recommend this sort of lesson if you're the type of person who likes one-on-one direction.

- **You can both play.** That way, you get the chance to receive instruction and the opportunity to observe an expert player in action. If you typically learn more by watching and copying what you see, this type of lesson is effective. Pay particular attention to the rhythm of the pro's swing, the way he manages his game, and how you can incorporate both into your own game.
- **The pro can manufacture typical on-course situations for you to deal with.** For example, the pro may place your ball behind a tree, point out your options, and then ask you to choose one and explain your choice. Your answer and the subsequent advice from the pro help make you a better player. Imagine that you have two escape routes — one easy, one hard. All the easy one involves is a simple little chip shot back to the fairway. Trouble is, because you won't be gaining any distance, you may feel like you wasted a shot. The difficult shot — through a narrow gap in the branches — is tempting because the reward will be so much greater. But failure will be disastrous. Hit the tree, and you could take nine or ten shots on the hole. Decisions, decisions! ***Remember:*** There's more to golf than just hitting the ball.

Gary's favorite teachers nationwide

Many famous teachers will teach absolutely anybody who wants to be taught — male or female, young or old. They're expensive — $100 to $400 an hour and up. Some teach at schools, and some (like Mac O'Grady) you can't find anywhere. Here are some of the best instructors:

- **Chuck Cook:** Chuck Cook Golf Academy in Austin, Texas (phone: 800-336-6158; Web: `www.chuckcookgolfacademy.com`; e-mail: `golfacademy@bartoncreek.com`)
- **Jim Flick:** Jim Flick Golf in Scottsdale, Arizona (phone: 888-546-3542; Web: `www.jimflickgolf.com`)
- **Hank Haney:** Hank Haney Golf Ranch in McKinney, Texas (phone: 972-542-8800; Web: `www.hankhaneygolf.com`)
- **Butch Harmon:** Rio Secco Golf Club in Las Vegas, Nevada (phone: 888-867-3226; Web: `www.butchharmon.com`; e-mail: `info@butchharmon.com`)
- **Peter Kostis:** Kostis/McCord Learning Center in Scottsdale, Arizona (phone: 888-506-7786; Web: `www.kostismccordlearning.com`; e-mail: `kmlc@grayhawkgolf.com`)
- **David Leadbetter:** David Leadbetter Golf Academy in Orlando, Florida (phone: 888-633-5323; Web: `www.davidleadbetter.com`; e-mail: `info@davidleadbetter.com`)
- **Jim McLean:** Doral Golf Resort & Spa in Miami, Florida (phone: 305-591-6409; Web: `www.golfspan.com/instructors/jmclean/welcome.asp`)
- **Mac O'Grady:** Planet Earth (sometimes — don't even try to make contact)
- **Dave Pelz:** Dave Pelz Scoring Game Schools in Austin, Texas (phone: 800-833-7370; Web: `www.pelzgolf.com`)

- **Rick Smith:** Rick Smith Golf Academy at Treetops Resort in Gaylord, Michigan (phone: 888-873-3867; Web: www.ricksmith.com) and Rick Smith Golf Academy at Tiburón in Naples, Florida (phone: 877-464-6531; Web: www.ricksmith.com)
- **Stan Utley:** Stan Utley Tour-Tested Golf in Scottsdale, Arizona (Web: www.stanutleygolf.com)

Getting the Most from Your Lessons

Much has been written about the relationship between Nick Faldo and his former teacher, David Leadbetter. Under Leadbetter's guidance, Faldo turned himself from a pretty good player into a great player. In the process, Leadbetter — quite rightly — received a lot of praise and attention. More recently, Tiger Woods switched teachers and retooled his game. After Woods won the 2005 Masters and British Open, his teacher Hank Haney got some of the credit.

Ultimately, however, the teacher is only as good as the pupil. Faldo, with his extraordinary dedication and total belief in what he was told, may have been the best pupil in the history of golf. And Tiger is nothing less than the best — and most focused — golfer of our time.

When you take lessons, you need to keep the faith. There's no point in going to someone you don't believe in. If you find yourself doubting what you're being told, you're wasting everybody's time. Change instructors if that happens — that is, if your instructor doesn't tell you to go elsewhere first.

Be honest

Okay, so you're on the lesson tee with your pro. What's the drill? The first thing you need to be is completely honest. Tell your instructor your problems (your *golf* problems, that is), your goals, the shots you find difficult. Tell him or her what style of learning — visual, auditory, or kinesthetic — you find easiest. For example, do you like to be shown how to do something and then copy it (which would make you a visual learner)? Do you prefer to have that same something explained in detail (making you an auditory learner)? Or do you prefer to repeat the motion until it feels natural (which would make you a kinesthetic learner)?

Gratuitous solicitation: At the Kostis/McCord Learning Center at Grayhawk Golf Club in Scottsdale, Arizona, our sports psychologist, Dr. Don Greene, has each student take a personality test of about 100 questions. He compiles the information on a computer and then personalizes a lesson plan for each student. Our instructors save valuable time because they know which teaching technique is best for each golfer. By using this type of information, they develop a much better teacher-student relationship.

No matter which technique you prefer, the instructor needs to know what it is. How else can the instructor be effective in teaching you something new? The bottom line is that the pro needs to know anything that helps create an accurate picture of you and your game. Don't be shy or embarrassed. Believe me, there's nothing you can say that your instructor hasn't heard before!

Listen up

Now that you've done some talking, make sure that you let the pro reciprocate. Listen to what the pro has to say. After the pro has evaluated both you and your swing, he or she will be able to give you feedback on where you should go from there. Feedback is part of every good lesson. So keep listening. Take notes if you have to.

Don't rate the success or failure of a session on how many balls you hit. You can hit very few shots and have a very productive lesson. It depends on what you need to work on. An instructor may have you repeat a certain swing in an attempt to develop a *swing thought,* or feel. You'll notice when the suggested change is becoming more effective.

Don't do what a lot of people do — don't swing or hit while the pro is talking. Imagine that you're a smart chicken crossing the road: Stop, look, and listen!

Drop your doubts

Take it from me: Five minutes into every lesson, you're going to have doubts. The pro will change something in your swing, grip, or stance, and you'll feel weird. Well, think about this: You *should* feel weird. What you've been doing wrong has become ingrained into your method so that it feels comfortable. Change what's wrong for the better and, of course, it'll feel strange at first. That's normal.

Don't panic. You'll probably get worse before you get better. You're changing things to improve them, not just for the heck of it. So give what you're told to do a proper chance. Changes rarely work in five short minutes. Give them at least a couple of weeks to take effect. More than two weeks is too long; go back for another lesson.

Ten rules to follow while learning

- Find a good teacher and stick with that person.
- Follow a timetable. Discipline yourself to work on what you've been told.
- Concentrate.
- Learn from your mistakes. You'll make them, so you may as well make them work for you.
- Relax. Take your time, and you'll learn and play better.
- Practice the shots you find most difficult.
- Have goals. ***Remember:*** Golf is a target game.
- Stay positive. Golf is hard enough. A bad attitude only hurts you.
- Stop practicing when you get tired. That's when sloppy habits begin.
- Evaluate yourself after each lesson: Are you making progress?

Ask questions

The pro is an expert, and you're paying good money, so take advantage of the pro's knowledge while he or she belongs to you. Don't be afraid of sounding stupid. Again, your question won't be anything the pro hasn't heard a million times before. Besides, what's the point of spending good money on something you don't understand?

The professional is trained to teach, so he or she will know any number of ways to say the same thing. One of those ways will push your particular button. But if you don't tell the pro that you don't get it, the pro won't know. Speak up!

Be cool

Finally, stay calm. Anxious people make lousy pupils. Look on the lesson as the learning experience it is, and don't get too wrapped up in where the balls are going. Again, the pro will be aware of your nervousness. Ask him or her for tips on swinging smoothly. Nervous golfers tend to swing too quickly, so keep your swing smooth. Give yourself time during your swing to make the changes. What's important at this stage is that you make the proper moves in the correct sequence. Get those moves right and understand the order, and good shots are a given.

Other Sources of Golf Info

There's little doubt that the golf swing is the most analyzed move in all of sports. As such, more has been written — and continues to be written — about the golf swing than just about any other athletic move. Take a look in any bookstore under "Golf," and you'll see what I mean. Maybe you have, because you're reading this book. (You made a great choice!)

Golf books that are almost as good as this one

So where should you go for written advice? Lots more books are out there, and some are quite good. But most books, sad to say, are the same old stuff regurgitated over and over. ***Remember:*** There hasn't been any original thought since the 15th century!

Here's another secret: Stay away from many of the books "written" by the top players. There's nothing inherently wrong with the information they impart, but if you think you're going to get some stunning insight into how your favorite plays, think again. In all likelihood, the author has had little to do with the text. Exceptions exist, of course, but the input of the "name" player is often minimal.

Monthly magazine fixes

The best instructional magazines are *Golf Digest, Golf Magazine,* and *Golf Tips.* They're published monthly and owe most of their popularity to their expertise in the instructional field. Indeed, most people buy these magazines because they think that the articles will help them play better. They all do a good job of covering each aspect of the game every month. If you're putting badly, for example, every month you'll find a new tip that you can try. Best of all, these magazines use only the best players and teachers to author their stories. So the information you receive is second to none.

But is the information in golf magazines the best? *Sometimes.* The key is to be careful of what you read and subsequently take to the course. Top teacher Bob Toski once said, "You cannot learn how to play golf from the pages of a magazine." And he's right. Use these publications as backups to your lessons — nothing more. Don't try everything in every issue, or you'll finish up hopelessly confused. Be selective.

Gary's favorite golf-instruction books

An amazing number of books have been written on golf. Historians have tried to track every hook and slice throughout golf's existence. Many have documented the footsteps of the great players throughout their careers.

But instruction is the main vein of golf books nowadays. There are books on every method of golf instruction, from household tools used as teaching aids to scientific data compiled by aliens used on the planet Blothar. (Okay, so the data compiled by aliens is a stretch.)

Anyhow, here are my favorite golf-instruction books, listed alphabetically by author. I've tried to help by reducing the list to my ten favorites, but I know that there are many more that should be included. The material is inexhaustible, so take your time and peruse this golf library with an open mind.

- *How to Play Your Best Golf All the Time* by Tommy Armour (Simon & Schuster, 1953)
- *On Learning Golf* by Percy Boomer (Knopf, 1992)
- *Natural Golf* by John Duncan Dunn (Putnam's, 1931)
- *The Mystery of Golf* by Arnold Haultain (Houghton Mifflin Co., 1908 — and now totally out of print, but still my favorite)
- *Five Lessons: The Modern Fundamentals of Golf* by Ben Hogan (Barnes, 1957)
- *Golf: The Badminton Library* by Horace Hutchinson (Longmans, Green, 1890)
- *Swing the Clubhead* by Ernest Jones (Dodd, Mead, 1952)
- *Down the Fairway* by Robert T. Jones, Jr., and O. B. Keeler (Minton, Balch, 1927)
- *Golf My Way* by Jack Nicklaus (Simon & Schuster, 1974)
- *Harvey Penick's Little Red Book* by Harvey Penick (Simon & Schuster, 1992)

Don't get the idea that I don't like these magazines. I've authored a few instruction pieces for *Golf Digest* over the years myself. But, by definition, these articles are general in nature. They aren't aimed specifically at *your* game. Of course, some of them may happen to work for you. But most won't. You have to be able to filter out those that don't.

Videos and DVDs: Feel the rhythm

Instructional videos and DVDs seem to get more popular every day. Because they can convey movement and rhythm so much better than their print counterparts, they're perfect for visual learners. Indeed, watching a video of a top professional hitting balls before you leave for the course isn't a bad idea. The smoothness and timing in an expert's swing has a way of rubbing off on you.

Gary's favorite golf-instruction videos

A bountiful supply of golf videos and DVDs is on the market. They range from *Dorf on Golf* by Tim Conway to very sophisticated features on the do's and don'ts of your golf swing. Here's a list of my favorites:

- **Fred Couples's *Couples on Tempo:*** Who could tell it better than Freddie for tempo?
- **Ben Crenshaw's *The Art of Putting:*** A must-see for golfers of any caliber.
- ***Nick Faldo's Tips and Drills:*** Faldo shares his secrets about what to do when your swing needs help.
- **David Leadbetter's *Faults and Fixes:*** Pause the video and find your fault and cure.
- ***Leadbetter's Simple Secrets:*** This one provides easy-to-understand explanations.
- **David Leadbetter's *The Full Golf Swing:*** An overview from the master.
- **Gary McCord's *Golf For Dummies* DVD:** How could I resist?
- ***Harvey Penick's Little Red Video:*** The video that was born out of one of the most popular golf books ever written, *Harvey Penick's Little Red Book.*
- ***Harvey Penick's Little Green Video:*** More of the late Harvey Penick's homey style of instruction.
- ***Rick Smith's Range Tips:*** One of the best young swing doctors gives his best prescriptions.
- ***Donna White's Beginning Golf for Women:*** Simple, easy to understand, and well produced.

You can buy golf instruction videos and DVDs at thousands of outlets, including video stores and golf shops, and you can order some of them from the back of your favorite golf magazines.

Instructional gizmos

A quick look at the classified section of any golf magazine will tell you that lots of little instructional gizmos are available. Most aren't very good. Some are okay. And a few are excellent. In Table 3-1, I outline my favorites for you.

Table 3-1 Gary's Favorite Instructional Gizmos

Gizmo	*Function*	*Where to Find It*
A 2-x-4 board	Lies on the ground to aid your alignment.	Hardware store or lumberyard
Balance board	A platform with a balance point in the middle. The only way you can swing and hit the ball is by staying in balance.	Mail order or Internet
Chalk line	A builder's tool used to help your putting stroke. The line is caked in chalk. You snap it to indicate the line you want to the hole.	Hardware store
Flammer	A harness across your chest with an attachment for a shaft in the middle. When you turn as if to swing, you get the feeling of your arms and body turning together because a telescopic rod connects the club to your chest.	Mail order or Internet
Head freezer	Attaches to your cap. You look through a rectangular frame so that you can check the amount your head is moving during your swing/stroke.	Mail order or Internet
Path-Pro	A training aid that helps you hit longer, straighter shots.	Mail order or Internet
Perfect swing trainer	A large, circular ring that helps keep your swing on plane.	Mail order or Internet
Plane Truth	A new putting aid that keeps your stroke consistent.	Mail order or Internet — soon

(continued)

Table 3-1 *(continued)*

Gizmo	*Function*	*Where to Find It*
Putting connector	A device that fits between your arms, keeping them apart and steady during the stroke.	Mail order, Internet, or a few golf shops
Spray paint	A can of paint enables you to spray lines on the ground, which helps with alignment and swing path.	Hardware store
Swing straps	Hook them to your body to keep your arms close to your sides during the swing.	Mail order, Internet, or most golf shops

Chapter 4

Getting Fit for Golf

In This Chapter

- Understanding why physical fitness is important in golf
- Finding a golf-specific fitness-training program for you

Both hands on the club, my body tense in anticipation of flush contact. Eyes preoccupied with a distant stare of the uncertainty of the golf ball's destination. I realize that the swing sequence has begun, and I put all available resources into sending the ball on a wanton mission of distance collection. I sense the fluid nature of Fred Couples's swing, the mass chaos of Tiger Woods's hips as they rotate through the hitting area, the silent stare of John Daly's gallery as they try to interpret what they just saw. I'm awakened from my trance by the dull thud of contact: It hurts, it's sickly, and I hear voices from nearby, questioning my masculinity. Impact has all the compression of a gnat flying into a wall of warm butter. My body is vibrating like a marked-down, used Ford Escort, and I nearly pass out from the physical exertion.

Once I get back on my feet to review the moment and wait for the laughter to die down, I realize that the instrument swinging this club has been totally neglected and is in a state of sad disrepair. My "exercise regimen" up to this point has been to get in a bathtub filled with lukewarm water, pull the drain cord, and then fight the current. It's time to end this madness. I'm going to exercise!

—Fairway Louie, circa 1987, after hitting his opening tee shot in the La Fiesta Restaurant's annual Dos Gringos Alternate (Tequila) Shot Tournament

My expertise in regard to exercise is minimal at best, and the area of physical therapy is beyond my scope of knowledge. Therefore, I would like to introduce you to a friend of mine: Paul Callaway, a licensed physical therapist. I met Paul in 1984 when he was the first Director of Physical Therapy we had for the PGA Tour. On the PGA Tour and senior tour, we have large vans that accommodate physical conditioning apparatuses supervised by physical therapists. This program was started for the betterment of physical conditioning on the tour. Paul is a guy I go to frequently when my senior-tour body heads out of bounds.

Paul created Body Balance for Performance, a complete golf health and fitness-training program. The Illinois Section of the PGA has endorsed his program and techniques. If you'd like more information about this subject, have other questions related to golf health and fitness training, or are interested in locating anofficially licensed Body Balance for Performance center near you, call ProDynamics, Inc. (a division of Callaway Physical Therapy, Ltd., in Oak Brook, Illinois) at 888-348-4653, or refer to the Body Balance for Performance Web page at www.fitgolf.com.

Why So Many New Golfers Give Up

Golf is a trendy thing to do. More than 26 million Americans are now screwing up their lives by playing this game. There will be no sanity left for them after they start playing golf. But then again, for bowling you have to rent shoes, tennis is good if you're 17 years old, and I still don't understand squash, so golf seems like the right thing to do if I've got the rest of my life in which to do it.

This game is very hard, and if you take it too seriously, it frustrates you enough that you'll start wearing your shoes backward. Believe me, I know. . . . Also, any lingering pain you have while playing discounts your ability to play well and sends you to the snack bar to pick up an adult beverage more often than you should. A lot of attrition is going on in golf, for two main reasons, as I see it:

- Frustration from lack of improvement
- Injury

If you're going to have fun playing this game, you have to get your body ready to play golf for a lifetime. So let's get physical.

The purpose of this chapter is to embarrass you into getting into shape so that you can hit a little white ball around 150 acres of green grass without falling down. How tough can that be? I identify five essential elements of golf performance and elaborate on the physical requirements for performing at your best while reducing your risk of getting hurt. The motivation here is to get you out of the chair where you watch the Golf Channel and into a program that helps you feel better, hit the ball farther, and run circles around your kids in front of their friends. Well, the last one may be a stretch, but the other ones are a go.

Five Secrets to Success

Here's a list of five things that you should utilize for good performance in anything you do (yes, anything!):

- **A customized and sport-specific physical training program:** ***Note:*** Beer curls are not considered specific.
- **Professional instruction in your chosen sport:** I personally have an après-ski instructor.
- **Proper mental skills:** Enough said.
- **Training equipment:** Please, no Speedos.
- **Talent to enjoy the sport**

All of these have to be blended into reaching your goal of playing your best. When this process is learned and practiced, it is called *integrated performance enhancement,* or "you da man," as I call it.

If you're going to play on the highest level, you have to have some balance between talent, physical conditioning, mental awareness, instruction, and good ol' perseverance. Simply going out and buying new drivers that are touted to hit the ball 50 yards farther is not going to cut it. ***Remember:*** You have to have proper mental skills; use them in this case. Promise me.

Today's golfers are getting into great physical shape. Gary Player was the first guy on the tour who I saw preaching the benefits of being in good shape. Even as he approached 70 years old, a milestone he reached in November 2005, he could do most things the kids on the regular tour can do, except perhaps catching some big air on a snowboard.

Tiger Woods, Vijay Singh, and other top pros are into rigorous physical-exercise programs that will keep them strong into the later stages of the year, when a lot of players tire from so much wear and tear on the body. Both Tiger and Vijay can hit the ball into the next zip code, and that's not bad for incentive either.

The Keys to Golf Fitness

Now that I've defined the elements of integrated performance enhancement (you da man), take a look at three concepts that are crucial to a good training program.

Structure governs function

This heading, simply put, translates to: Your physical structure affects the way you play this game. If your range of motion is like the Tin Man's, your golf swing will not look very athletic and could actually rust. You need to address problem areas with physical conditioning. It's that simple, so get off your wallet and do something, now!

Here are five areas you can address to help your golf game:

- Balance
- Control
- Flexibility
- Posture
- Strength

If you're deficient in one of these areas, you may develop some bad habits in your golf swing to compensate. Not only will your golf game suffer, but also your body may break down from bad swing mechanics. Fix it now or fix it later; it's your choice.

Several things can cause structural imbalances. Typical factors include inherited body characteristics and the natural aging process. Imbalance can occur over a long period of time from consistent thumping of the golf ball.

Regardless of the causes of your body's structural imbalances, the connective-tissue system in your body, called the *fascial system,* can develop restrictions that compress and/or pull on muscles, tendons, ligaments, nerves, bones, everything. Left uncorrected, these imbalances in your fascial system will leave you in a mangled mess and adversely affect your performance.

You'll start to compensate for these restrictions in your golf swing, and pretty soon your golf game will stink. So go see a health and performance expert who is specifically trained to work with golfers, and cut out the middleman: bad golf.

Physical training improves structure

How can you improve your structure to play better and safer golf? A quick physiology lesson is at hand.

Earlier, I talk about fascia. More specifically, your body's fascial system contributes to your flexibility, mobility, posture, and function. Fascia, or connective tissue, is everywhere; it is the net that holds your body together.

Fascia's main job is to retain your body's normal shape, providing resistance to various stresses. In order to change your body structure and improve your ability to play golf, you benefit most by following a specific sequence of physical training, called "Release, Reeducate, and Rebuild," or, "The Story of Gary McCord's Career":

- **Release:** First, you must release your connective-tissue restrictions. Specially designed flexibility exercises help reduce tension in the inelastic portion of the fascial system that resists lengthening. You must perform these stretching exercises at low intensity but for a prolonged duration. Many people with significant fascial tightness need to sustain a single flexibility exercise for a minimum of three to five minutes before the layers of fascia begin to relax. A gentle, sustained stretching technique is far more effective than a short-duration, intense stretch because it more effectively and permanently lengthens the tough connective tissue of the body.
- **Reeducate:** As the fascial restrictions are being reduced, you need to reeducate your structure by doing specialized exercises aimed at improving posture, balance, stability, and control. These reeducation exercises help you capitalize on your improved flexibility by teaching you how to feel the positions in which your body is most functional. The goal for each golfer is to develop a new postural identity that produces a posture at address and swing mechanics that are safe, efficient, reproducible, and highly effective.
- **Rebuild:** Last, you undergo a program of rebuilding exercises, or strengthening exercises designed to solidify and then reinforce your physical structure and dynamic swing motion. These exercises can also improve your swing speed for added distance and improve muscular endurance for better swing control and performance toward the end of a round and/or during longer practice sessions.

This is a must for you prospective golfers: Enhance your structure and improve your game!

Exercise programs must be golf-specific and, ideally, customized

In order for an exercise program to be most helpful, it must be golf-specific. Warming up by throwing a shot put is not going to help your golf game. Fitness programs for other sports aren't designed around the specific muscles, movement patterns, and physical-performance factors that support the golf swing.

Of equal importance to golf-specific training is customized fitness training. If you start an exercise program that isn't designed around your personal physical weaknesses, isn't tailored to the special demands of golf, and isn't designed to accomplish your personal performance goals, then the chance that the exercise program will help is nil.

Go out and find a specialist to work with and then ask what sort of initial physical performance evaluation will be performed. The specialist will design your program from his or her findings. The elements of the evaluation should include at least the following:

- Health history of past medical problems, pain problems, injuries related to golf, and so on
- Tests to identify postural, structural, or biomechanical imbalances that may interfere with your ability to swing
- Balance assessment
- Muscle and joint flexibility testing
- Muscle strength, endurance, and control testing
- Biomechanical video analysis of the golf swing
- Golf skills evaluation (measurement of current swing and scoring performance potential, including elements of the swing such as clubhead speed and swing path, as well as driving distance, greens and fairways in regulation, handicap, and so on)
- Goals assessment (evaluation of performance goals, purpose for playing golf, and deadlines for reaching goals)

I'm proud of you. Following these steps helps you and your specific golf muscles perform better, and it beats watching *Judge Judy* during the day. Your physical abilities and conditioning will merge, and you'll become a force to be reckoned with out on the links. Enjoy your new outlook on golf!

Tests and Exercises

I'm going to give you the sample "laboratory white mice" tests before the initial performance tests you'll be consulting a specialist for. From these tests, you'll be able to tell how much serious conditioning you need.

Please remember, if you are unable to perform any portion of these simple tests or recommended corrective exercises easily and comfortably, you're not alone. I seized up during most of them! Go about it slowly, and if you can't perform one or the other, stop and turn on *Judge Judy*.

Test 1: Club behind the spine

The club-behind-the-spine test is a very helpful evaluation tool because it can identify several areas of physical weakness and/or imbalance. First, you know that having adequate rotation flexibility in the spine is one of the most essential requirements to performing a good golf swing. The area of the spine from which most rotation should come is the middle section known as the *thoracic spine.* To have maximal flexibility to turn during the swing, you must also have the physical potential to achieve a straighter thoracic spine at address, which is the way you set up to the ball (see Figure 4-1). In contrast, a bent thoracic spine at address blocks your ability to turn (see Figure 4-2). Therefore, one important purpose of this test is to determine your ability to achieve and maintain the ideal, straighter thoracic spine angle at address through adequate chest and middle-spine flexibility.

Figure 4-1: A straight thoracic spine gives you flexibility to turn during your swing.

Figure 4-2: A bent thoracic spine hinders your ability to turn.

In addition, this test measures (to a degree) the muscle strength of your lower abdominals, hips, thighs, middle and upper back, and shoulder blades — all essential to achieving and maintaining proper posture at address. Furthermore, this test can identify tightness in your *hamstring muscles* (the muscles in the backs of your legs).

Perform the club-behind-the-spine test as follows:

1. **Stand upright while holding a golf club behind your back.**
2. **In one hand, hold the head of the club flat against your tailbone. In your other hand, hold the grip of the club against the back of your head. (See Figure 4-3.)**
3. **Bend your hips and knees slightly (10 to 15 degrees) and contract your lower abdominal muscles, as needed, to press the small of your back into the shaft of the club.**
4. **While keeping your lower back in complete contact with the clubshaft, straighten the middle and upper portions of your spine and neck.**

   The goal is to make as much complete contact between the shaft and the entire length of your spine and back of your head as possible. (See Figure 4-4.)

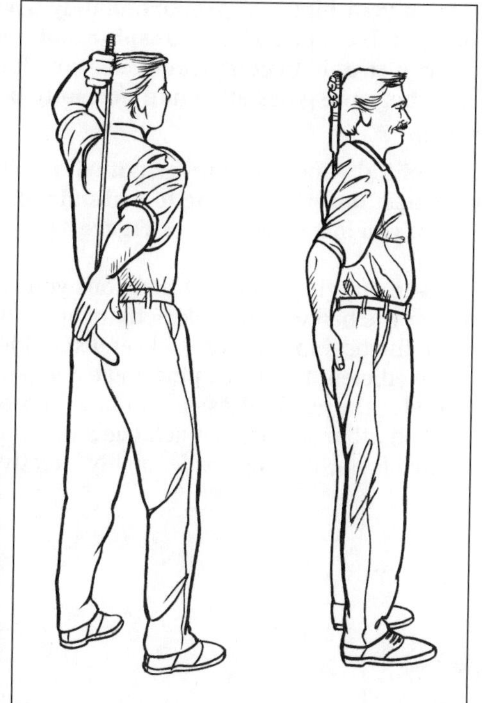

Figure 4-3: The beginning position of the club-behind-the-spine test.

Figure 4-4: Keep as much of your spine and back of your head in contact with the clubshaft as possible.

5. **Try to bend forward from your hips and proportionately from your knees while maintaining club contact with your spine and head. Keep bending forward until you're able to comfortably see a spot on the ground in front of you where the golf ball would normally be at address. (See Figure 4-5.)**
6. **Remove the club from behind your back and grip it with both hands in your normal address position while trying to maintain all the spine, hip, and knee angles that you just created. (See Figure 4-6.)**

If properly executed, the club-behind-the-spine test positions you so that you feel comfortably balanced over the ball with muscle activity appropriately felt in your lower abdominals, thighs, hips, upper back, and shoulder blades. You achieve a straighter, more efficient thoracic-spine angle and a neutral, more powerful pelvic position for the golf address position with proper degrees of hip and knee bend. In other words, you achieve a posture at address with the most potential for producing a safe, highly effective golf swing.

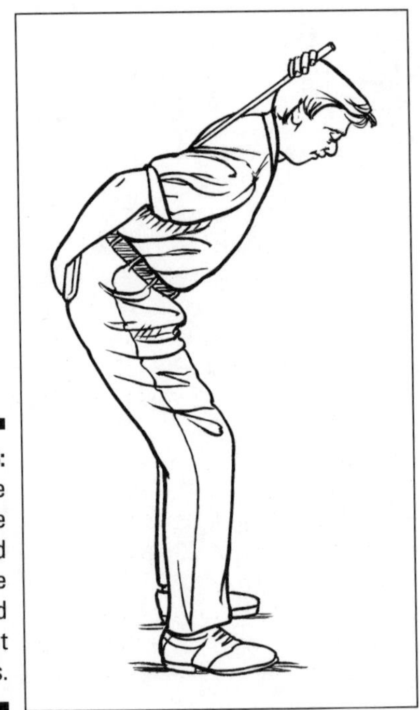

Figure 4-5: Look for the spot on the ground where the ball would be at address.

Figure 4-6: The ideal address position.

If you're unable to achieve the positions of this test easily and comfortably, you may find the next three simple exercises helpful. Nevertheless, please consult your physician before attempting to perform these or any of the other exercises suggested in this chapter. Although these exercises are generally safe for most individuals, if you notice *any* discomfort while performing them, you should stop and consult your physician *immediately* before continuing.

Exercise 1: Recumbent chest-and-spine stretch

The recumbent chest-and-spine stretch can help golfers perform a vital function within the initial phase of any proper exercise progression, called the *releasing phase.* This exercise specifically releases the tightness in your chest, in the front of your shoulders, and in your lower back. After you've mastered this exercise, you should have flexibility to perform the club-behind-the-spine test and, therefore, much better posture at address.

Perform this releasing exercise as follows:

1. **Lie on a firm, flat surface with your hips and knees bent at a 90-degree angle. Rest your lower legs on a chair, couch, or bed, as shown in Figure 4-7.**

   Depending on the degree of tightness in your chest, spine, and shoulders, you may need to begin this exercise on a softer surface (an exercise mat, blankets on the floor, or your bed), and place a small pillow or rolled-up towel under your head and neck to support them in a comfortable, neutral position. You may also need to place a small towel roll under the small of your back to support its arch.

2. **As shown in Figure 4-8, bend your elbows to approximately 90 degrees and position your arms 60 to 80 degrees away from the sides of your body so that you begin to feel a comfortable stretch in the front of your chest and shoulders.**

   This arm position looks a lot like a waiter's arms do when he carries a tray in each hand.

   If you feel any pinching pain in your shoulders, try elevating your arms and resting them on a stack of towels or a small pillow so that your elbows are higher above the floor than your shoulders.

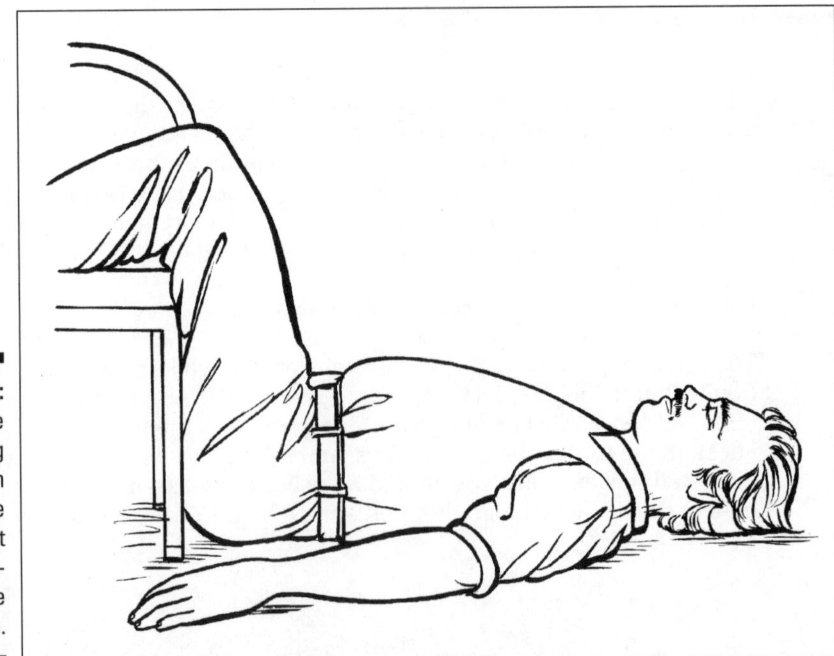

Figure 4-7: The beginning position for the recumbent chest-and-spine stretch.

Figure 4-8: Place your arms like this so that you feel a comfortable stretch.

3. **Relax into this comfortable stretch position for at least three to five minutes or until you experience a *complete* release of the tightness in your chest, front of your shoulders, and lower back.**

   You're trying to get your back, spine, and shoulders completely flat on the floor.

Repeat this exercise daily for five to ten days until you can perform the exercise easily, feeling no lingering tightness in your body.

You may want to increase the degree of stretch in your body by removing any support or padding from under your body and/or arms — or even by adding a small towel roll under the middle portion of your spine (at shoulder-blade level) in a position perpendicular to your spine (see Figure 4-9). Remember *always* to keep the degree of stretch comfortable and to support your head, neck, spine, and arms so that you don't put excessive stress on those structures while you perform this exercise.

Figure 4-9: Place a small, rolled-up towel under the middle of your spine to increase the stretch.

Exercise 2: Recumbent abdominal-and-shoulder-blade squeeze

The recumbent abdominal-and-shoulder-blade squeeze is designed to help reeducate your golf posture and begin rebuilding two key areas of muscle strength necessary for great posture at address: your lower abdominals and your shoulder-blade muscles.

Perform this reeducation and rebuilding exercise as follows:

1. **Assume the same starting position as for the recumbent chest and spine stretch (refer to Figure 4-8).**
2. **Contract the muscles of your lower abdominals and middle and lower shoulder-blade regions so that you can feel the entire length of your spine, neck, and shoulders flattening firmly to the floor.**

   If you're performing this exercise properly, you should feel a comfortable degree of muscle contraction while you maintain a normal, relaxed breathing pattern (see Figure 4-10).

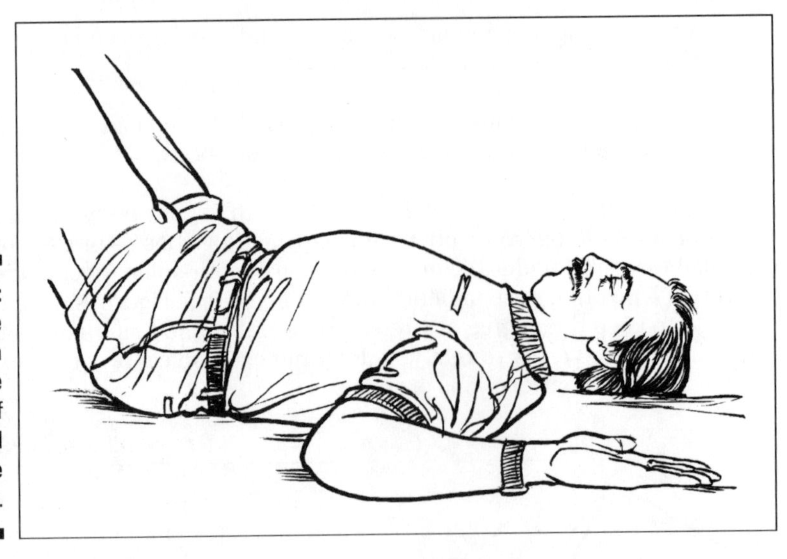

Figure 4-10: Make sure you feel a comfortable degree of stretch and can breathe normally.

3. **Hold this contraction for three to five breaths, relax, and then repeat the exercise.**

Perform this exercise at least once every other day for 2 to 3 weeks, starting with one set of 10 repetitions and building up gradually to one set of 50 repetitions as needed.

Exercise 3: Prone torso lift

To advance the recumbent abdominal-and-shoulder-blade squeeze exercise, you can further challenge your abdominal, spine, and shoulder-blade muscles by trying the prone torso lift. This exercise provides the same golf-specific benefits as the preceding exercise but to a more advanced degree.

Perform this exercise as follows:

1. **Turn over on your stomach, place several large pillows under your body, and place your arms in the double "tray position" with your forehead resting on a towel roll, as shown in Figure 4-11.**

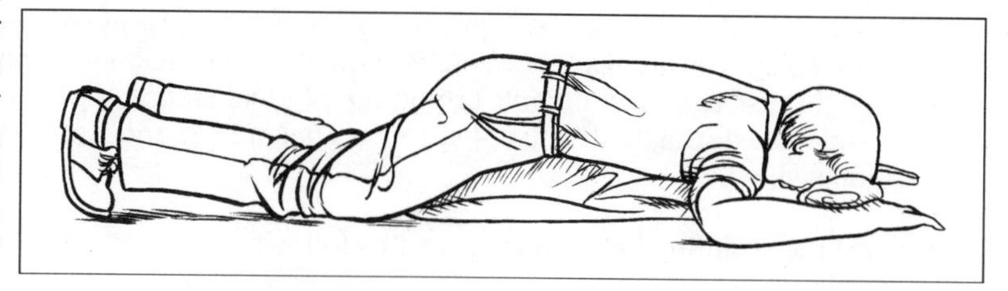

Figure 4-11: Lie on your stomach with your forehead on a towel roll for the prone torso lift.

2. **Perform a pelvic tilt by squeezing your lower abdominal muscles, and rotate your pelvis forward.**
3. **Place your arms in the double "tray position," keeping your neck long and your chin tucked, and lift just your upper torso comfortably off the pillows until you have achieved a straight spine (see Figure 4-12).**

   Be sure to keep your neck tucked in and your lower back flat by contracting your lower abdominal muscles. Also remember to breathe comfortably throughout the exercise. If you perform it properly, you should be able to achieve a lift position such that someone could place a golf club flat along your spine and have virtually no space between your spine and the clubshaft.
4. **Hold the lift for three to five breaths, and then slowly relax and repeat.**

Do this exercise at least every other day for 1 to 2 sets of 8 to 12 repetitions, and for about 2 to 3 weeks or until the exercise becomes very easy.

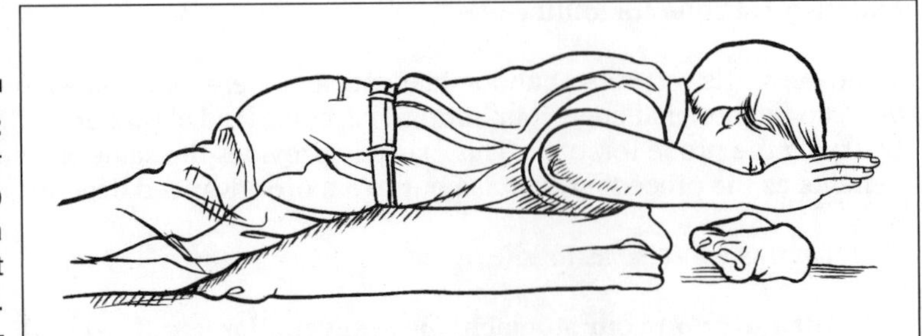

Figure 4-12: Lift your upper torso to achieve a straight spine.

Test 2: Standing balance sway

After posture, the next most important physical characteristic required to make an optimal and consistent golf swing is balance. The purpose of the standing balance-sway test is to help you identify muscle and connective tissue tightness that may be pulling you out of ideal standing posture and balance, thus interfering with your posture and balance at address and during your full swing.

Perform the standing balance-sway test as follows:

1. **Remove your shoes and stand on a level surface with your arms hanging relaxed by your sides.**

   If you've been prescribed customized *orthotics* (arch supports) for your shoes, repeat this test with your orthotics in place and your shoes on.

2. **Close your eyes and gently relax your body so that you can attempt to feel which direction your body would tend to drift, tip, or sway if you let it.**
3. **After 5 to 10 seconds, open your eyes and identify the predominant direction of sway.**
4. **Repeat the test several times to determine whether you have a consistent direction of sway.**

Much like a tent's center pole leaning toward a support wire that has been staked into the ground too tightly, the direction that you consistently feel is the first and/or strongest direction of sway is probably caused by connective tissue and muscle tightness pulling your body in that direction. If left uncorrected, this tightness will also pull you out of posture and balance at address as well as during your swing. Any attempts to correct your swing motion without first reducing the physical causes of your posture and balance dysfunction can lead to inconsistent performance and/or injury.

Exercise 4: Single-leg balance drill

Many exercises can improve your standing balance as a golfer. One simple balance reeducation exercise is called the single-leg balance drill.

Perform this balance reeducation exercise as follows:

1. **Stand on a firm, flat surface in your bare or stocking feet.**

   If you have been prescribed customized *orthotics* (arch supports) for your shoes, repeat this exercise with your orthotics in place and your shoes on.

2. **Place a club behind your spine as though you were trying to perform the club-behind-the-spine test (refer to Figure 4-4).**
3. **With your eyes open, try to stand and balance on your right leg by lifting your left knee to approximately 90 degrees so that your left thigh is parallel to the floor (see Figure 4-13). In this position, do your best to maintain your balance for 10 to 15 seconds.**
4. **Repeat the exercise with your left leg down, lifting your right knee to 90 degrees.**

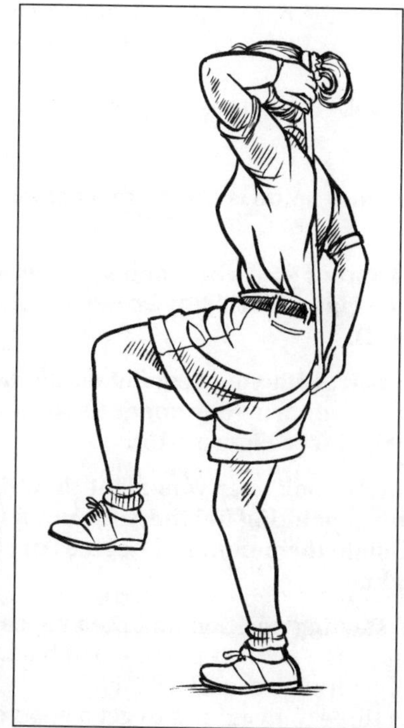

Figure 4-13: Try to balance in this position for 10 to 15 seconds.

Do this exercise 10 to 20 times with each leg at least once each day for 2 to 3 weeks or until you can easily perform the exercise without losing your balance on one foot for 15 seconds.

To increase the difficulty of this exercise and improve your golf balance even more, try the exercise with your *eyes closed!* You can imagine how much more balanced you'll feel over the ball at address and during your full swing when you can master this exercise with your eyes open and then with your eyes closed.

Test 3: Seated trunk rotation

Rotation flexibility in the spine and hips is essential for optimal and safe golf. Without it, you can't make a complete, well-balanced backswing and follow-through. Furthermore, compensations that you'll most certainly make as a result will force biomechanical swing flaws such as reverse pivots, lateral sways, and coming over the top. Compensations from a lack of spine and hip-rotation flexibility can also create stress in other body areas that aren't designed to rotate. If left uncorrected, this physical limitation will eventually spell disaster by causing an injury.

The next two tests can help you evaluate your rotation flexibility in the spine and hips.

The first test is called the seated trunk-rotation test. Perform this test as follows:

1. **Sit forward in a chair so that your spine is not resting against the back of the chair.**
2. **Place a golf club across the front of your chest and shoulders (at the collarbone level) and hold the club securely by crossing both hands in front of you (see Figure 4-14).**
3. **Sit as tall as possible in the chair, with your feet flat on the floor, both knees pointing straight ahead, and turn your upper torso as far as comfortably possible to the right (see Figure 4-15).**
4. **When you've turned completely, look over your right shoulder and see where the end of the club is pointing behind you. Mentally mark the spot on the wall and estimate the number of degrees of rotation that you've turned to the right.**
5. **Slowly return to the neutral starting position and then repeat the trunk-rotation test to the left.**

Repeat this test in both directions three to five times to get a good estimate of the amount of trunk rotation in each direction and which direction you can rotate farther and/or easier.

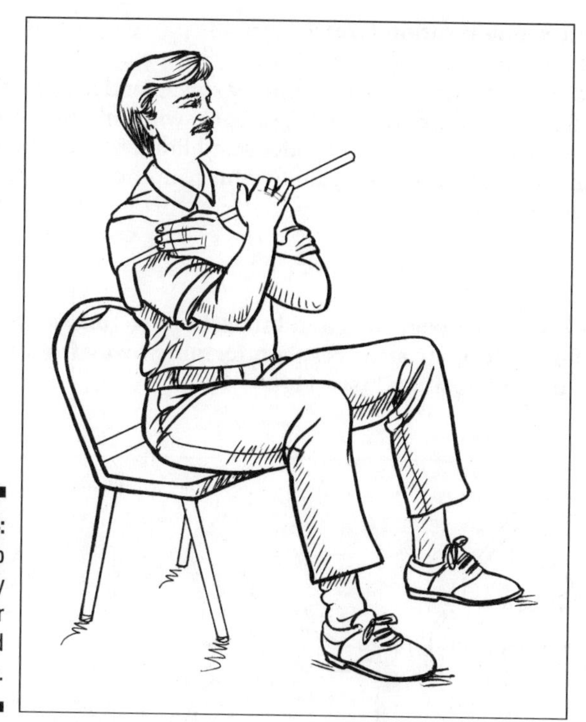

Figure 4-14: Hold a club securely to your chest and shoulders.

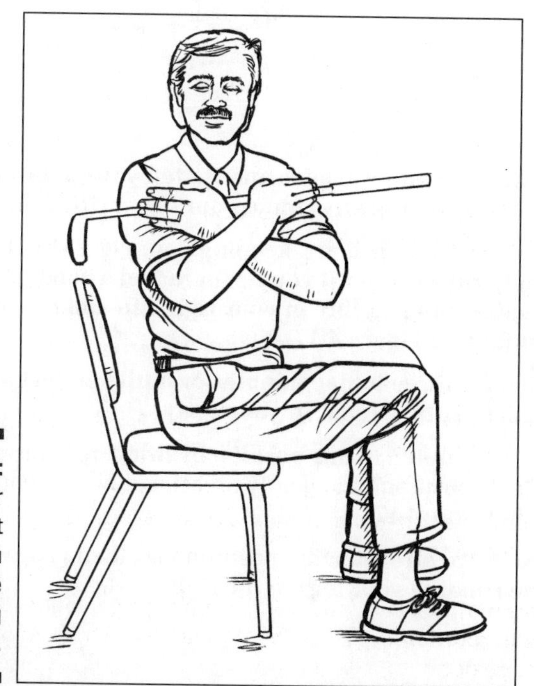

Figure 4-15: Turn as far to the right as you can while remaining comfortable.

Exercise 5: Supine trunk-rotation stretch

The supine trunk rotation stretch is a good releasing exercise to help improve your ability to complete a stress-free backswing and follow-through. If the seated trunk-rotation test (Test #3) identified limitations in one or both directions, this exercise can help you gain flexibility in the proper region of your spine and enable a better turn.

Perform this releasing exercise as follows:

1. **Lie on your back with your hips and knees bent so that your feet are flat on the floor and your arms rest comfortably away from your sides in the double "tray position" (see Figure 4-16).**

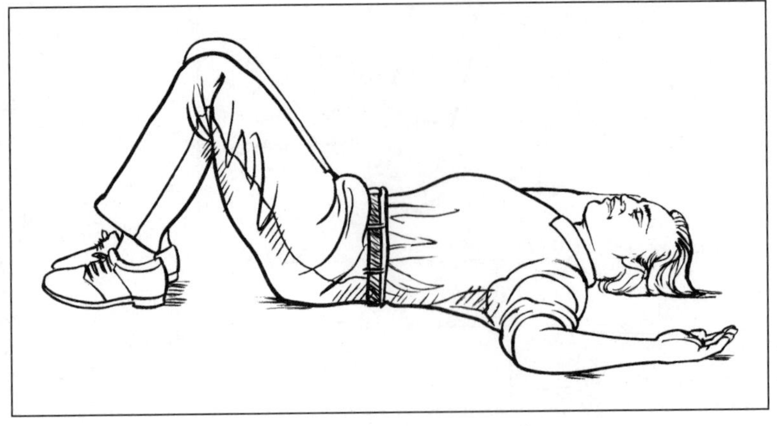

Figure 4-16: Lie on your back with your knees bent and your arms in the double "tray position."

2. **Gently squeeze your shoulder blades and flatten your neck to the floor while you slowly and gently rotate your legs to the left.**
3. **Continue to slowly twist your body, keeping your right shoulder blade and forearm flat to the floor until you begin to feel a comfortable stretch in your spine and possibly in your right hip and the front of your right shoulder (see Figure 4-17).**
4. **Hold this position for three to five minutes or until you feel a *complete* release of the gentle stretch in your body.**

   You can enhance the stretch in this position by bringing your left hand down from the "tray position" and gently pressing down on your right thigh, as shown in Figure 4-17.
5. **Slowly return to the neutral starting position and then repeat the stretch, this time rotating your legs to the right.**

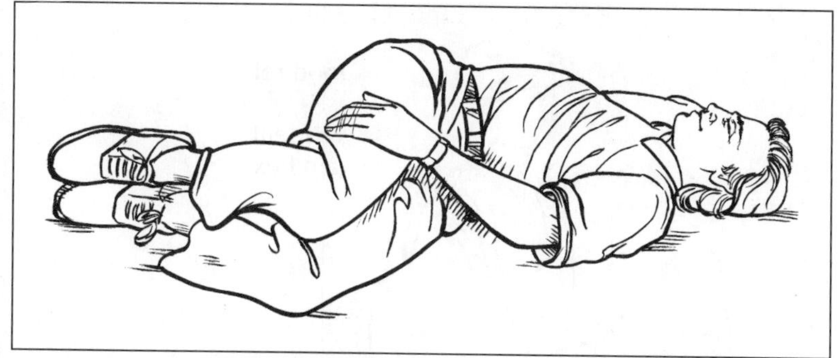

Figure 4-17: Twist your legs to the left until you feel a comfortable stretch.

Practice this releasing exercise at least once a day for two to three weeks until you can stretch equally well in both directions. If your spine was more stiff or limited in rotation when turning to your right during the seated trunk-rotation test, you should spend more time initially rotating your legs to the left. Likewise, if your trunk-rotation flexibility was more limited when turning to your left, then initially rotate your legs to the right in this exercise. Your ultimate goal is *balanced* rotation in both directions.

Test 4: Seated hip rotation

The seated hip-rotation test is designed to measure the relative degree of rotation flexibility in your hips. This test can identify whether you have significant tightness in one or both hips that may be interfering with your ability to rotate your hips during your golf swing. Poor hip rotation is one of the major causes of low back pain for golfers and can cause poor full-swing performance and inconsistency.

Perform the seated hip-rotation test as follows:

1. **Sit forward in a chair so that your spine is not resting against the back of the chair.**
2. **Sit as tall as possible with your spine straight. Cross your right leg over your left knee so that the outer part of your right ankle rests on the top of your left knee (see Figure 4-18).**
3. **Without losing your sitting posture, take both hands and gently apply downward pressure to the top of your right knee until you cannot comfortably push your shin any closer to a position parallel to the floor (see Figure 4-19).**

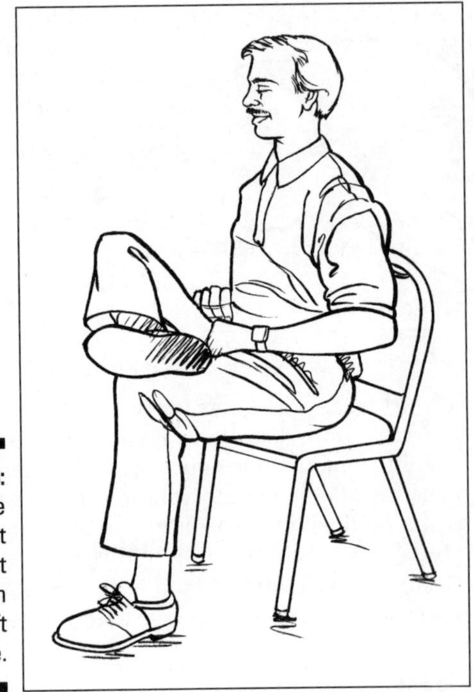

Figure 4-18: Rest the outer part of your right ankle on your left knee.

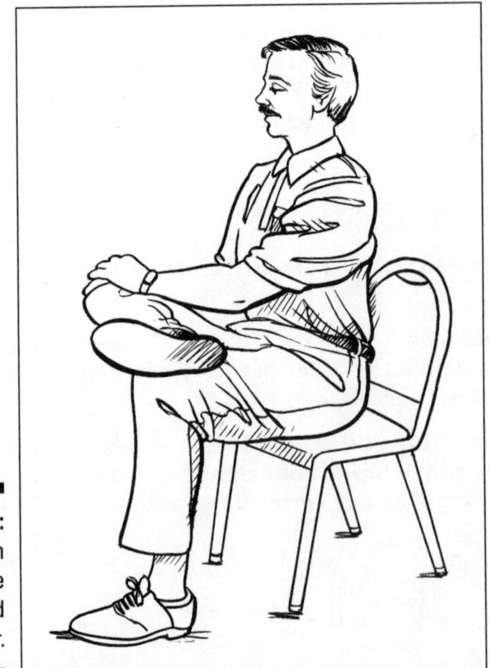

Figure 4-19: Gently push your knee toward the floor.

4. **When you've reached the limit of stretch for your right hip, observe your relative difficulty in achieving this position, the specific location and degree of tightness in your body, and the relative angle of your right shin in relation to the floor.**
5. **Slowly release your right knee and repeat the test with your left ankle resting on your right knee.**
6. **Compare the results of testing both hips and determine whether one or both hips have rotation-flexibility limitations.**

Exercise 6: Supine hip-rotation stretch

The supine hip-rotation stretch is a safe and effective exercise to help you reduce hip-rotation tightness and, therefore, improve your ability to make a full turn around your hips during a full golf swing.

Perform this releasing exercise as follows:

1. **Lie on your back close to a wall. Place both feet on the wall so that your hips and knees are bent about 90 degrees. (See Figure 4-20.)**
2. **Cross your right foot over your left knee and rest both hands on your right knee.**

Figure 4-20: Put your feet against a wall with your knees bent at a 90-degree angle.

3. **Gently apply pressure to your right knee with your hands in a direction down and away from your right shoulder (see Figure 4-21) until you feel a light, comfortable stretch in the outer portion of your right hip and/or groin.**
4. **Hold this stretch for three to five minutes or until you feel a complete release of the original stretch in your right hip.**
5. **After the stretch is complete, slowly release the pressure on your right knee and repeat the stretch on your left hip.**

Practice this releasing exercise at least once a day for two to three weeks or until you can stretch equally well in both hips. If you found one hip to be tighter than the other during the seated hip-rotation stretch, then initially spend more time stretching the tighter hip. Your ultimate goal is *balanced rotation* for both hips. Only by achieving complete and balanced hip-rotation flexibility can you accomplish a full backswing and follow-through with each and every swing.

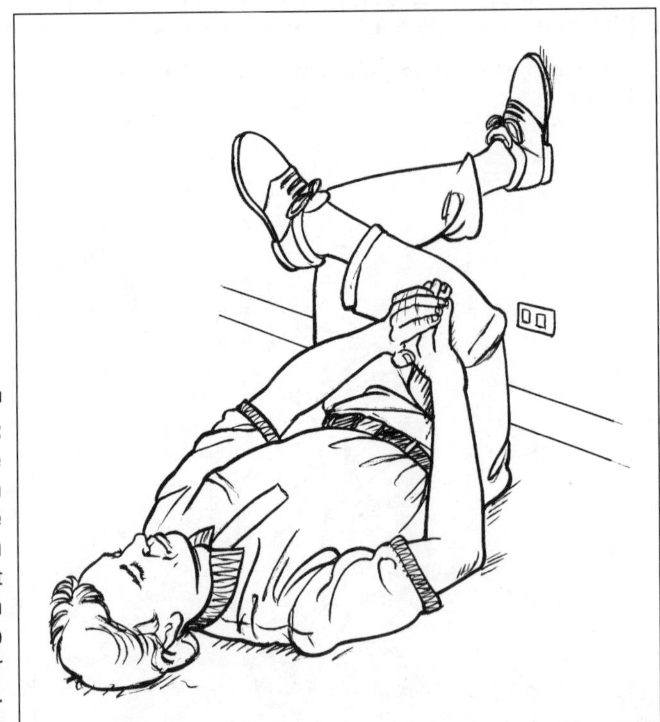

Figure 4-21: Put gentle pressure on your knee until you feel a light stretch in your hip and/or groin.

After you're balanced, you can advance this stretch simply by moving your body closer to the wall at the start. This allows your hips and knees to bend at an angle greater than 90 degrees, for a greater degree of stretch in your hips.

Chapter 5

Where to Play and Who to Play With

In This Chapter

- Practicing at driving ranges
- Reserving tee times on public courses
- Fitting in at country clubs and golf resorts
- Blending into a golf foursome
- Surviving a round with a jerk

Golf is played in three places: at public facilities, at private clubs, and on resort courses. In this chapter, I tell you the basics about all three, from the scuzziest range to the fanciest country club. I also share tips on how to fit in wherever you play — how to walk, talk, tip, practice and accessorize like a *real* golfer. I even tell you how to make the best of a round with a jerk. There aren't many jerks in golf, but you've gotta be ready for anything.

Let's start with the basics: Where in the world can you play this game?

Some courses have only 9 holes, while a few resorts offer half a dozen 18-hole courses, or even more. At the famous Pinehurst Resort in North Carolina, you'll find eight great 18-hole layouts — that's 144 chances to drive yourself nuts!

You can also hit balls at driving ranges, which is where you should start. If you rush to the nearest course for your first try at golf, tee off, and then spend most of the next few hours missing the ball, you won't be very popular with your fellow golfers. Believe me, instead of watching you move large clumps of earth with every swing, they'd prefer to enjoy a cool beverage in the clubhouse.

Driving Ranges

Driving ranges are fun. You can make all the mistakes you want. You can miss the ball, slice it, duff it, top it — do anything. The only people who'll know are the ones next to you, and they're probably making the same mistakes.

Driving ranges are basically large fields, stretching as far as 500 yards in length — which means, of course, that even long hitters like Tiger Woods and John Daly can "let the shaft out" and swing for the fences. But you don't have to hit your driver. Any good driving range will have signs marking off 50 yards, 100 yards, 150 yards, and so on. You can practice hitting to these targets with any club.

Some driving ranges will lend or rent you clubs, but most expect you to bring your own. As for balls, you purchase bucketsful for a few dollars — how *many* dollars depends on where you are. In some parts of the United States, you can still hit a nice big bucket of balls for a dollar. But on weekends at Chelsea Piers Golf Club in New York City, it's a lot more: up to 20 times as much. (At least you get a great view of New Jersey. . . .)

Public Courses

As you'd expect from their name, public courses are open to anyone who can afford the greens fee. They tend to be busy, especially on weekends and holidays. At premier public courses like Bethpage Black, the site of the 2002 U.S. Open, some golfers sleep in their cars overnight so they'll be first in line for a tee time the next morning. Sleeping in a car may not sound like much fun, but I'm told it's a great bonding experience.

Tee-time policies

Each course has its own tee-time policy. Many let you book a time up to a week in advance. Others follow a strange rule: You must show up at a designated time midweek to sign up for weekend play. And some courses you can't book at all. You just show up and take your chance (hence, the overnight gang sleeping in their cars). My advice is simple: Phone ahead and find out the policy at the course you want to play.

Okay, I'll assume that you've jumped through whatever hoops are necessary and you know when you're supposed to play. So you pull into the parking lot about an hour before your tee time. What next? Most courses have a clubhouse. You may want to stop inside to change clothes, and maybe buy something to eat or drink.

By all means, make use of the clubhouse, but don't change your shoes in there. If you're already dressed to hit the greens, put on your golf shoes in the parking lot. Then throw your street shoes into the trunk. Don't worry about looking goofy as you lace those spikes with your foot on the car bumper. Everyone does it!

I'm here! Now what?

The first thing to do at the clubhouse is to confirm your time with the pro or starter, and then pay for your round. The pro is sure to be in one of two places: teaching on the practice range or hanging out in the pro shop. If the pro doesn't take the money, the starter adjacent to the first tee usually will. As for cost, the price depends on the course and its location. You can pay anything from $10 to more than $150. At gorgeous Pebble Beach Golf Links in California, the greens fee is more than $400!

After the financial formalities are out of the way, hit some balls on the driving range to warm up those creaky joints of yours.

Your practice sessions may not be as long as mine, but then you're not trying to figure out how to beat Hale Irwin on the Champions Tour!

Here's what I do when I'm playing in a pro event: I get to the course one hour before my starting time. I go to the putting green and practice short shots — chip shots and short pitches. (Chapter 9 covers these shots in detail.) This gives me an idea how fast the greens are and slowly loosens me up for full-swing shots.

Make sure that you're allowed to pitch to the practice green on your course — some courses prohibit it.

Then I wander over to the practice tee and loosen up with some of the exercises that I describe in Part II. Start with the wedges and work your way up to the driver.

Next, I hit my 3-wood (some players call this titanium club the *3-metal* — a more accurate term, but it clangs in my ears). Then I proceed to bomb the driver. (If John Daly is next to me, I quietly wait for him to finish, and *then* I hit my driver.) Immediately after hitting practice drives — ten balls at most — I hit some short sand-wedge shots to slow down my metabolism.

I visit the putting green next, usually 15 minutes before I tee off. (See Chapter 8 for more about putting.) I start with simple 2- to 3-foot putts straight up a hill, to build my confidence. Then I proceed to very long putts — aiming not for the hole, but for the far fringe of the green. I do this because I don't want to become target-conscious on long putts. Putting the ball to the fringe lets me work on speed. It's the last thing I do before going to the tee. (Well, if it's a big tournament and my knees are shaking, I'll make a detour to the restroom.)

Country Clubs

In your early days as a golfer, you probably won't play much at country clubs. But if you *do* play at a country club, don't panic. You're still playing golf; it's just that the "goal posts" have been shifted slightly.

To avoid committing any social faux pas, remember a few formalities:

- **Before you leave home, make sure you're wearing the right clothes.** A sweat shirt announcing you as an avid follower of the Chicago Bulls or those cool (in your mind, anyway) cutoff jeans won't work in this environment. Wear a shirt with a collar and, if shorts are allowed, go for the tailored variety that stops just short of your knees. Short shorts are a no-no at most country clubs. In the fall and winter, slacks are acceptable for women. In the summer, shorts cut just above the knees are fine.
- **Get good directions to your destination.** It won't do your heart rate or your golf game any good to have a stressful journey full of wrong turns.
- **Time your arrival so that you have just an hour to spare before you tee off.** When you drive your car up the road toward the clubhouse, don't make the simple mistake of turning sharply into the parking lot. Go right up to the clubhouse. Look for a sign that reads "BAG DROP." A person will no doubt be waiting to greet you. Acknowledge his cheery hello as if this is something you do every day. Tell him who you're playing with — your host. Then get out of your car, pop the trunk, remove your spikes and hand him your keys. Tip him a few bucks (or a $5 bill at a fancy club like Trump International), and stroll into the clubhouse.

  Don't worry about your car or your clubs. The car will be parked for you, and the clubs will either be loaded onto a cart or handed to a caddie.
- **When you're inside the clubhouse, head for the locker room.** Drop your street shoes off next to your host's locker and then ask for directions to the bar, or to wherever your host is waiting. Don't offer to buy your host a drink. First, he or she is the host. And second, you probably won't be able to buy anything anyway. Your host will most likely sign the tab and be billed at the end of the month. (The only place where your cash/plastic will be accepted is the pro shop. The pro will sell you anything, but take my advice: Skip the purchase of that neat-looking shirt with the club logo on it. Every time you wear it, people will assume you're a member there. The questions will soon get old.)
- **If you have a caddie, remember that he or she is there to help you.** Trust your caddie's advice — he or she knows the course better than you do. Caddie fees at fancy clubs average about $50, which is added to your greens fee. You should tip your caddie half the caddie fee at the end of the round, so that's another $25. (Savvy golfers sometimes tip the caddie master before a round — slipping him a $10 bill can get you the best caddie he's got.)

- **On the course, be yourself.** And don't worry about shooting the best round of golf you've ever played. Your host won't expect that. Even if you happen to play badly, he won't be too bothered as long as you look as if you're having fun and keep trying. Just don't complain or make excuses. Nobody likes a whiner.
- **After your round, your clubs will probably disappear again — but don't worry: They'll be waiting at the bag drop when you finish your refreshing post-round beverage.** Don't forget to tip the bag handlers. Again, a few bucks is usually fine, but be generous if your clubs have been cleaned.
- **When you change back into your street shoes, you'll often find them newly polished — that means another few dollars to tip the locker-room attendant.** And when you leave, your golf shoes will have been done, too. Aren't country clubs grand?
- **One more tip to go: Give a few bucks to the person who delivers your car back to you and loads your clubs into the trunk.**

Resort Courses

You're on vacation, and you're dying to play golf. Where to go? To a resort course, of course. Some of my favorites are Kapalua Resort (Maui, Hawaii), Doral Golf Resort & Spa (Miami, Florida), and Sea Pines Resort (Hilton Head Island, South Carolina).

The great thing about resort courses is that you don't have to be a member or even have one in tow. The only problem arises when you aren't staying in the right place. Some courses are for certain hotel guests only. And again, prices vary, depending on the course and its location. Generally, though, resort courses cost a good deal more than public courses.

Phone ahead of time to find out when you can play.

Resort courses are a lot like public courses, but some have bag handlers and other employees who expect you to tip them. Tip as you would at a private club.

You'll probably have to rent a cart, too. Carts are mandatory at almost every resort golf course in the world. So enjoy the ride! You'll drive to your drive, then hop back behind the wheel and putt-putt to your putt.

How to Fit in on the Course

It starts at the first tee. I cover the gambling aspect of this initial get-together in Chapter 15, but you should know some other things as well.

If you're playing with friends, you don't need any help from me. You know them, and they know you. You should be able to come up with a game by yourselves. And you'll be able to say anything to them, with no risk of offending anyone.

That's not the case if you show up looking for a game. Say you're at a public course and you've asked the starter to squeeze you in (a few bucks will usually get you going sooner rather than later). Tell the starter your skill level, and be honest. If you're a beginner, you don't want to be teaming up with three low-handicap players. Forget all that stuff about how the handicap system allows anyone to play with anyone. That propaganda doesn't take human nature into account.

Golf, like life, has its share of snobs. And some of the worst are single-digit handicappers. Most of them have no interest in playing with you, a mere beginner. They might say they do, but they're lying. They see 18 holes with someone who can't break 100 as four to five hours of torture. The same is true on the PGA Tour. Some pros genuinely enjoy the Wednesday Pro-Ams — Mark O'Meara comes to mind — but many would gladly skip them if they could. (They can't, because the tour *requires* pros to show up for pro-ams.) The only upside from their point of view is that it represents a practice round of sorts. Now that may seem like a rotten attitude, but it's a fact of golfing life. No one will actually *say* anything to you (golf pros are generally much too polite), but the attitude is there. Get used to it.

Maybe I'm being a little harsh, but it's a fact that golfers are more comfortable playing with their "own kind." Watch a few groups play off the first tee, and you'll soon spot a trend. Almost every foursome consists of four players of relatively equal ability. There's a reason for that. Make that two reasons: No one wants to be the weak link in the chain. And no one wants to play with "those hackers who can't keep up."

So let's say you're paired with Gary, Jack, and Arnold. Introduce yourself calmly but quickly. Tell them what you normally shoot, if and when they ask, and make it clear that you're a relatively new golfer. This fact is impossible to conceal, so don't try. They'll know within a couple of holes anyway. But don't volunteer any further information. Save that for during the round. Besides, you'll find that most golfers are selfish — they really don't care about your game. They'll make polite noises after your shots, but that's the extent of their interest. You'll soon be that way, too. There is nothing — *nothing* — more boring than listening to tales about someone else's round or game. Of course, boring your buddies that way is part of the social order of this game. Golf stories are endless, and most are embellished, but they promote the bonding done over beers in the clubhouse bar, which is also called the *19th hole.*

Beginners sometimes do things that mark them as misfits on the course. Avoid these blunders at all costs:

- **Don't carry one of those telescoping ball retrievers in your bag.** It suggests that you're planning to hit balls in the water.
- **Don't wear your golf cap backward.** Ever. No exceptions.
- **Don't do stretching exercises on the first tee.** Find a place a few yards away, where it won't look like you're auditioning for Richard Simmons.
- **Don't dawdle when it's your turn to hit!**

When You're the Worst in Your Group

Early in your golfing existence, almost everyone is better than you. So, chances are, you're going to be in a foursome in which you're the worst player. What do you do? This section gives you some tips for getting from the first hole to that cool beverage at the 19th.

Pick it up!

The worst thing you can do is delay play. After you've hit the ball, oh, ten times on a given hole, pick it up and quit that hole as a courtesy to your playing partners. There's always the next hole.

When you're actually scoring a game, you're required to finish out every hole — that is, you must post a score for each hole. But beginners should feel free to skip that technicality. While you're learning, don't worry about scores.

Find your own ball

This comes under the "don't delay" heading. If you happen to hit a shot into the highest spinach patch on the course, don't let your companions help you look for it. Tell them to play on, and you'll catch up after a "quick look." They'll see you as someone who, though having a bad day, would be worth playing with again. (If you don't find the ball within a couple of minutes, declare it lost and don't score that hole.)

Never moan

Don't be a pain in the you-know-what. Most golfers gripe and moan when they're playing poorly. That's bad — and boring for the other players, who don't want to hear about your woes. All they care about is the fact that you're slowing things up. So grit your teeth and keep moving.

Never analyze your swing

Here's another common trap: You hit a few bad shots — okay, more than a few. Then you start analyzing what you're doing wrong. Stuff like, "Maybe if I just turn a little more through the ball. . . ." This is the *last* thing your playing partners want to hear. I repeat: *They don't care about your game.* So don't analyze, and don't ask them for swing tips. If one is offered, try it, but keep it quiet.

When You're Not the Worst

Then there's the other side of the coin. How do you behave when another golfer in your group can't get the ball above shin height? Here are some pointers:

- **Zip that lip.** Whatever you do, don't try to encourage your pal as his or her game implodes. After a while, you'll run out of things to say. And your friend will be annoyed with you.
- **Never give advice or swing tips to the other player.** You'll only be blamed for the next bad shot he or she hits.
- **Talk about other stuff.** The last thing you should discuss is your pal's awful game. Find some common interest and chat about that. Try football, movies, or the stock market. Even politics and religion are safer topics than that 20-yard drive your friend just dribbled off the tee.

Jerk Management

Most golfers are princes — tall, smart and handsome (with or without handlebar mustaches). The game not only *tests* character, it *builds* character. I'm willing to bet there are fewer louts and scoundrels in golf than in any other major sport. But with more than 25 million American golfers out there, you're bound to encounter a few bad apples. Here's how to have a good day anyway.

Who not to play with

As I mention earlier, most foursomes are made up of players of roughly equal ability. That's what you want. In fact, the best possible scenario is to find three golfers who are just a little bit better than you. By trying to keep up with them, you'll probably improve your usual game.

Those are the sorts of people you *should* be playing with. The people you *shouldn't* be playing with are those who play a "different game." That means anyone who shoots more than 20 shots less than you on an average day. All someone like that will do is depress you, and your slower, less-expert play may irritate him or her. Such a situation can bring out the jerk in both of you. So stay away from the best golfers at your course — at least for now. When you get better, playing with them will help you improve.

How to survive

Sometimes you can't help it — you're stuck with a loud, cursing lunkhead who talks during your swing, jabbers on his or her cell phone, and gives everyone unsolicited advice. How to deal?

- **At first, ignore the jerk.** It's a beautiful day, and you're out on the course playing the best game in the world. Play your game and be glad you'll only be spending a few hours with Golfzilla. If the jerk's behavior annoys the other members of your group, let them be first to call him or her on it.
- **If the jerk keeps it up, speak up.** Say, "You walked on my putting line — please don't." Or, "You're distracting me by talking on your cell phone." Being firm but polite often works with jerks.
- **Treat the jerk as a hazard.** If all else fails, think of Golfzilla the way you think of a strong wind or a lousy lie in a bunker. Golf is all about dealing with adversity. If you can keep your head and make a good swing despite the jerk, you'll be a tougher, better golfer tomorrow.

Part II

You Ain't Got a Thing If You Ain't Got That Swing

In this part . . .

How can something that takes only slightly over 1 second to perform — the golf swing — be so complicated to learn? Do you need to go back to school and study theoretical physics? No. Just enroll here, and I'll make it easy for you.

This part shows you how to swing a golf club without falling down. I show you how to build your swing and then how to do everything from knocking your drive off the opening tee to brushing that 3-foot putt into the 18th hole for your par.

Chapter 6

Getting into the Swing of Things

In This Chapter

- Understanding the importance of balance
- Understanding different sorts of swings
- Getting into position
- Mastering your swing
- Swinging from head to toe

What is a golf swing? That's a very good question, one that has different answers for different people. For most people, a golf swing means "nonsequential body parts moving in an undignified manner."

In simple terms, though, a golf swing is a (hopefully) coordinated, balanced movement of the whole body around a fixed pivot point. If done correctly, this motion swings an implement of destruction (the club) up, around, and down so that it hits a ball with an accelerating blow on the center of the clubface.

I'm starting to feel dizzy. How about you?

It All Starts with Balance

Balance is the key to this whole swinging process. You cannot hit the ball with consistency if at any time during your swing, you fall over. In contrast, when your swing consists of a simple pivot around a fixed point, the clubhead strikes the ball on the same downward path and somewhere near the center of the clubface every time. Bingo!

You're probably wondering where this fixed point in your body is. Well, it isn't your head. One great golf myth is that you must keep your head perfectly still throughout the swing, which is very hard to do. I don't advise keeping your head still . . . unless your hat doesn't fit.

The fixed point in your golf swing should be between your collarbones and about 3 inches below them, as shown in Figure 6-1. You should turn and swing around that point. If you get that pivot point correct, your head will swivel a little bit as you turn back and then through on your shots. If your head appears to move like Linda Blair's did in *The Exorcist,* you've got it wrong.

Figure 6-1: What *doesn't* move in your golf swing.

Different Strokes for Different Folks

You can swing the golf club effectively in many ways. For example, there are long swings and short swings. Imagine that you backed into a giant clock. Your head is just below the center of the clock. If at the top of your swing your hands are at 9 o'clock and the clubhead is at 3 o'clock, you're in the standard position for the top of your backswing. The shaft is parallel to the ground.

At the top of John Daly's swing, which is a long swing, his hands are at 12 o'clock, and the clubhead is approaching 5 o'clock. (Does your chiropractor have a toll-free number?) Other swings have a shorter arc. John Cook succeeded on the PGA Tour with a short swing. His hands only go to 8 o'clock, and the clubhead goes to 1 o'clock. Adam Scott stops short of parallel because he feels that his swing gets too loose if he goes farther. Physical constraints dictate the fullness and length of your swing; the distance the club travels is unimportant.

Golf swings differ in other ways, too.

- Some players swing the club more around their bodies — the way you'd swing a baseball bat.
- Others place more emphasis on the role of their hands and arms in the generation of clubhead speed.
- Still others place that same emphasis on turning the body.

Physique and flexibility play a major role in how you swing a golf club. If you're short, you'll have a flatter swing — more around your body — because your back is closer to perpendicular at *address* (the motionless position as you stand ready to hit the ball). If you're tall, you must either use longer clubs or bend more from the waist at address so that your swing is more upright. Most tall players develop upright swings.

The left arm always swings about 90 degrees to the angle of the spine. Stand straight up and put your left arm straight out, away from your body. Now start bending at the waist. See how your arm lowers? It's staying 90 degrees to your back as you bend down. I wish I'd taken more geometry in school!

Flight School

Although you can swing a golf club in many ways, all good swings have a few common denominators. But before I get to that, I want to break down the factors of flight:

- First, you want to hit the ball.
- Second, you want to get the ball up in the air and moving forward.
- Third, you want to hit the ball a long way.
- Fourth, you want to hit the ball a long way while your friends are watching.
- And last, you become obsessed, just like the rest of us.

Hitting the ball

You would think hitting the ball would be easy. But golf isn't tennis or baseball, where you can react to a moving ball. In golf, the ball just sits there and stares at you, beckoning you to make it go somewhere.

Here's your first thought: "I won't turn my body too much; I'll just hit the thing with my hands." That's natural — and wrong. You're worried about losing sight of the ball in your backswing and hitting nothing but air. You're not alone. We've all been through this sweat-drenched nightmare of flailing failure. But don't worry. You will evolve! You will make contact!

Getting the ball airborne

Okay, after a few fairly fruitless attempts, you're finally hitting more ball than air in your search for flight. Now you need a lesson in the aerodynamics of the game. The only time you want the golf ball to be on the ground is when you're close to the hole. To have any kind of fun the rest of the time, you want air under the ball; you need the ball to fly! Then you can stare with horrified fascination at the ridiculous places the ball ends up, which is the essence of the game.

One of my *Golf For Dummies* secrets is that the only time you should lift something is when you rearrange your living-room furniture. *Never* try to lift a golf ball with your club. You should hit down with every club except the driver and the putter, as shown in Figure 6-2. And when you do hit down, don't duck or lunge at the ball; hit *down* but keep your head *up*.

When you use your driver, the ball is set on a tee about an inch above the ground; if you hit down, the ball will fly off the top edge of the club and the shot will be high and short — not my favorite combination! With the driver, you want the clubhead coming into the ball from a horizontal path, moving slightly up at impact.

When you putt, you don't want the ball airborne. A putter is designed to roll the ball along the ground, not produce a high shot. So you need to foster more of a horizontal hit with that club. (See Chapter 8 for information on putting.)

Figure 6-2: Hit down on all clubs except the driver and putter.

If the club in your hands is a fairway wood or an iron, hit down.

Generating power

As soon as the ball is in the air, your ego kicks in. Power with a capital *P* becomes your concern. Power intoxicates your mind. Power makes legends out of mere mortals. Power makes you want to get a tattoo. Power also sends the ball to the far corners of your little green world if you don't harness it.

Some professional golfers can create as much as 4½ horsepower in their swings. That's some kind of giddy-up. The ball leaves their drivers at speeds of more than 150 mph. This power comes from a blending of the body twisting around a slightly moving pivot point with a swinging of the arms and hands up and around on the backswing, and then down and around in the forward swing. All of which occurs in the space of about a second!

The key to optimum power is to try to turn your back to the target on your backswing (see Figure 6-3), which involves another *Golf For Dummies* must-do: On the backswing, turn your left shoulder under your chin until your shoulder is over your right foot. Make sure that you turn your shoulders far enough. Don't just raise your arms. Turning your shoulders ensures that you have power for the forward move. Turn for power. The unwinding of the hips and the shoulders on the downswing creates the power surge.

More power for women!

I've seen plenty of female golfers with tremendous power — women from Mickey Wright to Laura Davies to Michelle Wie. But for the most part, female golfers struggle to generate power. The average woman simply doesn't have the same upper-body, forearm, and wrist strength as a man. Much to her dismay, she finds it physically impossible to drive the ball 300 yards.

By doing a few simple strengthening and conditioning exercises (see Chapter 4), female golfers — or golfers at any level — can strengthen their upper bodies, wrists, and forearms enough to boost the power in their swings.

Here's one simple exercise that improves wrist strength — and you can do it almost anywhere. Take a tennis ball in your hand and squeeze until it hurts. Then switch hands and do the same thing. You don't have to give yourself carpal tunnel syndrome — just repeat this exercise for at least five minutes with each hand. You'll notice gradual improvement in your wrist and forearm strength, which will help you avoid wrist injury and arm fatigue — and will add yards to your drives.

Figure 6-3: At the top of the backswing.

The same swing principles apply for women. However, to build momentum and swing speed, ladies generally rely less on muscle and more on a longer backswing. A long backswing allows complete rotation in the left shoulder, which enables the left arm to extend fully and cocks the wrist to help release power.

Building Your Swing

To become a golfer, you must master the building blocks of your swing. How do you hold on to the club so that you can give the ball a good whack? After you have a good grip, how do you align yourself to the target so that the ball goes somewhere near where you aimed? What should your posture look like? How much knee flex should you have, and where in the world should the ball be placed in your stance? Should you look at the ball or somewhere near the sun? This section has the answers.

For natural left-handers, perfecting the golf swing can be tricky. In the past, not many clubs were designed for the lefty, and most course designs put left-handed golfers at a disadvantage. As a result, many lefties were taught to play right-handed. Today, however, technology has advanced to the point where lefties have little trouble finding clubs.

Whether you swing left-handed or right-handed, it basically all comes down to which side has the stronger, most natural-feeling swing. To find out what works best for you, try swinging the club like a baseball bat from each side (keeping a safe distance from all breakable objects and small children). The muscles used in swinging a bat are similar to those used in a golf swing. Which reminds me of what Sam Snead said when a baseball slugger told him that hitting a baseball was harder than playing golf. “Maybe,” said Sam, “but I have to play my foul balls.”

Of course, you may have trouble hitting straight shots on the golf course. If so, you can always blame the equipment. That’s what I do.

The grip

Although the grip is one of the most important parts of the game, it’s also one of the most boring. Few golfers who’ve played for any length of time pay much attention to hand placement. For one thing, your grip is hard to change after you get used to the way your hands feel on the club. For another, hand placement simply doesn’t seem as important as the swing itself. That kind of neglect and laziness is why you see so many bad grips — particularly among bad players.

Get your grip correct and close to orthodox at the beginning of your golfing career. You can fake just about anything, but a bad grip follows you to the grave.

Women tend to have smaller hands than men, so for them, it's important to have the right grip size on the club. Another tip for ladies is to use the closed-face grip position, which can help square the clubface during the swing.

Here's how to sleep well in eternity with the correct grip. Standing upright, let your arms hang naturally by your side. Get someone to place a club in your left hand. All you do now is grab the club and — *voilà!* — you've got your left-hand grip. Well, almost. The grip has three checkpoints:

1. **Place your left thumb and left index finger on the shaft.**

   I like to see a gap of about ¾ inch between the thumb and index finger. To get that gap, extend your thumb down the shaft a little. If extending your thumb proves too uncomfortable, pull your thumb in toward your hand. Three-quarters of an inch is only a guide, so you have some leeway. But remember: The farther your thumb extends down the shaft, the longer your swing. And the opposite is also true. Short thumb means short swing. (See Figure 6-4.)

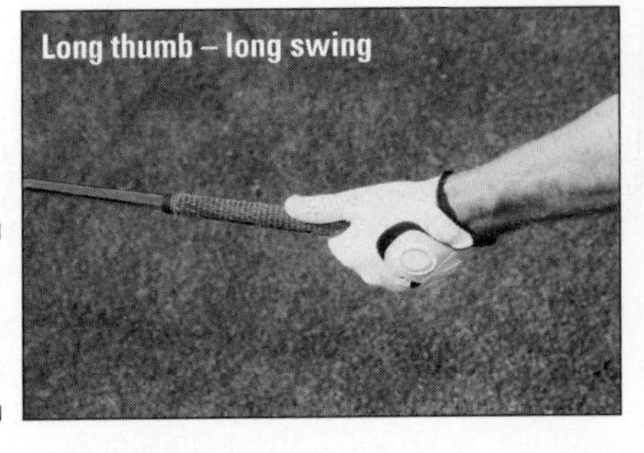

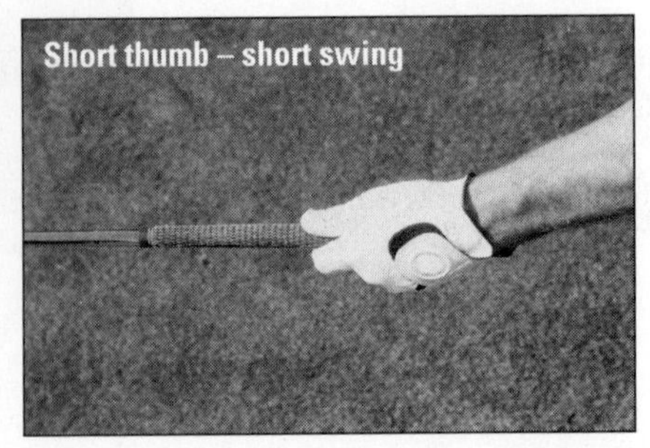

Figure 6-4: Long thumb, short thumb.

2. **Make sure the grip crosses the base of your last three fingers and the middle of your index finger, as shown in Figure 6-5.**

   This is important. If you grip the club too much in the palm, you hinder your ability to hinge your wrist and use your hands effectively in the swing. More of a finger grip makes it easy to cock the wrist on the backswing, hit the ball, and then recock the wrist on the follow-through. Just be sure that the *V* formed between your thumb and forefinger points toward your right ear.

3. **Complete your grip by placing your right hand on the club.**

   You can fit the right hand to the left in one of three ways: the overlapping (or Vardon) grip, the interlocking grip, or the ten-finger grip. I cover each of these grips in the following sections.

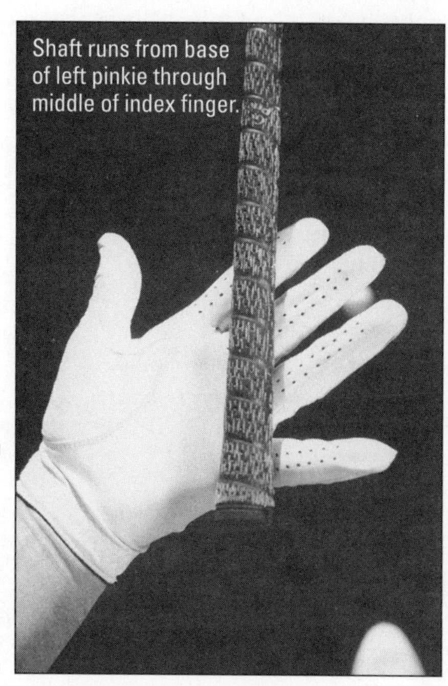

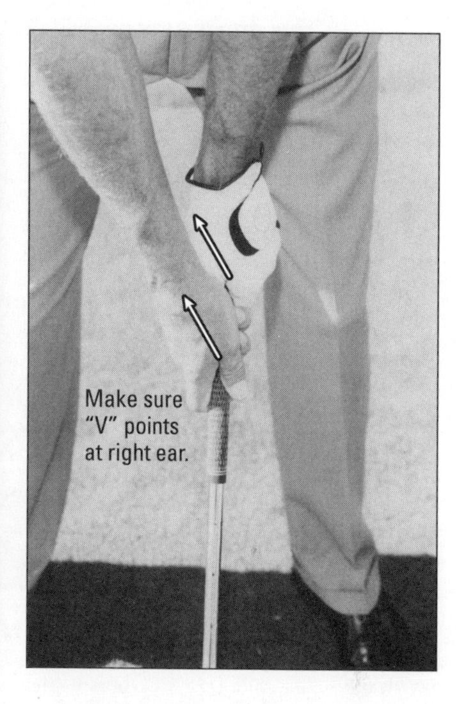

Figure 6-5: Grip more in the fingers of the left hand than in the palm.

Vardon grip

The Vardon grip is the most popular grip, certainly among better players. The great British player Harry Vardon, who still holds the record for British Open wins — six — popularized the grip around the turn of the century. Old Harry was the first to place the little finger of his right hand over the gap between the index and next finger of the left as a prelude to completing his grip, as shown in Figure 6-6. Harry was also the first to put his left thumb on top of the shaft. Previously, players kept their left thumbs wrapped around the grip as if they were holding a baseball bat.

Try the Vardon grip. Close your right hand over the front of the shaft so that the *V* formed between your thumb and forefinger points to your right ear. The fleshy pad at the base of your right thumb should fit snugly over your left thumb. The result should be a feeling of togetherness, your hands working as one, single unit.

This grip is very cool — probably 90 percent of tour players use the Vardon grip.

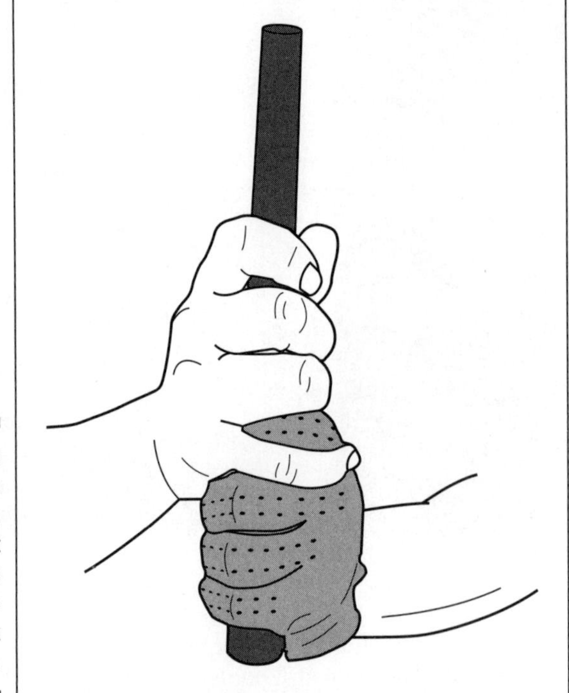

Figure 6-6: In the Vardon grip, the right pinkie overlaps the left index finger.

Interlocking grip

The interlocking grip is really a variation on the Vardon grip. The difference is that the little finger of your left hand and the index finger of the right actually hook together (see Figure 6-7). Everything else is the same. You may find this grip more comfortable if you have small hands. Jack Nicklaus, possibly the game's greatest player ever, uses this grip for that reason. Many top women players use this grip, too.

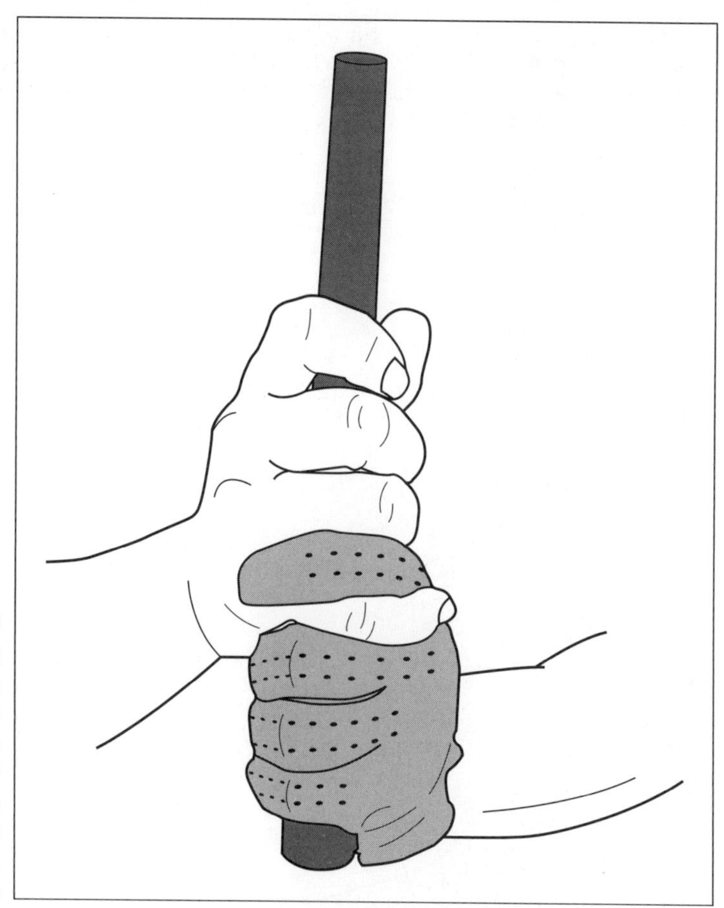

Figure 6-7: An alternative is to interlock the right pinkie and left index finger.

Ten-finger grip

The ten-finger grip used to be more common, and you still see it occasionally. Bob Estes has used it on the PGA Tour. Dave Barr — one of the best players ever from Canada — also uses this grip. The ten-finger grip is what the name tells you it is. You have all ten fingers on the club, like a baseball player gripping a bat. No overlapping or interlocking occurs; the little finger of the left hand and the index finger of the right barely touch (see Figure 6-8). If you have trouble generating enough clubhead speed to hit the ball as far as you want, or if you're fighting a slice, give this grip a try. Keep in mind that controlling the clubhead is more difficult with this grip because more "cocking" of the hands occurs.

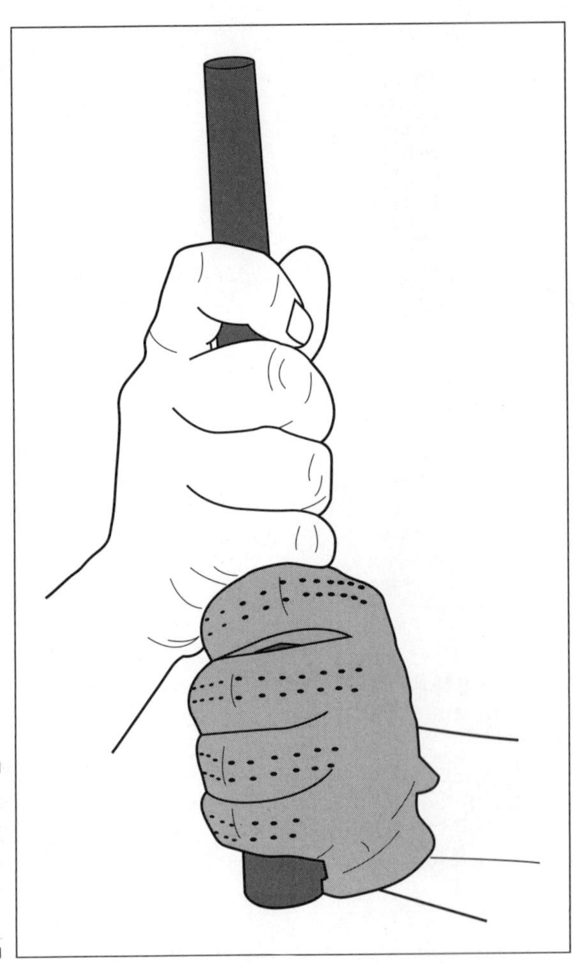

Figure 6-8: You can place all ten fingers on the club.

Completing your grip

Put your right hand on the club, with the palm directly opposite your left hand. Slide your right hand down the shaft until you can complete whatever grip you find most comfortable. Your right shoulder, right hip, and head lean to the right to accommodate the lowering of the right hand. Your right earlobe moves closer to your right shoulder.

Your grip pressure should never be tight. Your grip should be light. You should exert only as much pressure as you would when picking up an egg from a spotted owl. Lightly now! Spotted owls are becoming extinct!

Aiming

I've played pro golf for more than 25 years, which means taking part in a lot of pro-ams. (In a pro-am, each professional is teamed with three or four amateurs.) And in every single one of those rounds, I saw someone misaligned at address. Sometimes that someone was me! Aiming properly is that difficult.

Generally speaking, right-handed golfers tend to aim too far right of the target. I don't see many of them aiming left — even slicers, whose shots commonly start left and finish right. Invariably, people tend to aim right and swing over the top on the way down to get the ball started left. (For information on fixing common faults, see Chapter 11.)

What makes aiming so difficult? Human nature is part of it. Getting sloppy with your aim is easy when your mind is on other things. That's why discipline is important. Taking the time and trouble to get comfortable and confident in his alignment is one reason Jack Nicklaus was as great as he was. Watch him even now. He still works his way through the same aiming routine before every shot. And I emphasize *routine.* First, he looks at the target from behind the ball. Then he picks out a spot a few feet ahead of his ball on a line with that target. That spot is his intermediate target. Then he walks to the ball and sets the clubface behind it so that he's aiming at the intermediate point. Aligning the club with something that is 2 feet away is much easier than aiming at something 150 yards away.

How Nicklaus aims is exactly how you should work on your aim. Think of a railroad track. On one rail is the ball and in the distance, the target. On the other rail are your toes. Thus, your body is aligned parallel with — but left of — the target line. If you take nothing else away from this section on aiming, remember that phrase. Cut out Figure 6-9 and tape it onto the ceiling over your bed. Stare at it before you go to sleep.

Don't make the mistake that I see countless golfers making: aiming their feet at the target. If you aim your feet at the target, where is the clubface aligned? Well to the right of where you want the ball to go. This type of alignment will usually sabotage the flight of your ball.

Figure 6-9: Aiming correctly.

The stance

Okay, you're aimed at the target. But you're not finished with your feet yet. Right now, your feet are not pointing in any direction; you're just standing there. All the books tell you to turn your left toe out about 30 degrees. But what's 30 degrees? If you're like me, you have no clue what 30 degrees looks like or — more important — feels like, so think of 30 degrees this way:

You know what a clock looks like, and you know what the big hand is and what the little hand does. If you can read a clock, you can build a stance. Your left foot should be pointed to 10 o'clock, and your right foot should be at 1 o'clock. However, this does not work during daylight saving time. You're on your own then.

Figure 6-10 demonstrates this stance. Keep it simple and always be on time.

Width of stance is easy, too. Your heels should be shoulder-width apart, as shown in Figure 6-11. Not 14 inches, or 18 inches. Shoulder-width. Let the shape of your body dictate what's right for you.

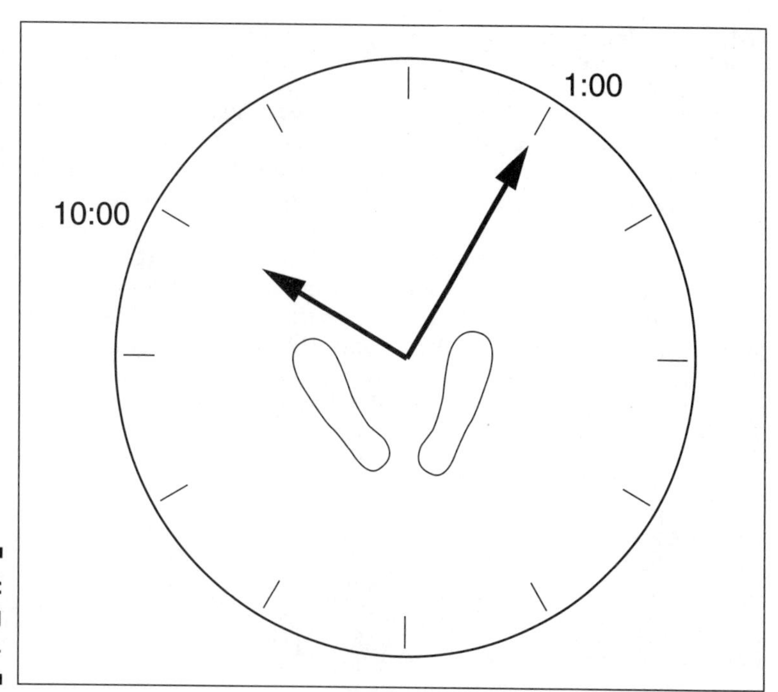

Figure 6-10: A standing start.

Figure 6-11: Your knees should be as wide as your shoulders.

Knee flex

Moving on up, our next stop is at your knees. Again, you can read all sorts of books that tell you the precise angle at which your knees should be flexed at address. But that knowledge won't do you much good when you're standing on the range without a protractor. What you need is a feel.

Think of your knee flex as a "ready" position. You've got to set yourself so that movement is easy. So, from an upright start, flex your knees and bend forward until your arms are hanging vertically, as shown in Figure 6-12. That's where you want to be. Just like a quarterback waiting for a snap. Or a soccer goalkeeper facing a shot. Or a shortstop ready for a ground ball. You're ready to move. Left. Right. Back. Forward. Whatever. You're ready. And remember, maintaining balance is the key.

Figure 6-12: Get "ready."

Ball position

Where is the ball positioned between your feet? It should be opposite your left armpit with a driver, which also should be opposite your left heel. For other clubs, the ball should be steadily moved back with each club until you get to the middle of your stance with a wedge (see Figure 6-13).

Figure 6-13: Ball position.

You're trying to hit up on the ball with your driver — that's why the ball is forward in your stance (toward the target). You want to hit down with all other clubs, which is why you move the ball back in your stance (away from the target) as the loft of your clubs increases. When the ball is played back in your stance, hitting down is much easier.

The bottom of the swing

The bottom of the swing is an important, frequently neglected aspect of golf. After all, that's usually where the ball is! The arc of the swing has to have a low point; hopefully, that low point is precisely where your golf ball will be as you swing an iron. (***Remember:*** The driver must be hit on the upswing.) If you don't know where the bottom of your swing is, how do you know where to put the ball in your stance? You can make the best swing in the world, but if the ball is too far back, you'll hit the top half of it. Too far forward is just as bad — you'll hit the ground before the ball.

Fear not; such shots are not going to be part of your repertoire. Why? Because you're always going to know where the bottom of your swing is: directly below your head.

Think about it. I've already discussed how the ball is positioned opposite the left armpit for the driver. That position automatically puts your head "behind" the ball whenever you swing your driver. In other words, the ball is nearer the target than your head is. Which means that you'll strike the ball on a slightly upward blow. The bottom of the swing is behind the ball, so the clubhead will be moving up as it hits the ball, as shown in Figure 6-14. That's all right because the ball is perched on a tee. The only way to make solid contact (and maximize your distance) is to hit drives "on the up."

Figure 6-14: Hit up.

The situation for an iron shot from the fairway differs from that of driver from the tee. Now the ball is sitting on the ground. Plus, the club you're using has more loft and is designed to give best results when the ball is struck just before the ground. So now your head should be over the ball at address and impact. In other words, something has to move.

That something is the ball. Start from the middle of your stance, which is where the ball should be when you're hitting a wedge, one of the shortest and most lofted clubs in your bag. Move the ball steadily forward — all the way to opposite your left armpit for the driver — as the club in your hands gets longer. (See Figure 6-15.)

Figure 6-15: The ball moves!

For me, the distance between my left armpit and chin is about 6 inches. With the driver, the ball is opposite my left armpit, and with the shorter irons, it's opposite my chin (that is, where my head is). In my case, the ball moves about 6 inches. Most golf courses are about 7,000 yards, so 6 inches shouldn't have much significance. Practice this part early in your development and you'll have more success with the other 7,000 yards.

You may be a little confused by all of that. It may sound weird that the more lofted clubs (which hit the highest shots) are back in your stance so that you can hit down on the ball more. But the explanation is a simple one: The more the clubface is angled back from vertical, the higher the shot will fly. Thus, the only way to move a ball from the ground into the air is by exerting downward pressure.

The eyes have it

I see too many players address the ball with their chins on their chests. Or, if they've been told not to do that, they hold their heads so high they can barely see the ball. Neither, of course, is exactly conducive to good play.

So how should you be holding your head? The answer is in your eyes. Look down at the ball, which is in what optometrists call your *gaze center.* Your gaze center is about the size of a Frisbee. Everything outside your gaze center is in your peripheral vision. Now lift or drop your head slightly. As your head moves, so do your eyes, and so does the ball — into your peripheral vision. Suddenly you can't see the ball so well. But if you hold your head steady enough to keep the ball inside that Frisbee-shaped circle, you can't go too far wrong (see Figure 6-16).

Figure 6-16: Stay focused.

One hand away

One last thing about your address position: Let your arms hang so that the butt end of the club is one hand from the inside of your left thigh, as shown in Figure 6-17. You should use this position for every club in the bag except for your putter.

The butt end of the club is a useful guide to check the relationship between your hands and the clubhead. With a wedge, for example, the butt end of the club should be in line with the middle of your left thigh. For a driver, it should be opposite your zipper. As before, every other club is between those parameters.

Well, I've covered a lot of stuff, and I haven't even taken a cut at the ball yet. Work hard on these pre-swing routines. After you get yourself in position to move the club away from the ball, forget your address position and concentrate on your swing. It's now time to do what you were sent here to do: Create some turbulence. Now I'll get on with the swing.

The club should be one hand from your body.

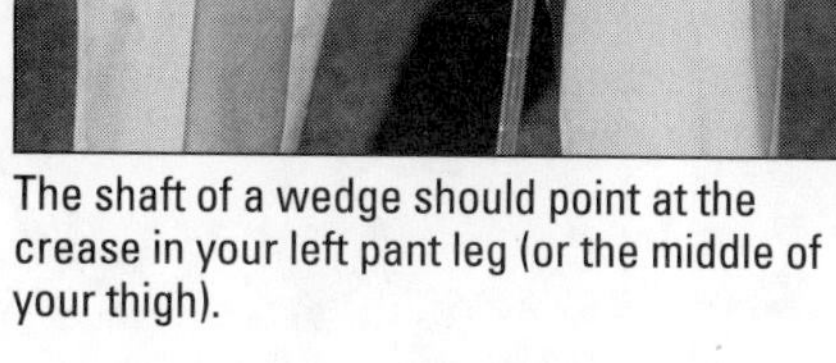

Figure 6-17: Your hands and the club.

The shaft of a wedge should point at the crease in your left pant leg (or the middle of your thigh).

A driver should point at your zipper.

Starting the Swing: First, Break It Down

Many people think that the most effective way to develop a consistent golf swing is to stand on the range whacking balls until you get it right. But the best way to develop a consistent golf swing is to break the swing down into pieces. Only after you have the first piece mastered should you move on to the next one. I start with what I call *miniswings.*

Miniswings: Hands and arms

Position yourself in front of the ball as I describe earlier in this chapter. Now, without moving anything except your hands, wrists, and forearms, rotate the club back until the shaft is horizontal to the ground and the toe of the club is pointing up. The key to this movement is the left hand, which must stay in the space that it's now occupying, in its address position (see Figure 6-18). The left hand is the fulcrum around which the "swing" rotates. The feeling you should have is of the butt of the club staying in about the same position while your hands lift the clubhead.

Figure 6-18: Push down, pull up.

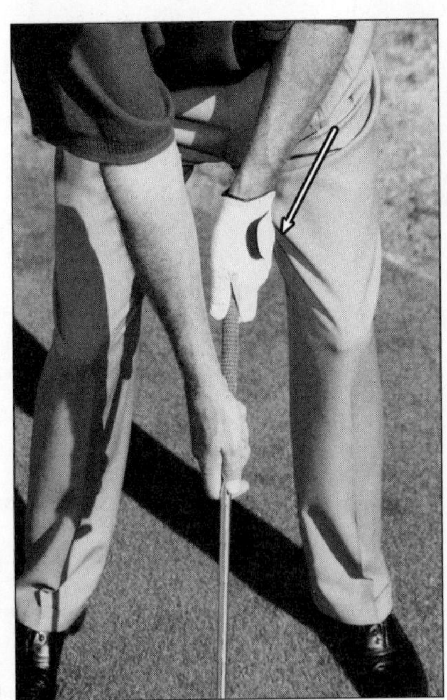

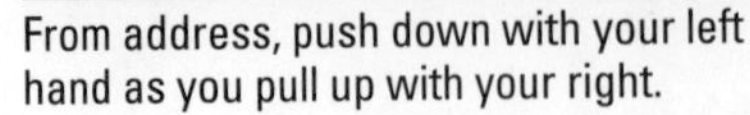

From address, push down with your left hand as you pull up with your right.

Rotate the club back until the shaft is horizontal, the toe pointing up.

After you get the hang of that little drill, try hitting shots with your miniswing. Let the club travel through 180 degrees, with the shaft parallel to the ground on the backswing and then back to parallel on the through-swing; your follow-through should be a mirror image of the backswing. The ball obviously doesn't go far with this drill, but your hands and arms are doing exactly what you want them to do on a full swing: Cock the wrists, hit the ball, recock the wrists.

After you have this move down, it's time to turn on the horsepower and get your body involved in the action.

Test your rhythm

One of the most effective ways for your brain to master something like the golf swing is to set the motion to music. We all learned our ABCs by putting the letters to song. I've played some of my best golf while humming a Hootie and the Blowfish tune. Music plays a valuable role in the learning process.

When you start to move the club and your body into the swing, think of a melody. Make the song real music. Rap, with its staccato rhythm, is no good. To me, that suggests too much independent movement. The golf swing should be a smooth motion, so your song should reflect that smoothness. Think of Tony Bennett, not Eminem.

Anyway, here's the first step toward adding body movement to the hands-and-arms motion described in the preceding section. Stand as if at address, with your arms crossed over your chest so that your right hand is on your left shoulder and your left hand is on your right shoulder. Hold a club against your chest with both hands, as shown in Figure 6-19.

Now turn as if you're making a backswing. Turn so that the shaft turns through 90 degrees, to the point where the shaft is perpendicular to a line formed by the tips of your toes. As you do so, let your left knee move inward so that it points to the golf ball. The real key here is keeping your right leg flexed as it was at address. Retain that flex, and the only way to get the shaft into position is by turning your body. You can't sway or slide to the right and still create that 90-degree angle.

Your backswing should feel as if you're turning around the inside of your right leg until your back is facing the target. That's the perfect top-of-the-backswing position.

Left hand on right shoulder, right hand on left shoulder, place a club across your chest.

Then turn the club with your shoulders through 90 degress.

Figure 6-19: Turn your body.

Unwinding

From the top, you must let your body unwind back to the ball in the proper sequence. (Note that your spine angle must stay the same from address to the top of the backswing.)

Uncoiling starts from the ground up. The first thing to move is your left knee. That knee must shift toward the target until your kneecap is over the middle of your left foot, where it stops. Any more shifting of the knee and your legs will start to slide past the ball. A shaft stuck in the ground just outside your left foot is a good check that your knee shift hasn't gone too far. If your left knee touches the shaft, stop and try again.

Next, your left hip slides targetward until it is over your knee and foot. Again, a shaft in the ground provides a good test — a deterrent to keep your hip from going too far.

Pay special attention to the shaft across your chest in this phase of the swing (work in front of a mirror if you can). The shaft should always parallel the slope of your shoulders as you work your body back to the ball.

Finishing: Go ahead and pose

"Swing" through the impact area all the way to the finish. Keep your left leg straight and let your right knee touch your left knee, as shown in Figure 6-20. Hold this position until the ball hits the ground — that way, you'll prove beyond doubt that you've swung in balance.

Wrong

Right

Figure 6-20: *Turn,* don't slide.

Get yourself together

Practice each of these exercises for as long as you need to. After you put them together, you'll have the basis of a pretty good golf swing, one that combines hands/arms and body motion.

- Practice your miniswing.
- Hum a mellow tune.
- Turn your shoulders so that your back is toward the target.
- Put a shaft in the ground — don't slide.
- At the finish, keep your left leg straight, with your right knee touching your left knee.

Coordinating all these parts into a golf swing takes time. The action of the parts will soon become the whole, and you'll develop a feel for your swing. But knowledge, in this case, does not come from reading a book. Only repetition — hitting enough balls to turn this information into muscle memory — will help you go from novice to real golfer. So get out there and start taking some turf!

Key on the rhythm of your swing. There comes a point in every golfer's life when he or she just has to "let it go." You can work on your mechanics as much as you want, but then the moment to actually hit a ball comes. And when that moment comes, you can't be thinking about anything except, perhaps, one simple swing key, or swing thought. That's why top golfers spend most of their time trying to get into that focused, wordless mental space they call the *zone*.

The *zone* is a state of uncluttered thought, where good things happen without any conscious effort from you. You know the kind of thing: The rolled-up ball of paper you throw at the trash can goes in if you just toss it without thinking. The car rounds the corner perfectly if you're lost in your thoughts. In golfing terms, getting into the zone means clearing your mind so that your body can do its job. The mind is a powerful asset, but it can hurt you, too. Negative thoughts about where your ball might go are not going to help you make your best swing.

Of course, getting into the zone is easier said than done.

So how do you get there? Perhaps the best way is to focus on the rhythm of your swing as opposed to mechanics or possible screw-ups. By *rhythm,* I don't mean speed. We've seen fast swings and slow swings and a lot in between, and all can have good rhythm. For example, three-time major winner Nick Price has a fast swing. Blink and you miss it. In contrast, 1987 Masters winner Larry Mize has an extremely slow motion. Congress works faster. Yet Price and Mize both have perfect rhythm. And that perfect rhythm is the key. The rhythm of your swing should fit your personality. If you're a fairly high-strung, nervous individual, your swing is probably faster than most. If your swing is slower, then you're probably more laid back and easygoing. The common factor is that the potential for great rhythm is within every golfer.

Swing triggers: What's a waggle?

Good rhythm doesn't just happen. Only on those days when you're in the zone can you swing on autopilot. The rest of the time, you'll need to set the tone for your swing with your waggle. A *waggle* is a motion with the wrists in which the hands stay pretty much steady over the ball and the clubhead moves back a foot or two, as if starting the swing (see Figure 6-21). In fact, a waggle is a bit like the miniswing drill I describe in the section "Miniswings: Hands and arms," earlier in this chapter.

Figure 6-21: Get in motion.

Waggling the club serves two main purposes.

- **Waggling is a rehearsal of the crucial opening segment of the backswing.**
- **Waggling can set the tone for the pace of the swing.** In other words, if you have a short, fast swing, make short, fast waggles. If your swing is of the long and slow variety, make long, slow waggles. Be true to your species.
- **Make that *three* main purposes: In golf, you don't want to start from a static position.** You need a running start to build up momentum and to keep your swing from getting off to an abrupt, jerky beginning. Waggling the clubhead eases tension and introduces movement into your setup.

But the waggle is only the second-to-last thing you do before the backswing begins. The last thing is your swing trigger. A swing trigger can be any kind of move. For example, 1989 British Open champion Mark Calcavecchia shuffles his feet. Gary Player, winner of nine major championships, kicks his right knee in toward the ball. A slight turning of the head to the right is Jack Nicklaus's cue to start his swing. Your swing trigger is up to you. Do whatever frees you up to get the club away from the ball. Create the flow!

Kevin Costner's pre-shot routine

When I started working with Kevin Costner on his golf game for the movie *Tin Cup,* one of the first things we talked about was a pre-shot routine. Teaching Kevin about the pre-shot routine this early in his golfing education got him to do the same thing every time he approached the ball. We had to get him to look like a real touring pro, and every pro has his own routine.

Kevin picked up the pre-shot routine really fast. He would get about 6 feet behind the ball and look first at the ball, and then at the target (seeing the target line in his mind's eye). He would then walk up and put his clubface right behind the ball and put his feet on a parallel line to his target line, which is the best way to establish the correct alignment. He would then look at the target once, give the club a little waggle, and then — *whack!* — off the ball went. I made him repeat this routine from the first day we started working on his swing.

By the time the golf sequences were shot for the movie, Kevin had the look of a well-seasoned touring pro. In fact, as we were walking down the second hole together in the Bob Hope Chrysler Classic, I asked Kevin where he got all his mannerisms — tugging on his shirt, always stretching his glove by pulling on it, and pulling his pants by the right-front pocket. He looked at me and said, "I've been watching you for the past three months." I had no idea I was doing all those things in my pre-shot routine! So I'm living proof that your mannerisms become automatic if you do them enough.

By the way, my pre-shot routine looks a lot better when Kevin Costner does it!

Visualizing shots

As you practice your swing and hit more and more shots, patterns — good and bad — emerge. The natural shape of your shots becomes apparent. Few people hit the ball dead-straight; you'll either *fade* most of your shots (the ball flies from left to right, as shown in Figure 6-22) or *draw* them (the ball moves from right to left in the air).

If either tendency gets too severe and develops into a full-blooded slice or hook (a *slice* is a worse fade, and a *hook* is a worse draw), you should stop playing. Go get a lesson. Such severe faults tend to be obvious to the trained eye. One session with your local pro should get you back on track.

Lessons are important. Faults left to fester and boil soon become ingrained into your method. When that happens, curing them becomes a lengthy, expensive process. The old adage comes to mind: "Pay me now, or pay me later." Pay your pro early, when your woes are easier to fix. (Chapter 3 offers valuable information on golf lessons. For a list of golf schools, see Appendix B.)

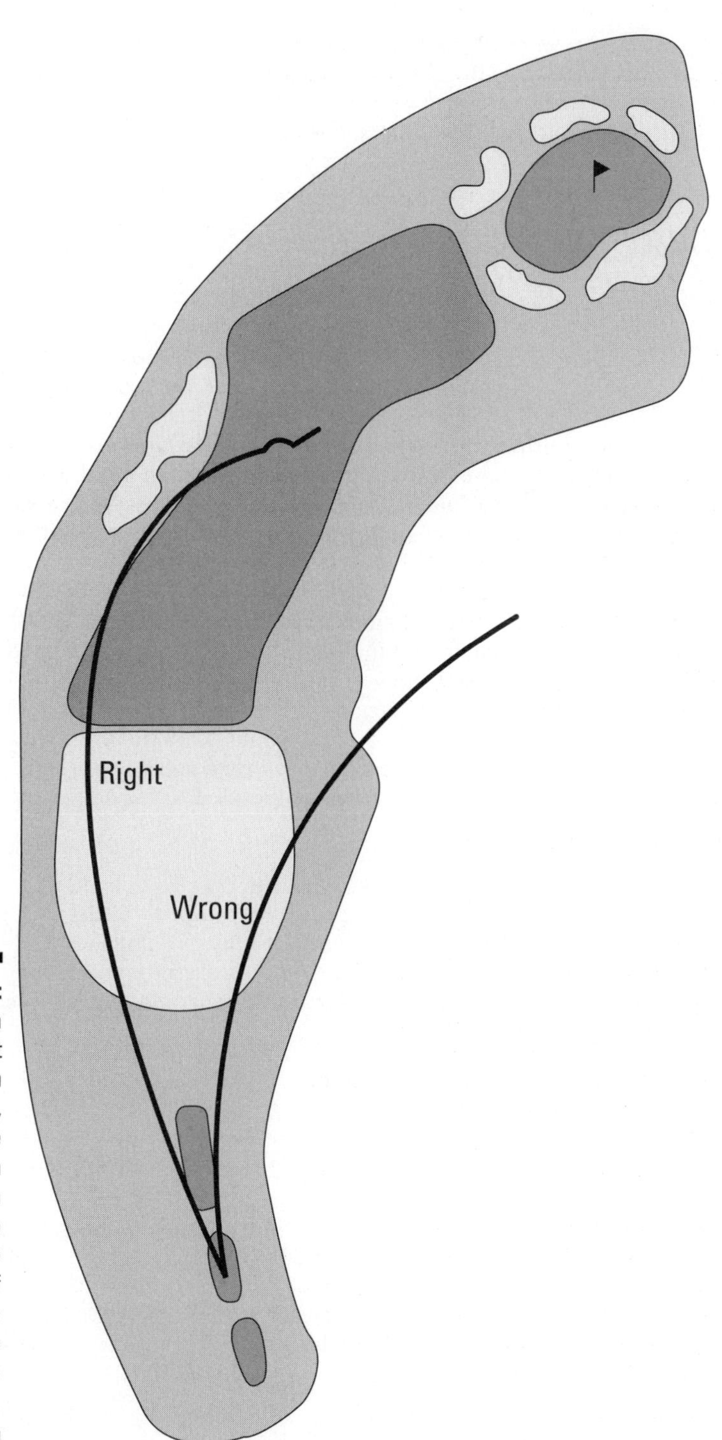

Figure 6-22: If you hit a ball that curves from left to right, make sure that you aim far enough to the left to allow the curve of your ball to match the curve of the hole.

Anyway, after you've developed a consistent shape of shot, you can start to visualize how that shape fits the hole you're playing. Then, of course, you'll know exactly where to aim whether the hole is a *dogleg right* (turns right), *dogleg left* (turns left), or straightaway. You're a real golfer.

A near-perfect swing — Hey, that's me!

When you put together all the connected parts I discuss in this chapter, they should flow into a swing. The first time you see yourself swinging in a series of photos, a video, or a DVD, you'll swear that that person is not you. What your swing feels like versus what really occurs can be deceiving.

The golf swing is nothing more than a bunch of little motions that are learned, becoming a total motion that is remembered. It's tempo and rhythm filtered through your personality. People who rush through life swing fast; those who go slowly swing like molasses. ***Remember:*** Your swing should suit your personality.

If you can master the basic mechanics described in this book and then apply them to your own personality, your swing should bloom into something unique. Work hard to understand your swing and watch how other people swing at the ball. The great Ben Hogan told me about how he watched other golfers: If he liked something they did, he would go to the practice tee and incorporate that particular move into his swing to see if it worked. What finally came out was a mix of many swings blended to his needs and personality. A champion works very hard.

My golf swing is not the one that got me to the PGA Tour. In 1986, at the age of 38, I started working with Mac O'Grady to revamp my entire swing. Mac gave me a model that I used and blended with my existing swing, shown in the nine photos of Figure 6-23. What came out is a pretty good-looking golf swing, if I do say so myself. Thanks, Mac, for at least making me look good!

Address: The calm before the chaos. All systems are go and flight is imminent.

Monitor your swing speed at this time. Checking to see if my seatbelts are fastened.

Turn and stay balanced over your feet. Feel the sun and breeze on your face.

I've reached the top. I'm in attack mode, my swing is growing teeth.

The start down is a slooooooow accumulation of speed. At this time, I've forgotten the sun and wind on my face.

I've organized my chaos. Liftoff is precise. My soul feels the ball.

Figure 6-23: Not a bad-looking golf swing!

The hit is relayed up from the shaft to my hands, through my arms into my command center. Post-impact, I feel I've been here forever.

My first glimpse at the sphere that is targetbound. The anxieties of flight and destination consume my brain.

Who cares where it went? I look good enough to be on the top of a golf trophy.

Chapter 7

Refining Your Swing

In This Chapter

- Defining your golf personality
- Checking out your swing plane
- Learning from the greats

This chapter comes with the golfing equivalent of a government health warning: The information on the next few pages isn't for everyone. That's not to say that anything in this chapter is incorrect; it isn't. But for many people — especially those at an early stage of development as golfers — it may be too much to assimilate. Little puffs of smoke will be coming from your ears.

So you need to know yourself psychologically. Say you ordered a computer and it's just arrived on your doorstep. You bring the boxes inside and start tearing them to pieces. You hook this cable to that port and put this on top of that. You're flying by the seat of your pants and have no idea what you're doing, but you do it anyway. Gone is the idea of looking at the instructions or reading any print data on how to assemble this new computer. If this scenario sounds like you, skip this chapter. You already know all you need to know about the golf swing — at least for now.

If, however, you're the type who takes a computer home, reads everything in the box, and goes from page 1 to the end of the instruction manual as you piece the components together, you're going to want to know more about the golf swing before you can play with confidence. Read on to better understand the complexities of the swing.

What Type of Golfer Are You?

My friend, renowned teacher Peter Kostis, breaks golfers into four types:

- **Analytics** are organized types. You can always spot their desks — the neat ones — in the office.
- **Drivers,** as you'd expect, like to work. They do whatever it takes to get something done.

- **Amiables** are easy to deal with. They accept whatever advice you offer without asking too many questions.
- **Expressives** don't mind any environment they happen to find themselves in; they adjust to whatever comes their way.

In recent golf history, an analytic is someone like Nick Faldo or Bernhard Langer. Jack Nicklaus, Tom Watson, and Annika Sorenstam are drivers. Nancy Lopez, Fred Couples, and Ben Crenshaw are amiables. And Fuzzy Zoeller and Lee Trevino are classic expressives.

Drivers and analytics don't play like amiables and expressives. For a driver or analytic to score well, he needs confidence in his mechanics. An amiable or expressive doesn't — if he feels like he's playing okay, then his swing must be okay, too.

The following situation clarifies these differences. Four of the greatest golfers of our era are playing an exhibition. Lee Trevino, Ben Crenshaw, Jack Nicklaus, and Nick Faldo are scheduled to tee off at Running Rut Golf Course precisely at 11 a.m. Because of a mix-up with the courtesy cars that pick up the players and deliver them to the golf course (Jack and Nick don't like the color of their car; Freddy and Ben couldn't care less), the players are late getting to Running Rut.

When they arrive, with only ten minutes to tee off, the analytic (Faldo) and the driver (Nicklaus) run out to hit balls before playing. Faldo has to swing to gain confidence, and Nicklaus has to hit balls because he likes to work at his game.

The other two guys are in the locker room putting on their golf shoes. Trevino is in deep conversation with the locker-room attendant about the virtues of not having to tune up his Cadillac for 100,000 miles due to the technologies of the Northstar system. Crenshaw is puffing on a cigarette, telling a club member that he was totally flabbergasted yesterday when three 40-foot putts lipped out and just about cost him his sanity. The expressive (Trevino) and the amiable (Crenshaw) don't have to hit balls to get ready. They just go about their business and don't worry about a thing.

By the way, the match is called off when Faldo and Nicklaus refuse to come to the tee because Nick finds something on the practice tee that he wants to work on and Jack ends up redesigning the practice range. I was told later that the locker-room attendant bought Trevino's old Cadillac.

At this stage of your development, being an amiable or an expressive is to your advantage. Because of the enormous amount of new information that you have to absorb, anything that prevents confusion is good.

Having said that, this chapter is for all you analytics and drivers out there. Amiables and expressives — I'll see you in Chapter 8.

Establishing Your Swing Plane

The *swing plane,* at its most basic, is the path the club's shaft follows when you swing. Unfortunately, many factors affect your swing plane, including your height, your weight, your posture, your flexibility, the thickness of your torso, and maybe even the dew point. Swing plane can get complicated — especially if you want to cover all the possible variations in the plane from address to the end of the follow-through.

At this point, for all you amiables and expressives, let me expound on the idea of thinking less about the plane of your swing than about the shape of your swing. Two of the best players in the game when I was on tour — Greg Norman and Bruce Lietzke — had totally different planes to their swings. The golf swing consists of different planes that shift during the course of the swing. For example, Greg shifted the plane of his swing a little to the outside on the backswing, and then shifted to the inside on the downswing to achieve his particular curve of the ball, a *draw.* Bruce shifted the plane of his swing a little to the inside on the backswing, and then shifted to the outside on the downswing to get his particular curve of the ball, a *fade.*

The plane of your swing is dictated to a large extent by the shaft's angle at address. The swing you make with a wedge in your hands is naturally more upright — or should be — than the swing you make with a driver. The driver has a longer shaft than the wedge and a flatter *lie* (the angle at which the shaft emerges from the clubhead), so you have to stand farther away from the ball.

For this book, I'm assuming that you maintain the plane you establish at address throughout the swing. For most players, this isn't always the case. If a player's favored shot is one that bends a great deal in the air, the swing plane is tilted either to the right or to the left to compensate for the ball's flight. But if you're trying to hit straight shots, one consistent plane is the way for you.

Mastering the checkpoints

The easiest way to keep your swing on plane is to have a series of checkpoints, as shown in Figure 7-1. By the way, I'm assuming that you're swinging a driver and that you're right-handed. Here are the checkpoints:

Start with the shaft at 45 degrees to the ground.

At the top, the shaft should be parallel with a line along your heels.

Impact should look a lot like address, except that the hips are opening to the target.

Figure 7-1: The swing plane.

- **Checkpoint #1:** The first checkpoint is at address. The shaft starts at a 45-degree angle to the ground.
- **Checkpoint #2:** Now swing the club back until your left arm is horizontal. At that point, the club's *butt end* (the end of the grip) points directly along the target line. (The *target line* is the line between the target and the ball. That line also continues forward past the target in a straight line and beyond the ball going in the opposite direction in a straight line. What I'm talking about in this case is one long, straight line.) If the end of the grip is pointing along the target line, you're *on plane.* If the end of the grip points above the target line, your swing is too flat, or *horizontal;* if the grip end is below the target line, your swing is too upright, or *vertical.*

- **Checkpoint #3:** At the top of your backswing, the club should be parallel with a line drawn along your heels. That's on plane. If the club points to the right of that line, you've crossed the line and will probably hook the shot. A club pointing to the left of that line is said to be *laid off.* In that case, expect a slice.
- **Checkpoint #4:** Halfway down, at the point where your left arm is again horizontal, the shaft's butt end should again point at the target line. This position and the one described in the second checkpoint on this list are, in effect, identical in swing-plane terms.
- **Checkpoint #5:** Impact is the most important point in the golf swing. If the clubface is square when it strikes the ball, what you do anywhere else doesn't really matter. But if you want to be consistent, try to visualize impact as being about the same as your address position, except your hips are aimed more to the left of the target than at the address position, and your weight is shifting to the left side.

To analyze your swing, use a video, a series of still photos, or a mirror — or have someone watch you.

Now remember, this method of mastering your checkpoints is a perfect-world situation. Your size, flexibility, and swing shape will probably produce different results. Don't be alarmed if you don't fit this model perfectly; no more than a dozen players on the PGA Tour do. As with anything else, there's room for deviation.

At the top

Take a closer look at the top of the backswing. If you can get the club on plane at the top, you'll probably hit a good shot.

Look for four things in your backswing:

- **Your left arm and your shoulders must be on the same slope.** In other words, your arm and shoulders are parallel.
- **The top of your swing is basically controlled by your right arm, which forms a right angle at the top of the swing (see Figure 7-2).** Your elbow is about a dollar bill's length away from your rib cage.

Figure 7-2: Check-point — get this angle right.

- **Your shoulders turn so that they're at 90 degrees to the target line.**
- **The clubface is angled parallel to your left arm and your shoulders.** Your left wrist controls this position. Ideally, your wrist angle remains unchanged from address to the top. That way, the relationship between the clubface and your left arm is constant. If your wrist angle does change, the clubface and your left arm will be on different planes — and that's a problem.

If your wrist angle changes, it's either bowed or cupped (see Figure 7-3). A *bowed* (bent-forward) left wrist at the top makes the clubface "look" skyward in what is called a *closed* position. From that position, a hook is likely. A *cupped* (bent-backward) wrist makes the clubface more visible to someone looking you in the face. A cupped wrist leads to an open position, which probably results in a slice.

Of course, playing good golf from an open or closed position at the top of the backswing is possible. It's just more difficult. To do well, your swing has to have some kind of built-in compensation that will square the clubface at impact. And compensations take a lot of practice. Only if you have the time to hit hundreds of balls a week can you ever hope to play well with an inherently flawed swing. Even then, that compensated swing is going to be tough to reproduce under pressure. For famous examples, watch Corey Pavin (open) and Lee Trevino (closed).

Figure 7-3: Wristy business.

Anyway, swing sequences tend to show three very different methods. The legendary Sam Snead crossed the line at the top and came over every shot to get the ball to go straight. Annika Sorenstam is the opposite: She lays the club off at the top. And 1995 PGA Champion Steve Elkington stays on plane. Make a swing like his your model, and you can't go too far wrong.

Going Where Others Have Gone Before

No matter what your skill level, a great way to improve is to watch other players, particularly those with some of the same characteristics that you have. Watch for similarities in body size, pace, and shape of swing — even the kinds of mistakes they make under pressure.

Start by identifying your goals. Do you want to emulate the masters of the long game, guys like John Daly, Ernie Els, and Davis Love III, who regularly blast drives beyond 300 yards? Or do you want to concentrate on following the short-game experts, such as all-time great Walter Hagen and tour veteran Brad Faxon? Phil Mickelson is long off the tee and has a great lob wedge. Tiger Woods, of course, does everything well.

If you want to follow some really fine putting, keep your eyes peeled for my Champions Tour colleague Isao Aoki of Japan, who has a unique putting stroke acutely tailored to Japanese grass. Some of the best putters in the world today are Faxon, Mickelson, and Jim Furyk. Nancy Lopez was another great putter in her heyday.

Maybe swing speed is your demon. Are you trying too hard to copy someone you admire, or are you making sure that the pace you use is as natural for you as tour golfers' swings are for them? Down through the years, Ben Crenshaw, Nancy Lopez, and Jay Haas have displayed slow-paced swings. Larry Mize's swing was always extremely slow. Davis Love III, Jack Nicklaus, Sam Snead, and Annika Sorenstam have all won with medium-paced swings. Ben Hogan, Lanny Wadkins, and Tom Watson all swung fast. One of the quickest swingers of all is Nick Price. And all those players have had great careers.

Hand size can affect grip; grip can affect your swing. Billy Casper was an all-time great putter who used his wrists to create momentum in the clubhead during his putting stroke. Fred Couples uses the cross-handed grip for putting. Jack Nicklaus uses the interlocking grip for his golf swing. Tom Kite uses the interlocking grip for full swings and the cross-handed grip for putting. Chris DiMarco, who was once such a poor putter he almost quit the tour, made it big with a grip called "the claw."

Maybe you want to keep tabs on golfers who have modified their games to see how a pro adapts his or her game, either to combat the yips, as did Bernhard Langer, who invented his own grip, and Sam Snead, who putted sidesaddle, or to accommodate a new tool, like the long putter Tom Lehman switched to. Vijay Singh used a *belly putter* — longer than a standard flatstick, shorter than a long putter — until he switched back to a standard model and played better than ever!

Notice how the attitudes of famous players affect not only how they play but also how much they enjoy the game. Arnold Palmer was a master of special shots, a bold golfer. Other daring players include Mickelson and John Daly, who are as fun and exciting to watch as expressive golfers Lee Trevino and Fuzzy Zoeller. Fred Funk is another fan favorite whose pleasure in playing is infectious. On the other end of the attitude spectrum, you'll find Hall of Famer Jackie Burke, who created intense drills for himself so that he knew all about pressure: His motivation was to win. Ben Hogan was another steely competitor, a perfectionist who surrendered finally not to any other player but to the yips. (See Chapter 8 for more on the yips.) Other hard-working perfectionists include Jack Nicklaus, Annika Sorenstam, and Tom Watson.

Whoever you choose to emulate, remember that golf is an individualist's game. You can mix and match facets of great players' styles, or develop your own — whatever works for *you*.

Chapter 8

Putting: The Art of Rolling the Rock

In This Chapter

- Finding your own putting style
- Visualizing putts
- Choosing the right putter
- Hitting good short and long putts
- Overcoming the yips
- Using optics to putt better

This chapter is one of the most important in the book. Statistically, putting is 68 percent of the game of golf, so you may want to take notes. You'd be smart to keep a "reminder book" full of putting tips from this chapter, because you can't score well if you can't putt — it's that simple. If you want proof, look at the top professionals on tour who average about 29 putts per round. In other words, these professionals are one-putting at least 7 of the 18 greens in a round of golf. The average score on tour isn't 7 under par, so even these folks are missing their fair share of greens. And where are they retrieving their mistakes? That's right: with their short games and putting.

Golfers often say they're *rolling the rock* on the green, rather than rolling the ball. Don't ask me why. I suspect it has to do with the difficulty of rolling a hard, irregular object that can hurt you. Or maybe *rock* and *roll* just go together.

No other part of golf induces as much heartache and conversation as putting. Many fine strikers of the ball have literally been driven from the sport because they couldn't finish holes as well as they started them. Why? Because putting messes with your internal organs. Every putt has only two possibilities: You either miss it or hole it. Accept that and you won't have nightmares about the ones that "should" have gone in.

You Gotta Be You

Putting is the most individual part of this individual game. You can putt — and putt successfully — in myriad ways. You can break all the rules with a putter in your hands as long as the ball goes in the hole. Believe me, you can get the job done by using any number of methods. You can make long, flowing strokes like Phil Mickelson and Ben Crenshaw. Or shorter, firmer, "pop" strokes like Corey Pavin and Gary Player. Or you can create the necessary momentum in the clubhead with your wrists — the great Billy Casper proved how well that can work. Or if none of these styles appeals to you, you can switch to a "belly putter" — Vijay Singh tried that — or go to a long, "witch's broom-handle" putter. Golfers from PGA Tour star Tom Lehman to former president George H. Bush have had success with long putters.

Putting is more about those ghostly intangibles — feel, touch, and nerve — than about mechanics. My feeling is that getting too involved with putting mechanics is a mistake. You can have the most technically perfect stroke in the world and still be like an orangutan kicking a football on the greens — if you don't have the touch, that is.

Even more than the rhythm and tempo of your full swing, your putting stroke should reflect your own personality. Your hands probably shouldn't be "behind" the ball at impact, but other than that, your style is up to you.

Be aware that if any aspect of this often-infuriating game were ever designed to drive you to distraction, it's putting. Putting may look simple — and sometimes it is — but on some days you just know that little ball at your feet will never make its way into that hole. You know it, your playing partners know it, your financial consultant knows it, everyone knows it. Putting is mystical; it comes and goes like the tide.

Because most women can't physically drive the ball hundreds of yards, they should focus on refining their short-game skills, such as chipping, pitching, and putting. ***Remember:*** A solid putt counts the same on the score card as a 200-yard drive.

Mind Games

In putting, visualization is everything. You can visualize in two ways: Either you see the hole as very small, or so big that any fool can drop the ball in. The former, of course, is infinitely more damaging to your psyche. When you imagine that the hole shrinks, the ball doesn't seem to fit. You can keep telling yourself that the ball is 1.68 inches in diameter and the hole 4.25 inches across, but the fact remains that the ball is too big. I know; I've been there. It just won't fit. It won't fit no matter what I do. When I start thinking that way, I usually seek psychiatric care and surround myself with pastel colors.

And on other days, happily, the hole is so big that putting is like stroking a marble into the Grand Canyon. Simply hit the ball, and boom, it goes in. When this happens to you, savor every moment. Drink in the feeling and bathe in it so that you don't forget it — because you may not take another bath like that for a *long* time.

The crazy thing is that these two scenarios can occur on consecutive days, sometimes even in consecutive rounds. I've even experienced both feelings on consecutive holes! Why? I have no idea. The answer is way beyond my feeble intellect. Try not to think too deeply about putting.

The Most Important Club in the Bag

Because putting is such a crucial part of the game, it follows that your putter is the most important weapon you've got. Club makers seem to have noticed: In recent years they've brought out a dizzying array of high-tech putters. Some are as sleek as a sports car, while others look more like anvils or spaceships. One new model has been likened to "a fire hydrant on a stick." How can you choose the putter that's best for your game? It's probably not as tricky as you think.

Your stroke shape tells you which putter you need

Although you have a lot of putters to choose from, you can eliminate many by knowing the type of putter you are. In other words, the shape of your stroke is the main factor in choosing a putter. Figure 8-1 shows two types of putters.

My good friend and noted teaching professional Peter Kostis explains that almost all putting strokes fall into one of two shapes. They either move "straight back and straight through" with the blade staying square, or "inside to inside," the blade doing a miniversion of the rotation found in a full swing. Conveniently, most putters are designed to suit a specific stroke shape. There are two main types: (1) face-balanced, center-shafted putters and (2) those that are not face-balanced, such as heel-shafted blades.

Figure 8-1: Which kind of putter?

The key to success is matching your putter to your stroke. If keeping the blade square throughout the putting stroke is your style, get a face-balanced, center-shafted model. You can test to see if a putter is face-balanced by resting the shaft on your finger. If the putterface stays parallel to the ground, it's face-balanced.

The inside-to-inside stroke is easier to make on a consistent basis with a heel-shafted putter. It will hang toe-down while resting on your finger.

Be warned, though. Some putters hang at an angle of 45 degrees. They're equally good — or bad! — for either stroke.

High-tech putters: From MOI to you

Don't be confused by all the high-tech (and high-priced) new putters on the market. Figure 8-2 shows several popular ones. Although they appear as colorful and as different as new cars, most offer only one or two features that may even make them worth the price.

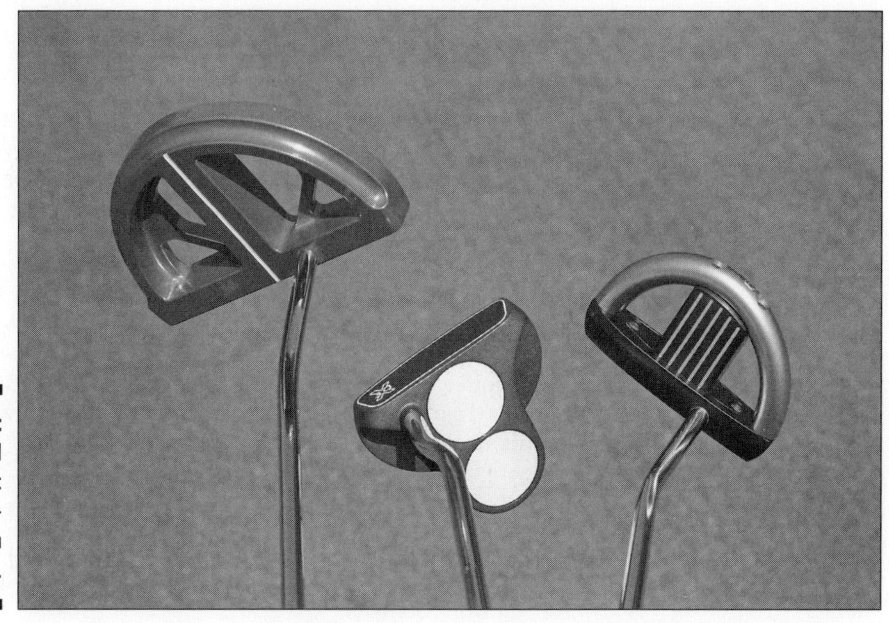

Figure 8-2: Weird science: A few new-millennium putters.

One term that puzzles most beginners is *MOI,* which is short for *moment of inertia.* It sounds scientific, and in fact there's a lot of science behind the new MOI putters, but you don't have to bother with that. All you need to know is that MOI putters resist twisting on off-center hits. That means that your bad putts turn out better than they would otherwise. How much better? That's hard to say, but a 2005 study cited in *Golf Digest* suggested that an MOI putter might make a 4-foot difference on a 22-foot putt. That's a massive difference — almost as massive as some of these putters.

Many modern putters also feature alignment aids, like the pair of white circles behind the face of Odyssey's popular 2-Ball putters. Other manufacturers put bold lines or arrows on their putters to help golfers start the ball on the target line. (For more on alignment, see "The Art of Aiming the Ball," later in this chapter.) Another new wrinkle is adding an insert to the face of the putter — often a panel of urethane, the same stuff golf balls are made of — for a softer feel when the putter strikes the ball.

As with other technological advances, from titanium drivers to graphite shafts to super-comfy golf shoes, such features have their benefits — especially if you *believe* they'll help your game. Because, as you know by now, this game is as mental as anything.

Still, the best feature of all is sound fundamentals. Without them, all the tech support in the world won't do you much good.

Long putters and belly putters — it's a long story

Some golfers swear by extra-long putters. Others swear *at* them, saying the long putter is bizarre and ought to be illegal. There is even talk of banning long putters. But if you're struggling to make putts, you may want give one of them a try.

The terminology can be confusing: What's the difference between a long putter and a belly putter? But it's simple if you know the crucial difference: Both are longer than a standard model, but a long putter is *lo-o-onnnger*. Its handle goes under the golfer's chin, while the handle of a belly putter is anchored to the belly. Both are used almost exclusively by players who've struggled to make putts the usual way.

Long putters

The long putter is the final refuge of the neurologically impaired. If you watch any Champions Tour event on TV, you'll see more than a few long putters. There are even a few on the PGA Tour.

Long putters range from 46 inches in length to 50 and up. They remove all wrist action from your putting stroke because your left hand anchors the club to your chest. Your left hand holds the club at the end of the shaft, and your fingers wrap around the grip so that the back of that hand faces the ball. The grip is the fulcrum around which the club swings. Your right hand is basically along for the ride. In fact, your right hand should barely touch the club. Its only role is to pull the club back and follow the club through.

Long putters are easy on the nerves, which is why these clubs enjoy such popularity on the Champions Tour. But to be fair, senior players are not alone. No fewer than three members of the European Ryder Cup team in 1995 used long putters. And all three members won their singles matches on the final afternoon, perhaps the most pressure-packed day in all of golf. So long putters definitely have something going for them. You've got nothing to lose by trying one.

Belly putters

A recent variation on the long putter is the midlength belly putter. You anchor it to your midsection, so that it looks like the club is stabbing you in the navel. Belly putters are 40 to 45 inches long. Like long putters, they're designed to minimize wrist action in the stroke. Vijay Singh, Fred Couples, and other pros have fought putting woes with these midlength mallets, though Singh putted better when he went back to a standard model.

If you're struggling with jumpy wrists on the greens, you may want to try the belly method. (Keep in mind that it takes patience.) But remember: Like the long putter, the belly putter is generally seen as a last resort. If you can make putts with a standard-length putter, that's what you should use.

Building Your Stroke

As I've already said, you can putt well by using any number of methods or clubs. But I'm going to ignore that for now. At this stage, you should putt in as orthodox a manner as possible. That way, when something goes wrong — which it will — the fault is easier to fix. The trouble with being unorthodox is that it's hard to find order in chaos.

The putting grip

The putting grip isn't like the full-swing grip. The full-swing grip is more in the fingers, which encourages your wrists to hinge and unhinge. Your putting grip's purpose is exactly the opposite. You grip the putter more in the palm of your hands to reduce the amount of movement your hands make. Although you may putt well with a lot of wrist action in your stroke, I prefer that you take the wrists out of play as much as possible. Unless you have incredible touch, your wrists are not very reliable when you need to hit the ball short distances. You're far better off relying on the rocking of your shoulders to create momentum in the putterhead.

Not all putting grips are the same — not even those grips where you place your right hand below the left in conventional fashion. But what all putting grips have in common is that the palms of both hands face each other so your hands can work together. The last thing you want is your hands fighting one another. Too much of either hand, and your ball has a bad experience. If your left hand dominates, your right hand sues for nonsupport. Both hands need to work together for a good experience with no legal hassles.

Your hands can work together in one of two ways, as shown in Figure 8-3. Start by placing the palms of your hands on either side of the club's grip. Slide your right hand down a little so that you can place both hands on the club. You should feel like you're going to adopt the ten-finger grip (see Chapter 6). Then do one of the following, depending on which grip you prefer:

- Place your left index finger over the little finger of your right hand. Known as the *reverse overlap,* this is probably the most popular putting grip on the PGA and LPGA tours.

- Extend your left index finger past the fingers of your right hand until the tip touches your right index finger. I call this grip the *extended reverse overlap.* The left index finger, when extended, provides stability to the putting stroke.

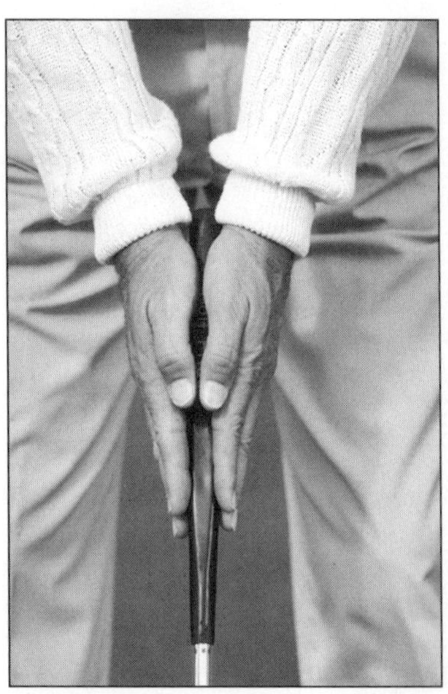

Place your palms on opposing sides of the grip.

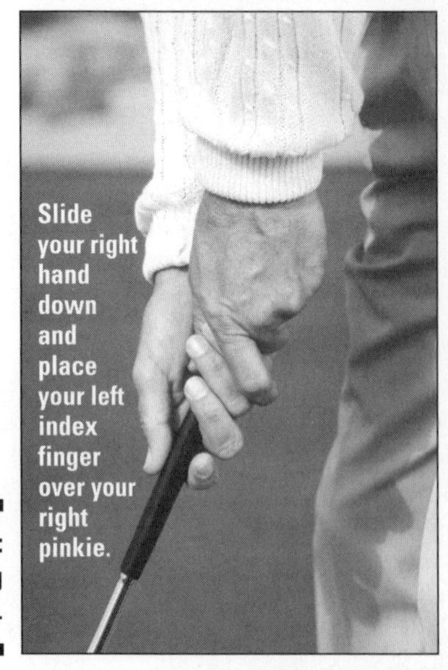

Figure 8-3: A gripping start.

Go with the grip that you find most comfortable. I describe other methods of gripping the putter in the following sections.

Left hand low

This method is commonly referred to as *cross-handed.* The left hand hangs below the right with the putter (or vice versa if you're a lefty). Many players use this method today because it helps keep the lead hand (the left, in this case) from bending at the wrist as you hit the ball. (See Figure 8-4.)

One of the biggest causes of missed putts is the breakdown of the left wrist through impact. When the left wrist bends through impact, the putter blade twists. This twisting causes the ball to wobble off-line, even if you've got an MOI putter. That's why you should maintain the bend of your left wrist from the address position all the way through the stroke.

Figure 8-4: Keep that left wrist firm.

The cross-handed grip can make it easier to maintain that wrist position. Great players — including Fred Couples and Tom Kite — have gone to this type of grip.

The few times I've tried the cross-handed grip, pulling with the left wrist seemed to be easier. It seems that pulling with the lead hand makes it harder to break down with the wrist.

Another reason you see many of today's pros using a cross-handed grip is that, with the left arm lower on the shaft, you pull the left shoulder more square to your target line. Pulling your left shoulder happens automatically with this grip. I tend to open my shoulders (aim to the left) with my putter. As soon as I tried a cross-handed grip, my left shoulder moved toward the target line, and I was more square to my line.

I think the best asset that this stroke has to offer is that you swing the left arm back and forth during the stroke. The trailing hand (right) goes along for the ride, which is a very good way to stroke your golf ball. I suggest that you try putting with your left hand low. You might stick with this method forever.

The "claw"

This weird-looking grip got a huge boost at the 2005 Masters, where claw-gripper Chris DiMarco took eventual winner Tiger Woods into a thrilling playoff. To try the claw, start with a standard putting grip. Turn your right palm toward you and bring it to the putter's handle so that the handle touches the spot between your thumb and index finger. Now bring your index and middle fingers to the shaft, leaving your ring finger and pinkie off, as shown in Figure 8-5.

DiMarco had gone through a spell of such terrible putting that he nearly gave up hope; with this grip he rejuvenated his career and clawed his way to the top.

Putting posture: Stand and deliver

As you crouch over the ball to putt, you need to be in the correct position. You should have a slight knee flex in your putting stance. If your knees are locked, you're straining your back too much. Don't bend your knees too much, though, because you may start to look like a golf geek!

Bend from your waist so that your arms hang straight down. This allows your arms to swing in a pendulum motion, back and forth from a fixed point. Hold your arms straight out from your body. Bend down with those arms outstretched from the waist until your arms are pointing to the ground. Now flex your knees a little bit, and you're in the correct putting posture.

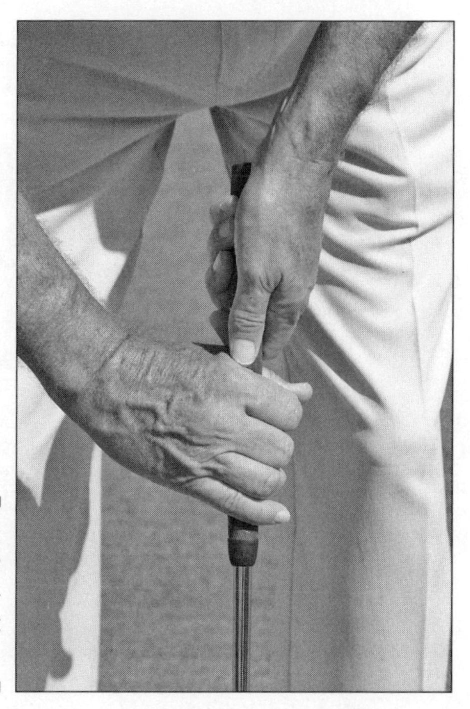

Figure 8-5: The claw grip — weird, but it may work.

You can break a lot of rules in how you stand to hit a putt (see Figure 8-6). Ben Crenshaw stands open to the target line, his left foot drawn back. Gary Player always did the opposite: He set up closed, his right foot farther from the target line than his left. But that's their style; I keep things simple with a square stance so that I don't need to make many in-stroke adjustments to compensate.

Toeing the line

As in a full swing, the line of your toes is the key. Regardless of which stance you choose, your toe line should always be parallel to your target line. Be aware that the target line isn't always a straight line from the ball to the hole — if only putting were that simple. Unfortunately, greens are rarely flat, so putts break or bend from right to left or from left to right. (See "Reading the break," later in this chapter.) So sometimes you'll be aiming, say, 5 inches to the right of the hole, and other times maybe a foot to the left (see Figure 8-7). Whatever you decide, your toe line must be parallel to your target line.

Figure 8-6: Putting stances are optional.

Figure 8-7: Playing the break.

Being parallel to your target line is vital. In effect, you make every putt straight. Applying a curve to your putts is way too complicated and affects your stroke. Imagine how you'd have to adjust if you aimed at the hole and then tried to push the ball out to the right because of a slope on the green. You'd have no way to be consistent. So keep putting simple. On breaking putts, aim your feet parallel to the line you've chosen, not toward the hole (see Figure 8-8).

Figure 8-8: Keep your feet parallel to your putting line.

Standing just right

Okay, now what about width of stance? Again, you have margin for error, but your heels need to be about shoulder-width apart at address, as shown in Figure 8-9.

Figure 8-9: Heels and shoulders are the same width.

You have to bend over to place the putter behind the ball. How far should you bend? Far enough to get your eye line (a much-neglected part of putting) directly over the ball. To find out how that position feels, place a ball on your forehead between your eyes, bend over, and let the ball drop, as shown in Figure 8-10. Where does the ball hit the ground? That's where the ball should be in relation to your body. It shouldn't be to the inside, the outside, behind, or in front of that point. It should be right there, dead center. This alignment places your eyes not just over the ball but also over the line that you want the ball to travel.

Getting up to speed

In the two decades–plus that I played on the PGA Tour, I saw a lot of golfers with a lot of different putting methods. The good putters came in all shapes and sizes, too. Some putted in what could be termed mysterious ways, and others were totally conventional. So analyzing different putting methods is no help. The best way to look at putting is to break it down to its simplest level. The hole. The ball. The ball fits into the hole. Now get the ball into the hole in the fewest possible strokes.

You want to get the ball rolling at the right speed. If you don't have the speed, you can't know where to aim. The right speed means hitting a putt so that if the ball misses the cup, it'll finish 14 to 18 inches past the hole, as shown in Figure 8-11. This distance is true no matter the length of the putt. Two feet or 40 feet, your aim must be to hit the ball at a pace that will see it finish 14 to 18 inches beyond the hole. If it doesn't go in, that is.

You're probably wondering why your ball needs the right speed. Well, the right speed gives the ball the greatest chance of going into the hole. Think about it: If the ball rolls toward the middle of the cup, you don't want it moving so fast that it rolls right over the hole. If it touches either side of the cup, it may drop in. Your goal is to give the ball every chance to drop in, from any angle — front, back, or side. I don't know about you, but I want that hole to seem as big as possible.

Figure 8-10: Align your eyes over the ball.

Figure 8-11: Just past: Here's how hard to hit your putts.

The only putts I know that *never* drop are the ones you leave short of the hole. If you've played golf for any length of time, you've heard the phrase "never up, never in." The cliché is annoying but true. As the Irish say, "Ninety-nine percent of all putts that come up short don't go in, and the other 1 percent never get there." Remember that saying! Also remember that you should try to make every putt that stops 10 feet from the hole or closer. I *hope* to make every putt from 10 to 20 feet, and I try to get every putt close from 20 feet and beyond.

Reading the break

After you have the distance control that a consistent pace brings, you can work on the second half of the putting equation: reading the break. The *break* is the amount a putt moves from right to left, or left to right, on a green. Slope, topographical features such as water and mountains, the grain of the grass, and, perhaps most important, how hard you hit the ball dictate the break. For example, if I am an aggressive player who routinely hits putts 5 feet past the cup, I'm not going to play as much break as you do. (***Remember:*** You should hit your putts only 14 to 18 inches past the cup.)

The firmer you hit a putt, the less the ball breaks on even the steepest gradient. So don't be fooled into thinking that there's only one way a putt can be holed. On, say, a 20-footer, you probably have about five possibilities. How hard you hit the ball is one factor.

The key, of course, is consistency. Being a bold putter is not a bad thing (if you're willing to put up with the occasional return 5-footer), as long as you putt that way all the time — and are still in your teens.

The first thing I do when I arrive at a golf course is to find the natural slope of the terrain. If there are mountains nearby, finding the natural slope is easy. Say the mountains are off to your right on the first hole. Any slope will run from right to left on that hole. In fact, the slope on every green is going to be "from" the mountain (unless, of course, a particularly humorless architect has decided to bank some holes toward the mountain). So I take that into account on every putt I hit.

If the course is relatively flat, go find the pro or course superintendent. Ask about nearby reservoirs or, failing that, the area's lowest point. This point can be 5 miles away or 20 — it doesn't matter. Find out where that point is and take advantage of gravity. Gravity is a wonderful concept. Every putt breaks down a hill — high point to low point — unless you're in a zero-gravity environment. But that's another book.

After you know the lowest point, look at each green in detail. If you're on an older course, the greens probably slope from back to front because of drainage. Greens nowadays have more humps and undulations than ever and are surrounded by more bunkers. And the sand tells a tale: Most courses are designed so that water runs past a bunker and not into it. Take that insight into account when you line up a putt.

And don't forget the barometric pressure and dew point — just kidding! (For fun and entertaining information about sand play, see Chapter 10.)

Reading the grain

Golf is played on different grasses (ideally, not on the same course). Climate usually dictates the kind of grass you find on a course. Grasses in hot, tropical areas have to be more resilient, so they typically have thick blades. *Bermuda grass* is the most common. Its blades tend to follow the sun from morning to afternoon — in other words, from east to west. Because the blade is so strong, Bermuda grass can carry a golf ball according to the direction in which it is lying. Putts "downgrain" go faster than putts "into" the grain. All that, of course, has an effect on where you have to aim a putt.

Look at the cup to find out which way the grass is growing. Especially in the afternoon, you may see a ragged half and a smooth, or sharp, half on the lip of the cup — that shows the direction in which the grass is growing. The ragged look is caused by the grass's tendency to grow and fray. If you can't tell either way, go to the *fringe* (the edge of the green). The grass on the fringe is longer, so you can usually see the direction of the grain right away.

Another common type of grass is *bent grass.* You see this strain of grass mostly in the northern and northeastern United States. Bent grass has a thinner blade than Bermuda grass, but it doesn't stand up to excessive heat as well.

Bent grass is used by many golf-course builders because it allows them to make the greens fast, and the recent trend for greens is to combine slope with speed. Try getting on the roof of your car, putting a ball down to the hood ornament, and making it stop. That's the speed of most of the greens on tour with bent grass.

I don't concern myself much with grain on bent greens. I just worry about the slope and the 47 things on my checklist before I putt. Putting could be so much fun if I didn't have a brain.

If you get the chance to play golf in Japan, you'll play on grass called *korai.* This wiry grass can be a menace on the greens because it's stronger than AstroTurf and can really affect the way the ball rolls on the green. If the blades of grass are growing toward you, you have to hit the ball with a violent pop.

Isao Aoki, a great Japanese player, developed a unique putting stroke in which he kept the toe of the putter way off the ground and then gave the ball a pop with his wrist to get it going — an effective way of dealing with the korai grass he grew up on.

When dealing with grasses, an architect tries to use the thinnest possible blade, given the climate, and then tries to get that grass to grow straight up to eliminate grain. Bent is better than Bermuda when it comes to growing straight, so grain is rarely a factor on bent greens.

Bobbing for plumbs

Plumb-bobbing is all about determining where vertical is. It lets you see how much break a putt will have. Plumb-bobbing is one reason — along with old-fashioned polyester pants and electric carts — that nongolfers laugh at golfers. When a plumb-bobbing golfer pops up on TV, all the nongolfer sees is a guy, one eye closed, standing with a club dangling in front of his face. Actually, the whole thing does look more than a little goofy. I can't honestly say that I'm a devotee of the method, although plumb-bobbing works for some people. I use plumb-bobbing only when I'm totally bored on the green or if I think that one of the condos on the course was built on a slant. But if Ben Crenshaw thinks that plumb-bobbing helps, who am I to argue?

The first step in plumb-bobbing is to find your dominant eye. You close the other eye when plumb-bobbing. Here's how to find yours.

Make a circle with the thumb and index finger of your right hand a couple of inches in front of your face, as shown in Figure 8-12. Look through the circle at a distant object. Keep both eyes open at this stage. Now close your right eye. Where is the object now? If the object is still in the circle, your left eye is dominant. If, of course, you can still see the object in the circle with your left eye closed, your right eye is dominant.

Figure 8-12: Find your dominant eye.

Okay, now you're ready to plumb-bob. Put some dancing shoes on and stand as close to the ball as possible. First, keeping your dominant eye open, hold your putter in front of your face and perpendicular to the ground so that the shaft appears to run through the ball. Now look to see where the hole is in relation to the shaft. If the hole appears to the right of the club, the ball will break from the shaft to the hole — from left to right. If the hole is on the left, the opposite will be true. (See Figure 8-13.) What plumb-bobbing shows is the general slope of the green from your ball to the hole.

Remember that this method is about as exact as weather forecasting, but it gives you a general idea.

Plumb-bobbing is not an exact science. But it is very cool. People who see you plumb-bobbing will think that you know something they don't. So, if nothing else, fake plumb-bobbing. People will be impressed.

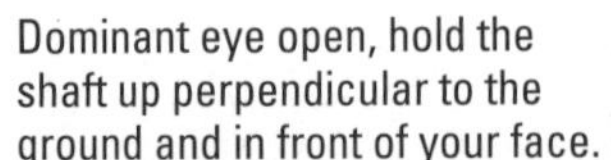
Dominant eye open, hold the shaft up perpendicular to the ground and in front of your face.

Where the hole is in relation to the shaft indicates how much a putt will bend.

Figure 8-13: Plumbing the depths.

Short Putts: Knee-Knockers

One of the greatest short putters of all time was former PGA champion Jackie Burke, who went on to help PGA Tour star Steve Elkington with his game. I was talking to Jackie one day about putting and asked how he developed his knack for making short putts. His reply seemed astonishingly simple. All Jackie did was analyze his game to identify his strengths and weaknesses. He concluded that his short game — his pitching and chipping — was where he could pick up strokes on his competitors. (See Chapter 9 for information about the short game.) Jackie knew that to score really well, he had to make a lot of putts in the 3- to 4-foot range. He thought that most of his chips and pitches would finish 3 to 4 feet from the cup.

So every day, Jackie went to the practice putting green with 100 balls. He stuck his putterhead in the cup and let the club fall to the green. Where the butt end of the putter hit the ground, he put a ball. Then he went over to the caddie shed and grabbed a caddie. Jackie handed the guy a $100 bill and told him to sit behind the cup. Jackie then putted 100 balls from that distance. If he made all 100, Jackie kept the money. If he missed even one, the caddie pocketed the cash.

Jackie followed this routine every day. All of a sudden, every short putt he hit meant something. All short putts counted. And when he got to the golf course and was faced with a short putt, he knew that he had already made 100 of them under a lot of pressure. (A $100 bill in those days was backed by real gold.)

The word *pressure* is the key. You must create a situation in which missing hurts. It doesn't have to hurt you financially. Any kind of suffering is fine. But you have to care about the result of every putt. If all you have to do after missing is pull another ball over and try again, you're never going to get better. You don't care enough.

So put yourself under pressure, even if you only make yourself stay on the green until you can make 25 putts in a row. You'll be amazed at how difficult the last putt is after you've made 24 in a row. It's the same putt in physical terms. But you're feeling nervous, knowing that missing means that you've wasted your time over the previous 24 shots. In other words, you'll have created tournament conditions on the practice green. Now that's pressure. Suck some air.

Because you don't want the ball to travel far, the stroke should be equally short, which doesn't give the putterhead much of an arc to swing on. But the lack of arc is okay. On a short putt, you don't want the putterhead to move inside or outside the target line (at least on the way back). So think "straight back, straight through." If you can keep the putterface directly toward the hole throughout the stroke and you're set up squarely, you're sure to make more knee-knockers than you miss.

My instructions sound easy, but as with everything else in golf, knowing how short putting feels helps. Place a two-by-four on the ground. Put the toe of your putter against the board. Hit some putts, keeping the toe against the board until after impact, as shown in Figure 8-14. Keep the putterhead at 90 degrees to the board so that the putter moves on the straight-back-and-straight-through path that you want. Practice this drill until you can repeat the sensation on real putts. And remember one of my *Golf For Dummies* secrets: Never allow the wrist on your lead hand to bend when putting. If you do, you'll end up in putting hell.

Keep the toe of your putter touching the board…

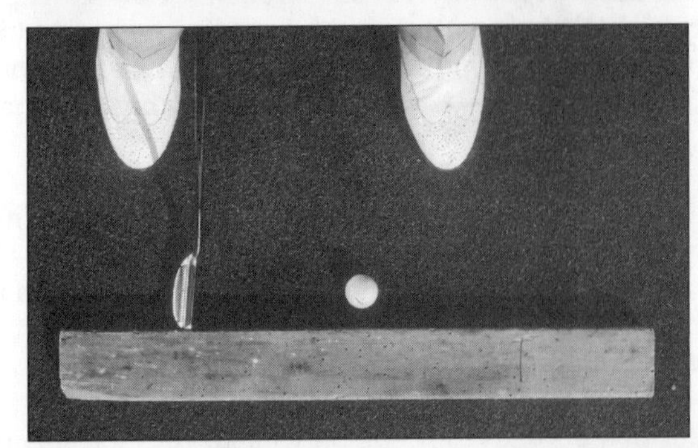

when you move the putter back…

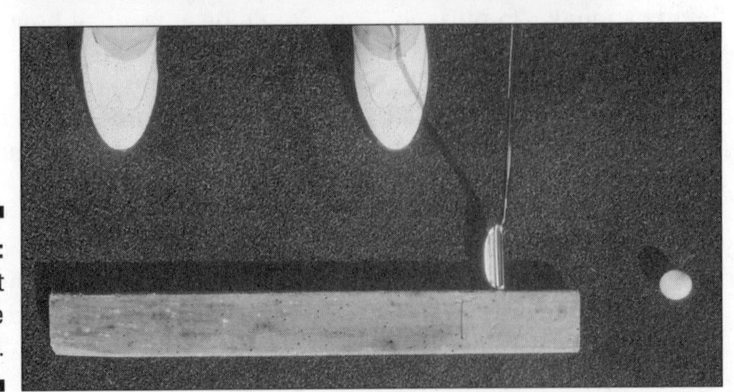

and through.

Figure 8-14: Wood that it could be this easy.

Long Putts: Lags

If short putts are a test of precision and technique, long putts are a test of your feel for pace. Nothing more. The last thing I want you thinking about over, say, a 40-foot putt is how far back to take the putter or what path the putter will follow. Instead, focus on smoothness, rhythm, and timing — all the things that foster control over the distance a ball travels. Or, as Chevy Chase said in the cult golf movie *Caddyshack,* "Be the ball."

Here's how I practice my long putting: First, I don't aim for a hole. I'm thinking distance, not direction. I figure that hitting a putt 10 feet short is a lot more likely than hitting it 10 feet wide, so distance is the key. I throw a bunch of balls down on the practice green and putt to the far fringe (see Figure 8-15). I want to see how close I can get to the edge without going over. I don't care about where I hit the putt, just how far. If you practice like this, you'll be amazed at how adept you become, to the point where you can predict at impact just how far the ball will roll.

One basic rule for a beginning golfer is to match the length of your golf swing to your putting stroke. That is, if you have a *short swing* (your left arm, if you're right-handed, doesn't get too far up in the air on your backswing), make sure that your putting stroke is a short one, too. If your full swing is *long,* make sure that your putting stroke is long also. This way, you're not contradicting yourself.

To get a feel for distance, putt a few balls to the far side of the practice putting green.

Figure 8-15: Find the pace.

Look at two of the greatest putters in the world today, Ben Crenshaw and Phil Mickelson. Both have long, slow swings, and their putting strokes are — you guessed it — long and slow. On the other hand, you have Nick Price and Lanny Wadkins, who have quick swings and quick putting strokes. They all keep a balance between golf swing and putting stroke.

Your swing tells a lot about your personality. If your golf swing is long and slow, you're probably an easygoing person. If your swing is short and fast, you're probably the type who walks around with his hair on fire.

I believe that a putting stroke that contradicts your full swing leads to problems. Sam Snead had a great long putting stroke that went with his beautiful swing, but as the years came on the golf course, the swing stayed long and the stroke got much shorter. The yips took over (see "Shh! Nobody Mentions . . . the Yips," later in this chapter). Johnny Miller had a big swing with his golf clubs and a putting stroke that was so fast you could hardly see it. There was a contradiction, and he had to go to the TV tower because he couldn't roll 'em in anymore. The change wasn't all bad; Johnny brings great insight to the game from his seat in the announcing booth.

So keep your two swings — the golf swing and the putting stroke — the same. Keep your mind quiet and create no contradictions between the two swings.

Another exercise to foster your feel for distance is what I call the ladder drill. Place a ball on the green about 10 feet from the green's edge. From at least 30 feet away, try to putt another ball between the first ball and the fringe. Then try to get a third ball between the second ball and the fringe and so on. See how many balls you can putt before you run out of room or putting gets too difficult. Obviously, the closer you get each ball to the preceding one, the more successful you are.

Shh! Nobody Mentions . . . the Yips

"I've got the yips" might be the most feared phrase in golf. Any professional golfer with the yips may as well be setting fire to dollar bills. Make that $100 bills. Simply put, *yips* is a nervous condition that prevents the afflicted from making a smooth putting stroke. Instead, the yipper makes jerky little snatches at the ball, the putterhead seemingly possessing a mind all its own.

Some of the best players in history have had their careers — at least at the top level — cut short by the yips. Ben Hogan, perhaps the steeliest competitor ever, was one such player. His great rival, Sam Snead, was another. Arnold Palmer has a mild case of the yips. Bobby Jones, winner of the Grand Slam in 1930, had the yips. So did Tommy Armour, a brave man who lost an eye fighting in the trenches during World War I and then later won a British Open and a PGA Championship, but whose playing career was finished by his inability to hole short putts. Peter Alliss, a commentator on ABC, found that he couldn't even move the putter away from the ball toward the end of his career.

Two-time Masters winner Bernhard Langer has had the yips not once, not twice, but three times. To Langer's eternal credit, he has overcome them each time, hence his rather unique, homemade style where he seems to be taking his own pulse while over a putt.

Langer, who beat the yips and is still considered one of the best putters in Europe, is the exception rather than the rule. As Henry Longhurst, the late, great writer and commentator, said about the yips, "Once you've had 'em, you've got 'em."

Longhurst, himself a yipper, once wrote a highly entertaining column on the yips, which opened with the following sentence: "There can be no more ludicrous sight than that of a grown man, a captain of industry, perhaps, and a pillar of his own community, convulsively jerking a piece of ironmongery to and fro in his efforts to hole a 3-foot putt." Longhurst is right, too. Pray that you don't get the yips.

So what causes this involuntary muscle-twitching over short putts? Mostly, I think it's fear of missing. Fear of embarrassment. Fear of who knows what. Whatever, it starts in the head. It can't be physical. After all, we're only talking about hitting the ball a short distance. What could be easier?

The yips spread insidiously through your body, like a virus. When the yips reach your hands and arms, you're doomed. Your only recourse is a complete revamping of your method. Sam Snead started putting sidesaddle, facing the hole, holding his putter with a sort of split-handed grip, the ball to the right of his feet. Other players have tried placing the left hand below the right on the putter. Langer invented his own grip and tried a long putter. The long putter (described earlier in this chapter) has saved several players.

When Mac O'Grady did his study on the yips, he mailed 1,500 questionnaires to golfers everywhere. When the doctors at UCLA's Department of Neurology looked over the results, they told us that the only way to "fool" the yips is to stay ahead of them. When you do something long enough, like bending over to putt a certain way, your body is in what the doctors call a *length tension curve.* The brain recognizes this posture, and after you've missed putts for a long period of time, the subconscious takes over and starts directing muscles to help get the ball into the hole. Your conscious and subconscious are fighting, and you're going to lose. Without your knowing it, your right hand twitches, or your left forearm has spasms trying to help you get the ball into the hole. You're in full *focal dystonia* (involuntary spasms) now, and that's no fun.

The remedy the scientists suggested was changing the length tension curve, or simply changing the way a yipper stands over a putt. The long putter surely makes you stand up to the ball differently, and maybe that's why golfers almost always putt better immediately after trying a long putter.

So if you get the yips, which usually come with age, simply change something drastic in the way you set up the ball, make your grip totally different, or go bowling.

The real key, however, is getting over the notion that using any of those methods immediately identifies you as a yipper, someone who is psychologically impaired. That, to my mind, is socially harsh. Don't be afraid to look different if you get the yips. Do whatever works.

The Art of Aiming the Ball

The golf swing is an assortment of trajectories flung around in time and space, with the golf club as the servant of the brain ill-equipped to do the directing in spatial darkness. Manifestations of your binocular acuity are the key to your pilgrimage. Are you in alignment with the parallel universe of focal obedience?

—Gary McCord, circa 1998, just after eating a lungfish tart

Golf is played with an assortment of physical skills and techniques. It is also played with the mind, which makes the final decisions and tells your motor system where and when things will happen, hopefully in some sort of harmony. It all starts with alignment.

Some golfers aim at a spot a few feet in front of the ball. When they place their putters down behind the ball, they aim the face of the putter or the lines on the putter at that spot. Aligning to a spot a foot or so in front of the ball is easier than aligning to the hole, which may be much farther away.

Bowlers use this same kind of alignment strategy. If you've ever bowled, you know about the spots that are a few feet in front of you on the lane. You look at the spots and then pick a line to roll the ball over. After I discovered this technique in my bowling league, the Gutter Dwellers, my average rocketed to 87. (Check out my bowling technique in Figure 8-16.)

You can use a couple of other strategies to help with alignment problems. The first is to take the logo of the golf ball and set it along the line that you want the putt to follow. This can help you get a better visual reference to the line. Some players, like Tiger Woods, take a Sharpie pen and make a line about an inch in length on the ball (see Figure 8-16). You can use this method in the same way as the logo tip — to achieve a better visual reference for directing the ball down the intended path. When you stand over the putt, the ball is already aimed. That easy.

Figure 8-16: Aim the logo of the ball down the intended line of the putt.

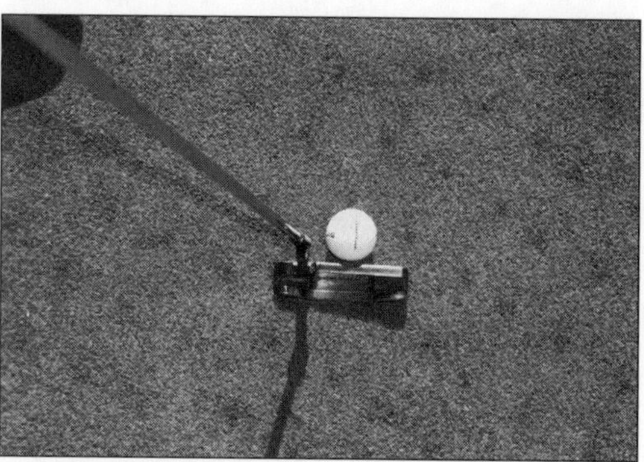

Or make a line on the ball with a Sharpie pen.

The eyes like lines

Players say that they putt better when they "see the line" of the putt. Some days when I play, the line seems so visible that I can't miss. Unfortunately, this happens about once every presidential-election year. Most of the time, I have to concentrate to "see" the line.

Another set of lines that can help your optics are the lines of your feet, knees, and shoulders. By keeping them *square* (at a right angle) to the target line, you help your eyes appreciate what is straight — and this helps keep your stroke on line.

Using the mind's eye

I remember one telecast when I commented on a putt that was caught on camera: "That putt must have taken 11 seconds." It was a long putt that went over a hill and then down a severe slope to the hole. The player had to perceive the roll in order to hit it with the proper speed; he had to visually rehearse the roll of the ball over all that terrain until it looked like an instant replay of the putt he was about to roll.

To help you keep the clubface square to your target line, use tape or a yardstick on the floor. Aim the tape at a distant target, like a baby grand piano at the far end of your ballroom. Now set up at the end of the tape as if you were going to hit an imaginary ball straight down the tape line. You're practicing visual alignment (which is a lot easier than practicing a 3-wood out of a fairway bunker with a large lip for three hours in a hailstorm). Give this drill a chance — it can really help your perception of straight lines.

When I'm having problems aligning my clubface, I take some of the gum that I've been chewing for the last three days and attach a tee to the putter with the fat end flush to the face, as shown in Figure 8-17. Then I aim that tee at the hole from about 3 feet away. (It's amazing how strong gum is after a three-day chew; in fact, I used it as mortar on my new brick mobile home.)

Your job is to stand there and visually process what a square clubface looks like as you look down the attached tee to the hole. Spend a couple of minutes appreciating this perspective. If it looks okay to you on your first try, you're in line for your Bachelor of Alignment degree. If not, repeat this drill daily until it looks okay the first time you place the club down. Use this drill to educate your eyes to a straight-line perspective and a square clubface.

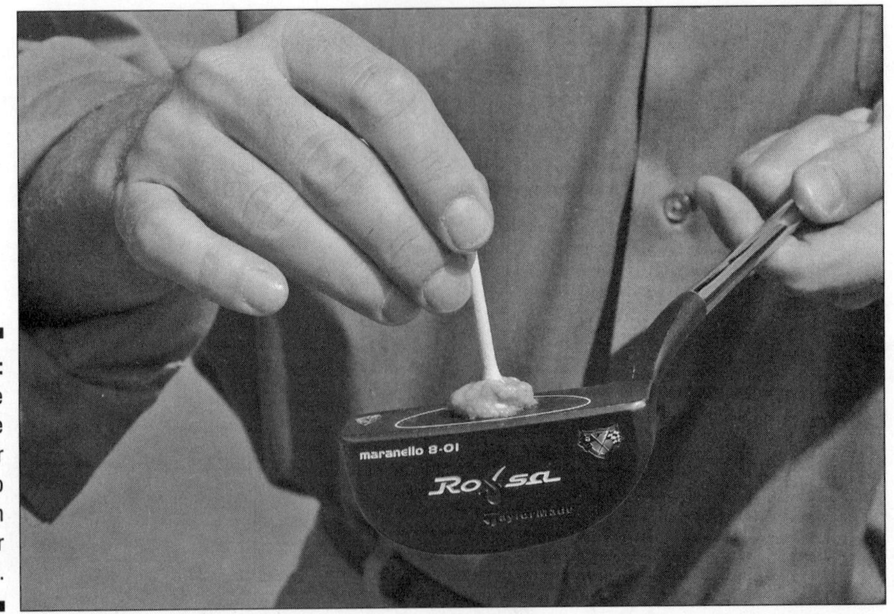

Figure 8-17: Stick a tee to the face of your putter to help align with your target.

Speed kills

Almost every putt is what I call a "depth charge launch." That means that it should have the speed to lurk around the hole and just maybe hit the hole and fall in. If you get it close, you might perform a burial with your ball. One of the best ways to develop a touch for the speed at which a putt should roll is to imagine things happening before they really do.

You must optically preview the putt's roll from its stationary point to a resting place near the hole — a tap-in is really nice. This optical preview activates the motor system to respond with the right amount of energy to hit the putt. You'd do the same thing if I told you to throw a ball over a bush and make it land no more than 5 feet beyond the bush. You'd decide at what arc and speed to toss the ball, and your mind's eye would relay this information to your muscles.

View a putt from a point off to the side of the target line, midway between the ball and the hole, as shown in Figure 8-18. This technique can give you a better feel for the distance. Some professionals swear that they can visualize the proper speed of a putt twice as well from the side.

A good rule of thumb: Don't change your mind about your strategy while you're over a putt. For one thing, putts look different from above than from the side! For another, the ground you stand on may not be sloped the same as it is near the hole. And unless the putt is all downhill, the ball will do most of its curving during the last third of the putt. (That's another reason to stand to the side of the putt — assessing the last third of the putt is easier from there.)

Figure 8-18: Viewing the putt from the low side can help you judge distance and speed.

Some quick tips you may want to write down in your reminder book:

- **Fast greens break more, so don't hit the ball too hard.** But keep in mind that hitting the ball softly means that the slope will affect it more.
- **Downhill putts act like fast greens, because the slope affects the roll of the ball for more than the last few feet.**
- **Slow greens break less, so you have to hit the ball harder.** That initial burst of speed will keep the ball from breaking as much.
- **Uphill putts act like slow greens.** Your challenge is to figure out how much uphill slope you're dealing with, and then adjust your putt accordingly — the steeper the slope, the more power it takes. Imagining the hole's being farther away than it really is can help.

Points of the roll

I give you information on some complicated stuff, so here are some key points:

- **Keep your alignment parallel to the target line.** All the following parts of you stay parallel to that line:
    - Feet
    - Knees
    - Shoulders
    - Eye line
- **Know what your putter blade looks like when it's square to the line.**
- **Use the ball's logo or a line you've marked on the ball to help you align putts.**
- **Follow the line of your intended putt with your eyes at the speed that you think the ball will roll.**
- **Stare at the line of your putt longer than you look at the golf ball.**

To putt well, you have to train yourself. Putting takes practice. The boys at the club practice putting less than anything else, but more than half the strokes you play in this silly game may be putts. Create some games on the putting green to enhance your desire to go there and practice. Your score card will thank you.

Chapter 9

Chipping and Pitching

In This Chapter

- Understanding the short game
- Noting the importance of the short game
- Chipping your way to success
- Pitching yourself out of tight spots

Five-time PGA champion Walter Hagen had the right approach. He stood on the first tee knowing that he'd probably hit at least six terrible shots that day. So when he did hit terrible shots, he didn't get upset. Hagen simply relied on his superior *short game* (every shot within 80 yards of the hole) to get him out of trouble. That combination of attitude and dexterity made him a feared match player. His apparent nonchalance — "Always take time to smell the flowers," he used to say — and his ability to get up and down "from the garbage" put a lot of pressure on his opponents. Opponents became depressed or annoyed and eventually downhearted. More often than not, Hagen won his matches without having hit his full shots too solidly. He proved that golf is more than hitting the ball well — golf is a game of managing your misses.

Golf Has Its Ups and Downs

As I mention earlier, the short game is every shot hit within 80 yards of the hole. That includes sand play (Chapter 10) and putting (Chapter 8). So what's left? Chipping and pitching — two versions of short shots to the green. The *chip* is a low shot, while the *pitch* is a higher flier.

Hang around golfers for only a short while, and you inevitably hear one say something like, "I missed the third green to the right but got up and down for my par." At this stage, you're probably wondering what in the world "up and down" means. Well, the "up" part is the subject of this chapter — chipping or pitching the ball to the hole. The "down" half of the equation, of course, is holing the putt after your chip or pitch (see Chapter 8). Thus, a golfer with a good short game is one who gets "up and down" a high percentage of the time (anywhere above 50 percent).

Now here's the weird thing: Although a good short game can erase your mistakes and keep a good round going, many amateurs tend to look down on golfers blessed with a delicate touch around the greens. They hate to lose to someone who beats them with good chipping and putting. Somehow a strong short game isn't perceived as "macho golf" — at least not in the same way as smashing drives 300 yards and hitting low, raking, iron shots to greens is macho. Good ball strikers tend to look down on players with better short games. This attitude is more than a snobbery thing — it's also a missing-the-point thing.

In golf, you want to move the ball around the course while achieving the lowest score you can. How you get that job done is up to you. No rule says that you have to look pretty when you play golf. Your round isn't going to be hung in an art gallery. As someone once said, "Three of them and one of those makes four." Remember that saying. You can make up for a lot of bad play with one good putt.

You don't hear professionals downplaying the importance of a good short game. We know that the short game is where we make our money. Here's proof: If you put a *scratch* (zero-handicap) amateur and a tournament pro on the tee with drivers in their hands, the two shots don't look that much different. Sure, you can tell who is the better player, but the amateur at least *looks* competitive.

The gap in quality grows on the approach shots, again on wedge play, and then again on the short game. In fact, the closer the players get to the green, the more obvious the difference in level of play. And the green is where a mediocre score gets turned into a good score and where a good score gets turned into a great score. (Take a look at the sample score card in Figure 9-1. It wouldn't hurt to keep that kind of record for yourself once in a while.)

Okay, I've convinced you of the importance of the short game in the overall scheme of things. Before you go further, you need to know the difference between a chip and a pitch. In the United States, this question is easy to answer. A *chip* is a short shot that's mostly on the ground. A *pitch,* in contrast, is generally a longer shot that's mostly in the air.

Men's Course Rating/Slope
Blue 73.1/137
White 71.0/130

Women's Course Rating/Slope
Red 73.7/128

Blue Tees	White Tees	Par	Hcp	JOHN				HOLE	HIT FAIRWAY	HIT GREEN		No. PUTTS	Hcp	Par	Red Tees
377	361	4	11	4				1	√	√		2	13	4	310
514	467	5	13	8				2	√	0		3	3	5	428
446	423	4	1	7				3	0	0		2	1	4	389
376	356	4	5	6				4	0	0		2	11	4	325
362	344	4	7	5				5	0	√		3	7	4	316
376	360	4	9	6				6	√	0		2	9	4	335
166	130	3	17	4				7	0	√		3	17	3	108
429	407	4	3	5				8	√	√		3	5	4	368
161	145	3	15	5				9	0	0		2	15	3	122
3207	2993	35		50				Out	4	4		22		35	2701
			Initial										Initial		
366	348	4	18	5				10	0	0		2	14	4	320
570	537	5	10	7				11	√	0		3	2	5	504
438	420	4	2	5				12	√	0		2	6	4	389
197	182	3	12	4				13	0	0		2	16	3	145
507	475	5	14	5				14	√	√		2	4	5	425
398	380	4	4	5				15	0	√		3	8	4	350
380	366	4	6	5				16	√	0		2	10	4	339
165	151	3	16	4				17	0	0		2	18	3	133
397	375	4	8	5				18	0	0		2	12	4	341
3418	3234	36		45				In	3	2		20		36	2946
6625	6227	71		95				Tot	7	6		42		71	5647
		Handicap											Handicap		
		Net Score											Net Score		
		Adjust											Adjust		

Scorer Attested Date

Figure 9-1: A score card with putts and chips highlighted.

Chips Ahoy!

Chips are short shots played around the greens with anything from a 5-iron to a sand wedge. The basic idea is to get the ball on the green and rolling as soon as you can. If you get the ball running like a putt, you'll have an easier time judging how far it will go.

Pick your spot

Your first point of reference is the spot where you want the ball to land. If at all possible, you want that spot to be on the putting surface. The turf there is generally flatter and better prepared, which makes the all-important first bounce more predictable. You want to avoid landing chips on rough, uneven, or sloping ground.

Pick a spot about 2 feet onto the green (see Figure 9-2). From that spot, I like to visualize the ball running along the ground toward the hole. Visualization is a big part of chipping. Try to see the shot in your mind's eye before you hit the ball. Then be as exact as you can with your target. You can't be too precise.

Figure 9-2: Pick your spot.

Choose the right club

Your choice of club depends on the amount of room you have between your landing point and the hole. If you only have 15 feet, you need a more *lofted* club (one with a face that is severely angled back from vertical), like a sand wedge, so that the ball doesn't run too far.

If you've ever watched golf on TV, you've probably seen Phil Mickelson or Tiger Woods use a full swing to hit the ball straight up in the air and cover only a short distance on the ground. Phil can do another thing that's really astounding: You stand about 6 feet away from Phil and turn your back to him. You then cup your hands and hold them straight out from your chest. Phil takes a full swing with his sand wedge and lofts the ball over your head and into your sweaty, waiting hands — all from only 6 feet away. Now that's a lob wedge!

If that gap is bigger — say, 60 feet — then a straighter-faced club, like a 7-iron, is more practical. Figure 9-3 illustrates this concept.

Figure 9-3: Get the ball rolling.

Lies and instinct

Then you have the problem of how the ball is lying on the ground. When the ball is in longer grass, you need to use a more lofted club and make a longer swing, no matter where the hole is. (***Remember:*** Longer grass means a longer swing.) You need to get the ball high enough to escape the longer rough. If the ball is lying "down" in a depression and you can't get the ball out with the straight-faced club, which the situation normally calls for, you have to go to more loft and move the ball back a little in your stance — closer to your right foot — to make the shot work (see Chapter 12 for more on low shots). So this part of the game does require flexibility.

Use the philosophy that I've outlined as a starting point, not as holy writ that must be followed to the letter. Let your own creativity take over. Go with your instincts when you need to choose the right club or shot. The more you practice this part of your game, the better your instincts become.

Practice, and only practice, makes you better. Try all sorts of clubs for these shots. Sooner or later, you'll develop a feel for the short game. I stress that you should use as many clubs as possible when practicing. Using different clubs helps you work on the technique and not just a particular shot.

Now hit that chip

Short game guru Phil Rodgers taught me my chipping technique, which is basically the same one that I employ for putting. I use a putting stroke, but with a lofted club — and I want you to do the same. Take your putting grip and stroke, and go hit chip shots.

The key to chipping is the setup. Creating the right positions at address is essential.

You want your stance to be narrow, about 12 inches from heel to heel, and open — pull your left foot back from the target line. Your shoulders should be open to the target as well. Now place about 80 percent of your weight on your left side. By moving your hands ahead of the ball, you encourage the downward strike that you need to make solid contact with the ball. Place the ball on a line about 2 inches to the left of your right big toe, as shown in Figure 9-4.

During your stroke, focus on the back of your left wrist. Your left wrist must stay flat and firm, as in putting (see Figure 9-5). To keep your wrist flat, tape a Popsicle stick to the back of that wrist (slipping the stick under your watchband works almost as well). You'll feel any breakdowns right away. Now go hit some putts and chips.

Figure 9-4: Chipping.

Figure 9-5: No wrist break.

When I play a tour event, one of the first things I do is go to the putting green, where I hit putts and chips to get an idea of the speed of the greens. I find a flat spot on the green and drop some golf balls about 5 feet off the putting surface. Then I put a coin on the green 2 feet from the *fringe* (the collar of grass around the green — it's longer than the grass on the green but shorter than the grass on the fairway). Then I take an 8-iron, 9-iron, and wedge to my spot off the green and chip balls onto the green, trying to bounce each ball off the coin and letting it then run to the hole. I get a really good idea of how fast the greens are that week. You can also develop a touch for those shots — and when you miss as many greens as I do, the practice comes in handy.

Make Your Pitch

Pitch shots, which you play with only your wedges and 9-iron, are generally longer than chip shots, so, as you'd expect, you need to make a longer swing. That introduces wrist action into the equation, which introduces the problem of how long your swing should be and how fast. In other words, pitch shots need some serious feel.

Even the best players try to avoid pitch shots. They're "in-between" shots. You can't just make your normal, everyday, full swing — that would send the ball way too far. You're stuck making a half-type swing — which is never easy, especially when you're under pressure.

Anyway, here's how to build your pitching swing.

First, adopt the same stance that you did for the chip shot: same width, same posture, same ball position. The only difference is in the alignment of your shoulders, which should be parallel to your toe line and open to the target line, as shown in Figure 9-6.

Figure 9-6: Set up to pitch.

Now make a miniswing (which I describe in Chapter 6). Without moving the butt end of the club too far in your backswing, hinge your wrists so that the shaft is horizontal. Then swing through the shot. Watch how far the ball goes. That distance is your point of reference. Do you want to hit the next pitch 10 yards farther? Make your swing a little longer (see Figure 9-7). Shorter? Your swing follows suit. That way, your rhythm never changes. You want the clubhead accelerating smoothly through the ball. And that acceleration is best achieved if the momentum is built up gradually from address.

Figure 9-7: Think "tempo."

Poor pitchers of the ball do one of two things: Either they start their swings way too slowly and then speed up too much at impact, or they jerk the club away from the ball and have to decelerate later. Both swings lead to what golf columnist Peter Dobereiner christened "sickening knee-high fizzers" — low, thin shots that hurtle uncontrollably over the green, or complete duffs that travel only a few feet. Not a pretty sight. The most common cause of both is tension. So relax.

Imagine that you're swinging with a potato chip between your teeth. Focus on not biting down on it. That'll keep you relaxed.

Here's a game we play at the back of the range at our facility at Grayhawk Golf Club in Scottsdale, Arizona. We get five empty buckets and place them in a straight line at 20, 40, 60, 80, and 100 feet. We then have one hour to hit one ball into each bucket, starting at 20 feet. The winner gets the title to the other guy's car. We're still driving our own cars — we usually get frustrated and quit before the one-hour time limit expires, or we go to lunch. But at least we get some good pitching practice.

In golf, you get better by doing; you *don't* get better by doing nothing.

Last pitching thought: Although pitch shots fly higher than chips, apply the same philosophy to your pitching: Get the ball back to the ground as soon as possible. Pick out your landing area and let the ball roll. See the shot in your mind's eye before you hit the ball, and remember your *Golf For Dummies* secret: Hit down — don't try to lift the ball.

Chapter 10

It's Your Sandbox: Bunker Play

In This Chapter

- What is a bunker?
- Understanding sand play
- Achieving a sound bunker technique
- Dealing with a less-than-perfect lie

I have read countless articles and books on sand play, and they all say the same thing: Because you don't even have to hit the ball, playing from the sand is the easiest part of golf. Bull trap! If sand play were the easiest aspect of the game, all those articles and books would never be written in the first place. Everyone would be blasting the ball onto the putting surface with nary a care in the world. And that, take it from me, is certainly not the case.

In this chapter, I explain the equipment and techniques you need to get out of the sand. I tell how and why your sand wedge is different from any other club in your bag. At the end of the chapter, I even tell how you can hit a successful bunker shot from a terrible lie. Do *that* your next time out and your friends will be amazed.

Bunkers: Don't Call 'Em Sand Traps!

Bunkers, or sand traps (as I'm told *not* to call them on TV), provoke an extraordinary amount of "sand angst" among golfers. But sometimes, *aiming* for a bunker actually makes sense — on a long, difficult approach shot, for example. The pros know that the "up and down" from sand can actually be easier than from the surrounding (usually long and thick) grass.

Bunkers began life as dips in the ground on the windswept Scottish linksland. Because such areas were sheltered from cold breezes, sheep would take refuge in them. Thus, the dips expanded and got deeper. When the land came to be used for golf, the locals took advantage of what God and the sheep left behind and fashioned sand-filled bunkers. (No word on what the sheep thought of all this.)

On these old courses, the greens were sited so as to maximize the bunkers' threat to golfers' shots, which is why they came to be named *hazards* in the rules of golf. Later, course architects placed these insidious "traps" so as to penalize wayward shots. That's why you generally don't see bunkers in the middle of fairways — they're mostly to the sides.

As to how much sand you find in a typical bunker, that varies. I prefer a depth of about 2 inches. That stops balls from burying too much on landing but still provides a decent cushion for the escape shot.

I don't know too many amateurs who have ever aimed at a bunker. Mired in a bunker is the last place they want to be. Typifying the way in which amateur golfers look at bunkers is the experience the late Tip O'Neill had years ago during the first few days of the Bob Hope Chrysler Classic, a pro-am tournament. The former Speaker of the House, admittedly not the strongest golfer (even among celebrities), found himself in a very deep bunker. He then spent the next few hours (okay, it just *seemed* that long) trying to extricate first the ball, and then himself, from the trap — all on national television. You could almost hear millions of viewers saying to themselves, "Yeah, been there, done that."

Why is it that most amateurs are scared to death every time their shots end up in a greenside bunker? Just what is it about sand play that they find so tough? Well, after much research, some of it in a laboratory, I've come to the conclusion the problem is simple. (If it weren't simple, I would never have discovered it.) It all comes down to lack of technique and/or a lack of understanding.

Sorry, sand man

Getting the ball out of a bunker can be easy if you practice enough and get a feel for it. I knew at an early age that my scoring depended on getting up and down out of bunkers with a certain regularity, so I practiced bunker shots with a vengeance. As a result, I can get a ball out of a bunker with everything from a sand wedge to a putter.

One day I was playing in the Kemper Open in Charlotte, North Carolina, when I saw a notoriously bad bunker player who was on the tour practicing hard on his sand play. After a few moments of idle conversation and general harassing, a bet transpired. He would hit ten balls with his sand wedge; I would hit five balls with a putter. If I got my ball closer than his ball, he would have to go in the locker room and announce to everyone that I beat him with a putter out of a bunker. If he won, I would take him to dinner and then not bother him for the rest of the year.

The laughter from the locker room echoed throughout the clubhouse, and his reputation as the worst bunker player on tour remained intact. I cannot divulge his name because he is playing the senior tour now and is doing very well. He got much better getting out of the sand after some much-needed practice.

Faced with a bunker shot, many golfers are beaten before they start. You can tell by their constipated looks, sweaty foreheads, and hesitant body language. Their reaction when they fail is also interesting. After a couple of shots finish up back in the bunker, most people don't focus on their technique. They merely try to hit the shot harder, making more and more violent swings. Not good. Hitting the ball harder only makes them angrier, and then the ball sure isn't going to come out. Still, they dig a nice big hole, which is perfect if they want to bury a small pet but not much good for anything else.

Part of the reason for this all-too-human reaction is that long stretches of failure resign you to your fate. In your mind, you've tried everything, and you still can't get the damn thing out. So you trudge into the bunker expecting the worst, and you usually get it.

The Problem with Sand Play

A huge majority of golfers address the ball in a way that makes it all but impossible to create the correct angles in their golf swings. Golf, and especially bunker play, is only the creation of the proper angle that the clubhead must take into the ball. (The *clubhead* is the part that, when you hold the club in front of your face, hangs below the leading edge.) Sometimes, the root of the duffs, hacks, slashes, and any other sort of poor shot is ball position. If you have the ball positioned way back toward your right foot, as so many people seem to do, you won't ever get the ball out of the trap. You can't hit the ball high enough, for one thing. For another, the clubhead enters the sand at too steep an angle. In other words, the clubhead digs into the sand instead of sliding through it. When that happens, the ball usually stays in the bunker, sucking sand.

Poor bunker players suffer from a lack of understanding. They get into the sand and start "digging" as if they're having a day out at a quarantined beach. Sometimes I feel like throwing poor bunker players a bucket and shovel so that they can dig for clams. Then at least they'd have something to show for all their efforts.

To Be — Or Not to Be — Handy from Sand

To be a competent sand player, you must take advantage of the way your sand wedge is designed. The bottom of the club is wider than the top (see Figure 10-1). The *bounce* is the bottom of the clubhead. Believe me, if you can make the best use of the bounce, bunker play will be off your endangered-species list.

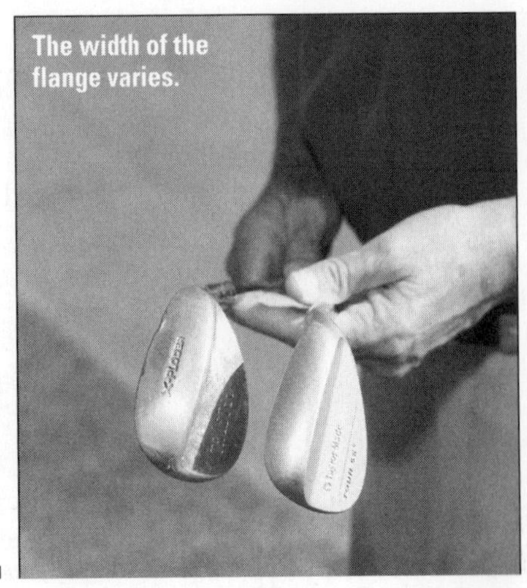

Figure 10-1: Sand wedges are different.

The bounce is the part of the clubhead that should contact the sand first. This encourages the sliding motion that's so crucial to good bunker play. Think about it: The sand is going to slow the club as you swing down and through, which is okay. But you want to keep the slowdown to a minimum. If the club digs in too much, the ball probably won't get out of the bunker. So *slide* the clubhead; don't use it to dig. Take note, however, that not every sand wedge has the same amount of bounce. The width of the sole and the amount that it hangs below the leading edge varies. This, of course, begs another question: How do you know how much bounce your sand wedge needs? The determining factor is the type of sand you play from. The bigger the bounce or the wider the sole on your sand wedge, the less it will dig into the sand.

If the sand at your home club is typically pretty firm underfoot, you need a sand wedge with very little bounce. A club with a lot of bounce does just that — bounce. And hard (or wet) sand only accentuates that tendency. So using that club is only going to see you hitting a lot of shots thin, the clubhead skidding off the sand and contacting the ball's equator. Either you hit the ball into the face of the bunker and don't get out at all, or the ball misses the face and finishes way over the green. Neither result is socially acceptable.

At the other end of the scale is really soft, deep sand. For that sort of stuff, you need a lot of bounce. In fact, because the clubhead digs so easily when the sand is soft, you can't have enough bounce.

But enough of this preamble. Take a look at how a sound sand technique is properly — and easily — achieved.

"Hoe-ly cow!"

Once, while in Vail, Colorado, I received an urgent phone call from director Ron Shelton while he was shooting the movie *Tin Cup.* He said, "Gary, we forgot to ask you this, but how do you hit a gardening hoe out of a bunker?"

"Gee, Ron," I said, "I haven't done that in a while; let me think. *What do you mean, how do you hit a gardening hoe out of a bunker?!!"* Ron told me that a scene had to be shot the next day with Kevin Costner hitting a ball out of a bunker, with a hoe, and that the ball had to land no more than 3 feet from the hole. Sure. Right.

I went to the practice green at Singletree Golf Course with my shag bag full of balls and a hoe. It was pouring down rain. It took me 40 minutes to get a single ball out of the bunker, and I *bladed* (hit the center of the ball with the leading edge) that one to get it out. I finally decided that the bottom edge of the hoe was too sharp and I needed some bounce to make it perform better in the sand. So I bent the hoe on the bottom and immediately started to get the ball up and out.

I called the movie set and gave directions on the technique of how to bend the hoe. They shot the scene, and Kevin Costner hit the first ball out of the bunker, with the hoe, 2 feet from the hole. That's a take; wrap it up, as they say.

So if the bounce can work to get a ball out of a bunker with a hoe, think what it can do for your sand wedge.

The Splash

Okay, you're in a greenside bunker. You want to get the ball out and onto the putting surface. Here's what to do: Open your stance by pulling your left foot back. Pull your foot back until you start to feel vaguely ridiculous. Your left foot's position must feel funny to you. If it doesn't, pull your foot back more. Next, open (turn to the right) your sand wedge to the point where the face is almost looking straight up at the sky, as shown in Figure 10-2. The ball should be positioned forward in your stance toward your left heel. (Do this even more if you're unlucky enough to be very close to the face of the bunker.) You should feel like you'll go right under the ball when you swing at it. This position should feel just as weird as your stance. Again, if it doesn't, turn your sand wedge to the right even more.

Your hands should be ibehi nd" the ball.

At address, pull your left foot back.

Turn the clubface clockwise until it looks skyward.

Figure 10-2: Open your stance until it feels ridiculous.

Most amateurs I play with don't do either of those things. They stand too square and don't open the clubface nearly enough. In effect, they don't take advantage of their sand wedges. This club is most efficient when the face is wide open (turned clockwise). Sand wedges are designed that way. The open face sends the ball up when you hit the sand.

Here's one other thing that you should know. When I go home to play, I notice that nobody practices bunker shots, not even my pal Sand Wedge Sam. (He got his nickname after demonstrating uncommon prowess in the much underestimated and neglected art of sand-wedge tossing.) Don't fall into that trap (I love bad puns); get into a bunker and *practice.* Besides, you never know, you may like bunkers.

Finally, remember that your club must not touch the sand before you hit the ball. That's *grounding* the club — illegal in a hazard.

Okay, you're over the shot, now what? You want to know where to hit the sand, right?

Aim about a credit-card length behind the ball. Swing at about 80 percent of full speed. Think of it as a sliding motion. Don't hit down. Let the clubhead throw a "scoop" of sand onto the green, as shown in Figure 10-3. Focusing on a full, uninhibited follow-through will help (see Figure 10-4). Forget the ball — all you're trying to do is throw sand out of the bunker. (The more sand you throw, the shorter the shot will be. So if you need to hit the shot a fair distance, hit maybe only 2 inches behind the ball.) If you can throw sand, the ball will be carried along for the ride. And that's why better players say that bunker play is easy — the clubhead never actually contacts the ball. Now go get some sunblock and spend some time practicing in the sand.

Figure 10-3: No digging allowed.

Figure 10-4: Keep going!

Buried Alive!

Unfortunately, not every lie (where the ball is sitting) in a bunker is perfect. Sometimes the ball *plugs* (embeds itself in the sand so that only part of it is visible). You'll hear other golfers call this sort of lie a *fried egg.* When that happens to your ball, and after you're through cursing your bad luck, you need to employ a different technique.

Or at least a different alignment of the clubface. You still need your open stance, but this time don't open the clubface. Keep it a little *hooded.* In other words, align the clubface to the left of your ultimate target. Now, shift nearly all your weight to your left side, which puts you "ahead" of the shot (see Figure 10-5). And play the ball back in your stance. This is the one time you want the leading edge of the club to *dig.* The ball, after all, is below the surface.

Figure 10-5: A buried lie in a bunker: Can you dig it?

Okay, you're ready. Swing the club up and down, and I mean *up* and *down* like you're chopping wood with a dull ax. Hit straight down on the sand a couple of inches behind the ball (see Figure 10-6). A follow-through isn't needed. Just hit down. Hard. The ball should pop up and then run to the hole. With little or no backspin, the ball will run like it just stole something. So allow for extra roll.

Figure 10-6: Hit down hard!

Just how hard you should hit down is hard for me to say — it depends on the texture and depth of the sand and on how deep the ball is buried. That old standby, practice, tells you what you need to know.

Second-to-last point: Practice with clubs of various lofts, and then use whatever works. Many times I use my pitching wedge (which has little bounce and a sharper leading edge and, therefore, digs more) with this technique.

Last point: Always smooth out your footprints when leaving a bunker. If there's no rake lying nearby, use your feet. Or if you're like my buddy Steamroller Ron, just roll around in the bunker until it's real smooth. Golfers used to gather to watch Ron smooth out the sand. We had very few rakes at the muni, and the Steamroller was the nearest thing we had to one. I miss Steamroller; he sold his gravel business and moved to Saudi Arabia.

Part III

Common Faults and Easy Fixes

"The book said I should place the ball opposite my left armpit. So I put it in my right armpit."

In this part . . .

This part covers common faults — and their cures. Have you ever had one of those days when nothing goes right? You're hitting the ball fat or thin, or when you *do* hit the thing it slices off the premises? I've got remedies for your ailments. You didn't know that we provided health care for golf, did you?

In this part, I also tell you how to play in bad weather, and how to deal with the bad breaks you're sure to encounter out there. I even give you tips on surviving a round with a loud, obnoxious, cell-phone-blabbing jerk — even if you're not a master of kung fu.

Chapter 11

Typical Problems and Simple Solutions

In This Chapter

- Skying your tee shots
- Slicing the ball to the right
- Hooking your ball to the left
- Topping the ball
- Shanking the ball
- Missing too many putts

If you're like everyone else who has ever played the game, golf is a constant battle against annoying faults in your full swing or putting stroke. Even the best golfers have some little hitch in their methods that they have to watch for, especially under pressure. Greg Norman once had a tendency to hit the ball well to the right of the target on the closing holes of big tournaments. Phil Mickelson and Tiger Woods went through periods when they drove the ball crooked at the wrong times. Watch your playing companions when they get a little nervous; you can see all sorts of unfortunate events. Putts are left short. Even simple shots take longer to play. Conversation all but stops. And best of all, from your point of view, any faults in their swings are cruelly exposed.

You're going to develop faults in your swing and game. Faults are a given, no matter how far you progress. The trick is catching your faults before they spoil your outlook on your game. Faults left unattended often turn into major problems and ruin your game.

The root cause of most faults is your head position. Your cranium's position relative to the ball as you strike it dictates where the bottom of your swing is. The bottom of your swing is always a spot on the ground relative to where your head is positioned. Test that assertion. Shift your weight and your head toward the target onto your left side. Leave the ball in its regular position. Now make your normal swing with, say, a 6-iron. The divot made by the club will be more in front of the ball. The bottom of your swing moves toward the target along with your head.

The opposite is also true. Shift your weight and head to the right, and the bottom of your swing moves in the same direction.

The bottom line: If your head moves too much during the swing, you have little chance to correct things before impact, and the result is usually some form of poor shot.

Don't get the idea that excessive head movement is responsible for absolutely every bad shot. Other poor plays can stem from improper use of your hands, arms, or body. But try to keep your head as steady as possible.

Anyway, that's the big picture. Now I'll get more specific. What follows is a discussion of the most common faults you are likely to develop, with cures for each fault. After you know what your tendencies are, you can refer to this chapter regularly to work on fixing them.

Skying Your Tee Shots: The Fountain Ball

One of the most common sights I see on the first tee of a pro-am or member-guest tournament is the skyed tee shot — the ball goes higher than it goes forward. It's usually hit on the top part of the driver, causing an ugly mark to appear, which is one reason why a tour player never lets an amateur use his driver. If the amateur hits a fountain ball (as my wife likes to call it, because she says that a skyed tee shot has the same trajectory as one of those fountains in Italy), he'll have a lot of apologizing to do.

At the municipal course where I nurtured my game, we had few rules, but one of them was that if you could catch your drive off the tee, you could play it over again with no penalty. We had so many guys wearing tennis shoes for speed that it looked like a track meet.

If you're hitting the ball on the top side of your driver, you're swinging the club on too much of a downward arc. What's that mean, you ask? It means that your head is too far in front of the ball (toward the target side of the ball) and your left shoulder is too low at impact — bad news for your driver.

Here's what to do:

1. **Go find an upslope.**
2. **Stand so that your left foot (if you're right-handed) is higher than your right.**
3. **Tee the ball up and hit drivers or 3-woods until you get the feeling of staying back and under the shot.**

   The uphill lie promotes this feeling.

I'll tell you a secret about this teaching trick: People who hit down on their drivers want to kill the stupid ball in front of their buddies. These golfers have a tremendous shift of their weight to the left side on the downswing. If you hit balls from an upslope, you can't get your weight to the left side as quickly. Consequently, you keep your head behind the ball, and your left shoulder goes up at impact. Practice on an upslope until you get a feel and then proceed to level ground. The next time I see you in the sky, it will be on Delta Airlines.

Slicing and Hooking

Most golfers *slice,* which means that the ball starts to the left of the target and finishes well to the right. I think slicing stems from the fact that most players tend to aim to the right of their target. When they do so, their swings have to compensate so that the resulting shots can finish close to the target.

In most cases, that compensation starts when your brain realizes that if you swing along your aim, the ball will fly way to the right. The resulting flurry of arms and legs isn't pretty — and invariably, neither is the shot. Soon this weak, left-to-right ball flight makes your life a slicing hell. Slices don't go very far. They're horrible, weak shots that affect your DNA for generations to come.

In general, slicers use too much body action and not enough hand action in their swings. Golfers who hook have the opposite tendency — too much hand action, not enough body.

Fear not, hapless hackers: Two variations of the same drill offer solutions.

If you're a slicer, you need to get your hands working in the swing. Here's how:

1. **Address a ball as you normally do.**
2. **Turn your whole body until your butt is toward the target and your feet are perpendicular to the target line.**
3. **Twist your upper body to the left so that you can again place the clubhead behind the ball.**

   Don't move your feet, however. From this position, you have, in effect, made it impossible for your body to turn to your left on the throughswing (see Figure 11-1).

   Try it. Should I call a chiropractor yet? The only way you can swing the club through the ball is by using your hands and arms.

If you slice, try this drill: Stand with your back to the target. Then turn your whole body until your butt is to the target and twist your upper body to address the ball.

Swing back…

and then swing your hands and arms through…

to finish. The ball should fly from right to left.

Figure 11-1: More hand action kills the slice.

4. **Hit a few balls.**

   Focus on letting the toe of the clubhead pass your heel through impact. Quite a change in your ball flight, eh? Because your hands and arms are doing so much of the rotating work in your new swing, the clubhead is doing the same. The clubhead is now closing as it swings through the impact area. The spin imparted on the ball now causes a slight right-to-left flight — something I bet you thought you'd never see.

After you've hit about 20 shots by using this drill, switch to your normal stance and try to reproduce the feel you had standing in that strange but correct way. You'll soon be hitting hard, raking *draws* (slight hooks) far up the fairway.

Golfers prone to *hooks* (shots that start right and finish left) have the opposite problem — too much hand action and not enough body. Here's a drill if you tend to hook the ball:

1. **Adopt your regular stance.**
2. **Turn your whole body until you're looking directly at the target.**
3. **Twist your upper body to the right — don't move your feet — until you can set the clubhead behind the ball (see Figure 11-2).**
4. **Hit some shots.**

   You'll find solid contact easiest to achieve when you turn your body hard to the left, which prevents your hands from becoming overactive. Your ball flight will soon be a gentle *fade* (slight slice).

After about 20 shots, hit some balls from your normal stance, practicing the technique I just described. Reproduce the feel of this drill, and you'll be on your way.

If you hit hooks, try this drill: Stand with both feet facing the target. Then turn your upper body until you are facing the target.

and then turn your body in concert with the club...

Figure 11-2: More body action will straighten your hook.

Topping the Ball

Topping isn't much fun. Plus, it's a lot of effort for very little return. *Topping* is when you make a full-blooded, nostrils-flaring swipe at the ball, only to tick the top and send the ball a few feeble yards.

Topping occurs because your head is moving up and down during your swing. A rising head during your downswing pulls your shoulders, arms, hands, and the clubhead up with it. Whoops!

To whip topping, you have to keep your head from lifting. And the best way to do that is to establish a reference for your eyes before you start the club back. Stick an umbrella in the ground just beyond the golf ball, as shown in Figure 11-3. Focus your eyes on the umbrella throughout your swing. As long as you stay focused on the umbrella, your head and upper torso cannot lift, which ends topped shots.

Figure 11-3: The umbrella drill can help you avoid topped shots.

Duffing and Thinning Chip Shots

Duffing and thinning are exact opposites, yet, like the slice and the hook, they have their roots in the same fault (see Figure 11-4).

Figure 11-4: The cure for chipping nightmares.

When you *duff* a chip (also called a *chili-dip,* or, as I like to say, *Hormel*), your swing is bottoming out behind the ball. You're hitting too much ground and not enough ball (also called hitting it *fat*), which means that the shot falls painfully short of the target and your playing partners laugh outrageously. Duffing a chip is the one shot in golf that can get you so mad that you can't spell your mother's name.

One shot that is rare to actually witness is the *double chip,* where you hit the chip fat, causing the clubhead to hit the ball twice — once while it's in the air. You could never do this if you tried, but sometime, somewhere, you'll see it performed and will stand in amazement.

I was playing a tournament in Palm Springs, California, when one of the amateurs, standing near the condos surrounding the course, hit a chip shot. He had to loft the ball gently over a bunker and then have it land on the green like a Nerf ball on a mattress. He hit the shot a little fat, the ball went up in the air slowly, and his club accelerated and hit the ball again about eye level. The ball went over his head, out of bounds, and into the swimming pool. The rule says that you may have only four penalty strokes per swing maximum, but I think he beat that by a bunch with that double-hit chip shot. When I saw him last, he was still trying to retrieve his ball with the homeowner's pool net.

Thinned chips (*skulls,* as they call it on tour, or *Vin Scullys,* as I call them, after the famous Dodgers baseball announcer) are the opposite of the Hormels (duffs). You aren't hitting enough ground. In fact, you don't hit the ground at all. The club strikes the ball above the equator, sending the shot speeding on its merry way, past the hole into all sorts of evil places. You need to hit the ground slightly so that the ball hits the clubface and not the front end of the club.

Again, start by sticking your club shaft in the ground beyond the ball.

If you continually hit Hormels (duffs), get your nose to the left of the shaft, which moves the bottom of your swing forward. Doing so allows you to hit down on the ball from the right position. Make sure that your head stays forward in this shot. Most people who hit an occasional Hormel move their heads backward as they start their downswings, which means that they hit behind the ball.

If you're prone to hit an occasional Vin Scully (a thin shot), set up with your nose behind or to the right of the ball, which moves the bottom of your swing back. When you find the right spot, you'll hit the ball and the ground at the same time, which is good. I've found that most people who hit their shots thin have a tendency to raise their entire bodies up immediately before impact. Concentrate on keeping your upper torso bent the same way throughout the swing. Hopefully, the next time you hear the name Vin Scully, it'll be on TV.

Can't Make a Putt?

Some people argue that putting is more mental than physical. But before you resort to séances with your local fortuneteller, check your alignment. You can often trace missed putts to poor aim.

My colleague Peter Kostis recently invented a device called the Plane Truth putting system to help straighten out troubled putters. It's similar to an old, tried-and-true putting aid, the string between two rods, which helped golfers keep the putter going straight back and straight through impact toward the hole. Straight as a string, get it?

But Peter had a better idea. The Plane Truth putting system features a Plexiglas panel and a metal bar that attaches to your putter (see Figure 11-5). Keep the bar in contact with the Plexiglas as you practice and you'll groove a smooth stroke that keeps the face of your putter square to the target. I'm convinced that plenty of tour pros are going to be using Peter's invention in the next few years.

Figure 11-5: The Plane Truth putting system keeps a putter's face square to the target.

Of course, you can't use such a device during a round of golf. But when you develop the right stroke on the practice green, you can repeat it on the course — and watch those putts roll straight and true.

An important lesson you can learn with devices like this is the crucial relationship between the putter's face and the target line. Putting takes a lot of imagination: If you can picture the line and keep the face of your putter square to it, you'll find it easier to stroke the ball along that line to the hole. With practice, you start to "see" the line on the golf course as you lurk over those 6-foot putts.

Shanking

Bet the man who has the shanks, and your plate will be full.

—Gary McCord

It must have started centuries ago. Alone with his sheep in a quiet moment of reflection, a shepherd swung his carved crook at a rather round multicolored rock, toward a distant half-dead, low-growing vine. The rock peeled off the old crook, and instead of lurching forward toward the vine, it careened off at an angle 90 degrees to the right of the target. "What was that?!" cried the surprised shepherd. "That was a shank, you idiot!" cried one of the sheep. "Now release the toe of that stick or this game will never get off the ground."

This story has been fabricated to help with the tension of a despicable disease. The *shanks* are a virus that attacks the very soul of a golfer. They can come unannounced and invade the decorum of a well-played round. They leave with equal haste and lurk in the mind of the golfer, dwelling until the brain reaches critical mass. Then you have meltdown. This sounds like one of those diseases that they're making movies about. And to a golfer, no other word strikes terror and dread like *shank*.

As a junior golfer, I was visiting the Tournament of Champions in 1970 when a bunch of the guys were watching the tournament winners hit balls on the driving range. I was completely mesmerized by Frank Beard as he hit shank after shank on the practice tee. My buddies wanted to go watch Nicklaus, but being somewhat of a masochist, I told them that I would follow Frank the Shank around and meet them afterward. I witnessed one of the greatest rounds I have ever seen. He shot a 64 and never missed a shot. How could a man who was so severely stricken by this disease on the practice tee rally and unleash a round of golf like he played? That is the mystery of this affliction. Can it be controlled? Yes!

Shanking occurs when the ball strikes the hosel of the club and goes 90 degrees to right of your intended target. (The *hosel* is the part of the club that attaches to the clubhead.) Shankers almost always set up too close to the ball, with their weight back on their heels. As they shift forward during the swing, their weight comes off their heels, moving the club even closer to the ball, so that the hosel hits the ball.

A shank is sometimes called a *pitch out,* a *Chinese hook, El Hosel,* a *scud,* or a *snake killer* — you get the idea. When you shank, the heel of your club (the *heel* is the closest part of the clubhead to you; the *toe* is the farthest) continues toward the target and then ends up right of the target. To eliminate shanks, you need the toe of the club to go toward the target and then end up left of the target.

Here's an easy exercise that helps cure the shanks (see Figure 11-6):

1. **Get a two-by-four board and align it along your target line.**
2. **Put the ball 2 inches from the near edge of the board, and try to hit the ball.**

   If you have the shanks, your club will want to hit the board. If you swing properly, the club will come from the inside and hit the ball. Then the toe of the club will go left of the target, the ball will go straight, and your woes will be over.

In a world full of new, emerging viruses, we have the technology to lash back at this golfing disease and eliminate it altogether from our DNA. Stay calm and get a two-by-four, practice the drill, and banish the shanks forever.

Release the toe and don't hit the board.

Figure 11-6: Just say, "No shanks!"

The Push

The *push* is a shot that starts right of the target and just keeps going. It isn't like a slice, which starts left and then curves to the right; the push just goes right. This shot happens when the body does not rotate through to the left on the downswing, and the arms hopelessly swing to the right, "pushing" the ball in that direction.

Hitting a push is like standing at home plate, aiming at the pitcher, and then swinging your arms at the first baseman. If this sounds like you, listen up. I'll show you how to hit one up the middle: Place a wooden two-by-four parallel to the target line and about 2 inches beyond the golf ball. You push the ball because your body stops rotating left on the downswing, and your arms go off to the right. If your arms go off to the right with that old two-by-four sitting there, splinters are going to fly. Naturally, you don't want to hit the board, so you will — hopefully — swing your hips left on the downswing, which will pull your arms left and stop the push.

The Pull

The *pull* is a shot that starts left and stays left, unlike a hook, which starts right of the target and curves left. The pull is caused when the club comes from outside the target line on the downswing and you pull across your body.

Hitting a pull is like standing at home plate and aiming at the pitcher, but swinging the club toward the third baseman, which is where the ball would go. This swing malady is a little more complicated, and it's more difficult to pick out one exercise to cure it, so bear with me.

Pulls are caused when your shoulders "open" too fast in the downswing. For the proper sequence, your shoulders should remain as close to parallel to the target line as possible at impact. Here's a checklist that will help you cure your pull:

- **Check your alignment.** If you're aimed too far to the right, your body will slow down on the downswing and allow your shoulders to open at impact to bring the club back to the target.
- **Check your weight shift.** If you don't shift your weight to your left side on the downswing, you'll spin your hips out of the way too fast, causing your shoulders to open up too quickly and hit a putrid pull. So shift those hips toward the target on the downswing until your weight is on your left side after impact.
- **Check your grip pressure.** Too tight a grip on the club will cause you to tense up on the downswing and come over the top for a pull.
- **Check your distance from the ball.** Too close and you'll instinctively pull inward on your forward swing — which means pulling to the left.

Power Outage

Everyone in the world would like more distance. John Daly and Michelle Wie would like more distance. I would like more distance, and I'm sure you would too. Here are some simple thoughts to help you add yardage:

- **Turn your shoulders on the backswing.** The more you turn your shoulders on the backswing, the better chance you have to hit the ball longer. So stretch that torso on the backswing — try to put your left shoulder over your right foot at the top of your swing.

  If you're having difficulty moving your shoulders enough on the backswing, try turning your left knee clockwise until it's pointing behind the ball during your backswing. This frees up your hips to turn, and subsequently your shoulders. A big turn starts from the ground up.

- **Get the tension out of your grip.** Hold the club loosely; you should grip it with the pressure of holding a spotted owl's egg. If there's too much tension in your hands, your forearms and chest will "tighten up," and you'll lose that valuable flexibility that helps with the speed of your arms and hands.

Turning your hips to the left on the downswing and extending your right arm on the through-swing are trademarks of the longer hitters. Here's a drill to help you accomplish this feat of daring:

1. **Tee up your driver in the normal position.**
2. **Place the ball off your left heel and/or opposite your left armpit.**
3. **Now reach down, not moving your stance, and move the ball toward the target the length of the grip.**
4. **Tee the ball up right there; it should be about 1 foot closer to the hole.**
5. **Address the ball where the normal position was and swing at the ball that is now teed up.**

   To hit that ball, you'll have to move your hips to the left so that your arms can "reach the ball," thereby causing you to extend your right arm.

Practice this drill 20 times and then put the ball back in the normal position. You should feel faster with the hips and feel a tremendous extension of your right arm.

The "Worm Burner"

Does your ball look like a duck trying to take off with a bad wing? Do your friends call you "Stealth"? Do worms fear your dreaded "worm-burner" drives? If you're having this problem with your driver, make sure that your head stays behind the ball at address and at impact. Moving your head back and forth along with your driver can cause too low a shot. Also, drivers come in different lofts. If you're hitting the ball too low, try a driver that has 11 to 12 degrees of loft.

If you're having a problem with low iron shots, you're probably trying to lift those golf balls into the air instead of hitting down. ***Remember:*** With irons, you have to hit down to get the ball up.

Spraying the Ball

If your golf ball takes off in more directions than the compass has to offer, check your alignment and ball position. Choose the direction you're going and then put your feet, knees, and shoulders on a line parallel to the target line. Be very specific with your alignment.

Ball position can play a major part in poor direction. If the ball is too far forward, it's easy to push it to the right. If the ball is too far back in your stance, it's easy to hit pushes and pulls. The driver is played opposite your left armpit. (As the club gets shorter, the ball should move back toward the middle of your stance.)

If nobody is around and you want to check your ball position, here's what you can do: Get into your stance — with the driver, for example — and then undo your shoelaces. Step out of your shoes, leaving them right where they were at address. Now take a look: Is the ball where it's supposed to be in your stance? Two suggestions: If it's a wet day, don't try this. And if your socks have holes in them, make sure nobody is watching.

Hitting from the Top

When you start cocking the wrist in your golf swing, the thumb of your right hand (if you're a right-handed golfer) points at your right shoulder on the backswing. That's good! When you start the downswing, you should try to keep that thumb pointing at your right shoulder for as long as you can, thus maintaining the *angle.* That's golfspeak for keeping the shaft of the club as close to the left arm on the downswing as possible. If your right thumb starts pointing away from your right shoulder on the downswing, not good! That is known as *hitting from the top.* In essence, you're uncocking the wrist on the downswing.

To stop hitting from the top, you must reduce your grip pressure. Too much tension in your hands will make you throw the clubhead toward the ball, causing you to hit from the top. After you've relaxed your grip pressure, get an old two-by-four and place it on the side of the ball away from you, parallel to the target line. The ball should be about 2 inches from the board. You'll find that if you keep pointing your right thumb at your right shoulder on the downswing, you won't hit the board with your club. If you point your thumb away from your shoulder on the downswing, your chances of chopping wood are very good. (See Figure 11-7.)

Figure 11-7: Hitting from the top.

The Reverse Pivot

A *reverse pivot* occurs when you put all your weight on your left foot on the backswing (shown in Figure 11-8) and all your weight on your right foot during the downswing. That is the opposite of what you want to do! Picture a baseball pitcher. Pitchers have all their weight on the right foot at the top of the windup, the left foot is in the air (for a right-hander), and on the follow-through, all the weight goes to the left foot. (The right foot is now in the air.) That's the weight transfer you need. Here's how you can achieve it:

1. **Start your backswing, and when you get to the top of your swing, lift your left foot off the ground.**

   Now you can't put any weight on that foot! You'll feel your whole body resist placing your weight over your right foot.

2. **Take your time and let your weight transfer to your right foot.**
3. **Start the downswing by placing your left foot back where it was and then transfer all your weight over during the swing.**
4. **When you've made contact with the ball (hopefully), put all your weight on your left foot and lift your right foot off the ground.**
5. **Stand there for a short time, feeling the balance.**

Figure 11-8: Reverse pivots.

This rocking-chair transfer drill lets you feel the proper weight shift in the golf swing. Take it easy at first. Practice short shots until you get the feel, and then work your way up to your driver.

Swaying Off the Ball

In a *sway,* your hips and shoulders don't turn on the backswing, but simply slide back in a straight line, as shown in Figure 11-9. Here's a good drill to help you stop swaying:

1. **Find a bare wall.**
2. **Using a 5-iron, place the club on the ground with the clubhead touching the wall and the shaft extending straight into the room.**
3. **Place your right foot against the end of the shaft with the little toe of your right shoe hitting the end of the club.**

   Now you're standing exactly one club length from the wall.
4. **Put your left foot in the normal address position for the 5-iron and, without moving your feet, bend over and pick up the club.**

Figure 11-9: Don't sway off the ball.

5. **Take a backswing.**

   If you sway with your hips 1 inch to the right on your backswing, you'll notice that you hit the wall immediately with the club.

Practice this until you can do it without hitting the wall. I put so many marks and holes in a motel room doing this drill, I could see the guy in the next room!

I suggest that you practice this drill in your garage at first to save the walls at home. You may want to use an old club, too.

The Belly-Button Twist

Another common fault is doing the belly-button twist: sliding your hips too far toward the target at the start of the downswing. How far should your hips slide before they start turning left? They must slide until your left hip and left knee are over your left foot. Then those hips turn left in a hurry!

Here's the best way to improve your hip position at the downswing:

1. **Get a broken club that has just a shaft and a grip on it.**

   You can find broken clubs in lost-and-found barrels, or just ask somebody at a driving range. Your golf pro can also help you find one.

2. **Stick the broken club into the ground just outside your left foot; the top of the grip should be no higher than your hip.**

3. **Now hit a few shots.**

   When you swing, your left hip should not hit the club stuck in the ground. It should turn to the left of the shaft. The key here is to straighten the left leg in your follow-through.

A Swing That's Too Long

If your swing is too long and sloppy (going beyond parallel to the ground at the top of the swing), here are two positions to work on:

- The right arm in the backswing (for a right-handed golfer) must not bend more than 90 degrees. It must stay at a right angle (refer to Figure 11-5).
- The right elbow must not get more than a dollar bill's length (6 inches) away from your rib cage at the top of the backswing (see Figure 11-10).

If you can maintain these two simple positions at the top of your swing, you won't overswing.

Figure 11-10: Do the right thing in your backswing.

A Swing That's Too Short

In most cases, a short swing comes from too little shoulder turn. Turn your left shoulder over your right foot at the top of your backswing. If you can't, lift your left heel off the ground until you can. Many players I see with short swings also keep their right elbows against their rib cages at the top of the swing. The right elbow should be away from the rib cage (6 inches) to allow some freedom in the swing and get the needed length to your swing arc.

Not Enough Backspin

How can you back up the ball like the pros on the tour? People ask me this question all the time. The answer: The more steeply you hit down on the ball and the faster you swing, the more spin you generate. People who play golf for a living hit short irons with a very steep angle of descent into the ball, which creates a lot of spin (along with the extra swing speed a pro generates). We also tend to play three-piece golf balls with relatively soft covers — balls that spin more than the two-piece ball most people play. (Chapter 2 explains the different types of golf balls in detail.)

We also play on grass that's manicured and very short so that we can get a clean hit with the club off these fairways. All this helps a bunch when you're trying to spin the ball. The bottom line is that we're trying to control the distance a ball goes. I don't care if the ball backs up to get to that distance or rolls forward to get there.

Consistency is knowing how far you can hit each club in your bag. Don't worry about how much spin you get; worry about how far each club travels.

Chapter 12

How to Beat Bad Luck and Bad Weather

In This Chapter

- Making shots that save your day
- Coping with Mother Nature's grumpy moods
- Playing through all four seasons

If you break golf down into its primal form, the sport is simple. All you have to do is hit a ball from a flat piece of ground (you even get to tee the ball up) to, say, a 40-yard-wide fairway, find the ball, and then hit the ball onto a prepared putting surface. Then the golf gods allow you to hit not one, but two putts. And even after all that stuff, you still get to call your score par.

However — you knew there had to be a catch, didn't you? — golf isn't often so straightforward. For one thing, you're going to make mistakes. We all do. Usually the same ones over and over. That won't change, by the way. Even the best players in the world have little glitches in their swings that give them problems. Everyone has a bad shot that he or she tends to hit when things go wrong. You may not hit that fairway with your drive or that green with your approach shot, or you may miss both. You may take three putts to get the ball into the hole now and again. And golf doesn't often take place on a level playing field. Not every shot is played from a perfectly flat piece of ground. Very seldom is the ball lying enticingly atop the grass. (Unless you're the guy at our course that we call "The Foot." He never has a bad lie.) Often wind or rain is in your face or at your back.

No two shots are ever exactly the same, particularly when you stray from the straight and narrow. When you start making friends with trees, rough, and all the other flora and fauna out there, your ball is going to land in places a lawn mower has never been. And you have to know how to escape from those and many other awkward spots (see Figure 12-1).

If you get into trouble on the course, you'll often be faced with a choice of escape routes.

Figure 12-1: Under or around?

Eat Your Roughage!

Well, Mom, if you knew that I was going to end up playing the PGA Tour and Champions Tour with a crooked driver, you probably wouldn't have left me with those words of wisdom. I've eaten a lot of rough getting from tee to green, but I think it's made me a better person.

Rough is the grass on the golf course that looks like it should be mowed. It's usually 2 to 3 inches in length and lurks everywhere but the tees, fairways, and greens. I grew up on a municipal golf course where the grass was short everywhere because the only thing they watered down was the whiskey.

When you try to hit a ball out of long grass, the grass gets between the clubface and the ball. The ball then has no backspin and goes off like a Scud missile, and direction can be a concern. But the real problem is that, with no backspin, the ball can take a longer voyage than you expected. The lack of backspin means less drag occurs while the ball is in the air. That's never been a problem with the driver off the tee, but it's a concern when you're trying to hit the ball a certain distance.

My philosophy is that if the lie is bad enough, just get the ball back into the fairway. If you can hit the ball, the technique for this shot is much the same as the shot out of a divot: Play the ball back in your stance and put your hands forward. A chopping-down motion allows the club to come up in the backswing and avoid the long grass; then you can hit down on the ball. Swing hard, because if you swing easily, the grass will wrap around the club and twist it, giving the ball an unpredictable trajectory.

The more you play this game, the more you'll hit these shots, and the more you'll understand how to play them. Keep your sense of humor and a firm grip on the club, and enjoy your roughage — your mother was right!

Tree Trouble

A walk in the woods can be a serene, soul-enhancing, mystical journey, blending one's spirit and body into nature and all her beauty. But when I'm walking into the trees to find my golf ball, I feel like I'm in a house of mirrors with branches and leaves. The trees seem to be laughing at my predicament, and I end up talking to them in less-than-flattering dialogue. You've got the picture by now.

The trees are playing games with me. And so, to extract my ball from this boundless maze of bark, I play a game with the trees. Usually, one lone tree is in my way as I try to exit this forest. All I do is take dead aim at that tree and try to knock it over with the ball. The key here is to not be too close to the tree in case you score a direct hit. You don't want to wear that Titleist 3 as a permanent smile.

My reasoning is that I got into these trees with something less than a straight shot. So if I now try to hit something that is 30 yards away from me and only 12 inches in diameter, what's the chance that I'll hit it? If I do hit it, what a great shot it was, and I turn a negative into a positive. I'm still in the trees, but I'm happy about my shot. Now you probably know why I'm in television and not on the regular tour anymore.

Special Shots

Because golf is a game of mistake management, you're going to get into trouble at least a few times in every round. How you cope with those moments and shots determines your score for the day and, ultimately, your ability to play well. Never forget that even the greatest rounds have moments of crisis. Stay calm when your heart tries to eject through the top of your head.

Special shots have diversity, too. Trouble lurks everywhere on a golf course. You have to know how to hit long shots, short shots, and, perhaps most important, in-between shots. All sorts of shots exist. You may be faced with a shot from 200 yards where a clump of trees blocks your path to the hole. Or you may be only 50 yards from the hole and have to keep the ball under branches and yet still get it over a bunker. Whatever the situation, the key is applying the magic word — time out for a drum roll — *imagination.*

A vivid imagination is a great asset on the golf course. If you can picture the way a shot has to curve in the air in order to land safely, you're halfway to success. All you have to do is hit the ball. And the best way to accomplish both things is through practice — practice on the course, that is. You can't re-create on the range most shots that you encounter out on the course. The range is flat; the course isn't. The wind constantly blows the same way on the range. On the course, the only constant about the wind is that it changes direction. That's golf — a wheel of bad fortune.

The best way to practice these weird and wonderful shots is to challenge yourself. See how low you can hit a shot. Or how high. Practice hitting from bad lies and see how the ball reacts. Play from slopes, long grass, and all the rest. Or play games with your friends. The first player to hit over that tree, for example, gets $5. The trick is to make practice competitive and fun — and also beat your friends out of five bucks.

Wait a minute, though. Hang on. I'm getting a little ahead of myself. I have to tell you that many of the trouble shots hit by the pros are not only very low-percentage plays but also way, way out of most people's reach. Even the pros miss the tough shots now and again. And when they do miss, the consequence means triple bogey (a score of 3 over par for one hole — for example, a 7 on a par-4) or worse. So admire them. But never, ever try to copy them — at least not yet.

The good news is that at this stage of your development, all you need is a couple of basic shots. Leave the really fancy stuff for another time, another book. All you need to know to score well is how to hit the ball low or high back onto the fairway. That's enough to cover 99 percent of the situations that you'll encounter. Better to give up one shot than risk three more on a shot that you couldn't pull off more than once in 20 tries.

Altitude adjustment

Because golf isn't played in a controlled environment, you're going to come across situations where a higher or lower shot is required. For example, when you have a strong wind in your face, a lower shot is going to go farther and hold its line better. The great thing is that you make all your adjustments before you begin. Then after you start your backswing, you can make your regular swing. You don't have to worry about adding anything else. Figure 12-2 illustrates the following shots.

Figure 12-2: The downs and ups of golf.

Hitting the ball lower

Hitting the ball low is easy. All you have to do is subtract from the effective loft of the club. And the best way to do that is to adjust your address position. Play the ball back in your stance, toward your right foot. Move your hands toward the target until they're over your left leg.

Now you swing, focusing on re-creating the positional relationship between your hands and the clubface as the ball is struck. In other words, your hands should be "ahead" of the clubface at impact, thus ensuring that the ball flies lower than normal.

This sort of technique is commonly employed when playing in Florida, Texas, and Hawaii, where golf swings get a little shorter and the divots get a little longer. When you play the ball back in your stance with your hands ahead, you come down into the ground with a more abrupt angle that takes more turf.

I remember one good story about a low shot. It happened years ago during the Bing Crosby tournament on the 7th hole at Pebble Beach (a downhill par-3 of 110 yards). From an elevated tee, you can just about throw the ball to the green. On this particular day, the wind was howling from the coast (the green sits on the ocean), and the 7th hole was impossible. Water was erupting from the rocks; wind was blowing water everywhere; seals were hiding; and seagulls were walking. Definitely a bad day for windblown golf balls.

Billy Casper arrived on the tee and surveyed the situation. Many players were using long irons (irons that go 200 yards) because the wind was so fierce. Billy went to his bag and got his *putter!* He putted the ball down a cart path into the front bunker. From there he got the ball down in two for his par-3. Now that's keeping it low into the wind and using your imagination!

Hitting the ball higher

As you'd expect, hitting the ball higher than normal involves making the opposite adjustments at address. Adjust your stance so that the ball is forward in your stance, toward your left foot. Then move your hands back, away from the target. Again, hitting the ball is that simple. All you have to do is reproduce that look at impact, and the ball takes off on a steeper trajectory.

Gyroscope golf: Sidehill lies

Not many golf courses are flat. Every now and again, you need to hit a shot off a slope. The ball may be below or above your feet. Both positions are *sidehill lies.* Or you may be halfway up or down a slope.

When you're faced with any or all of these situations, you need to make an adjustment. And again, if you can make most of your changes before starting your swing, things are a lot easier. The common factor in all these shots is the relationship between your shoulders and the slope. On a flat lie, you're bent over the ball in a certain posture. You should stand about 90 degrees to the ground.

In other words, if the ball is above your feet, you have to lean a little into the hill to keep your balance. If you stood at your normal posture to the upslope of the hill, you would fall backward. You're close to the ball because of the lean, and you need to choke up on the club.

The reverse is also true. With the ball below your feet, lean back more to retain your balance on the downslope. Because you're leaning back, you're a little farther away from the ball; grip the club all the way to the end and use the whole length of the shaft.

The main idea for sidehill lies is to stay balanced. I don't want you falling down the hills.

For uphill and downhill lies, it's a little different. Imagine that your ball is halfway up a staircase, and you have to hit the next shot to the top. Because your left leg is higher than your right, your weight naturally shifts to your right leg. Let that weight shift happen so that your shoulders are parallel to the banister. On a downslope, your weight shifts in the opposite direction, onto your left leg. Again, let that weight shift happen. Keep your shoulders and the banister parallel, as shown in Figure 12-3.

Finally, follow these three rules:

- **Adjust your aim when you're on a slope.** Off a downslope or when the ball is below your feet, aim to the left of where you want the ball to finish. Off an upslope or when the ball is above your feet, aim right.
- **As far as ball position is concerned, play the ball back toward the middle of your stance if you're on a downhill lie, or forward, off your left big toe, from an uphill lie.**
- **Take *more club* (a club that has less loft) if you're on an uphill lie because the ball tends to fly higher. Use *less club* (a club that has more loft) from a downhill lie because the ball has a lower trajectory in this situation.** For example, if the shot calls for a 7-iron, take your 8-iron instead. ***Remember:*** From these lies, swing about 75 percent of your normal swing speed to keep your balance. Practice with different clubs from different lies to get a feel for these shots.

Figure 12-3: Keep shoulders and slope parallel.

You can dig it: Hitting out of divots

Unfortunately for your blood pressure, your ball occasionally finishes in a hole made by someone who previously hit a shot from the same spot and forgot to replace the grass. These holes are known as *divots.* Landing in a divot may cause quiet muttering beneath your breath, but don't panic. To get the ball out, first set up with the ball farther back in your stance to encourage a steeper attack at impact. Push your hands forward a little, too. You need to feel as if you're really hitting down on this shot. A quicker cocking of the wrists on the backswing helps, too. I like to swing a little more upright on the backswing with the club (take the arms away from the body going back). This allows a steeper path down to the ball. (See Figure 12-4.)

Depending on the severity and depth of the divot, take a club with more loft than you would normally use. You need extra loft to counteract the ball being below ground level. Don't worry — the ball comes out lower because your hands are ahead of the ball. That makes up for the distance lost by using less club.

When you're feeling uncomfortable over the ball as it sits in that divot, remember that the ball will come out a lot lower and run along the ground more than a normal shot. So aim your shot accordingly.

Figure 12-4: Escaping a divot.

On the downswing of your shot out of a divot, there will be little or no follow-through. Because the ball is back in your stance and your hands are forward, your blow should be a descending blow. (When is the last time you had a follow-through when chopping wood?)

The one thought I've had in this situation is, *Don't swing too hard.* When you swing too hard, you move your head and don't hit the ball squarely. And when the ball is lying below the ground, you must hit it squarely.

Toupee Alert: Strong Winds Reported

When conditions are rough because of wind or rain, scores go up. You have to be ready for that occurrence. Adjust your goals. Don't panic if you start off badly or have a couple of poor holes. Be patient and realize that sometimes conditions make it difficult to play golf. And remember that bad weather conditions are equally tough on all the other players.

I've played professional golf for some 25-odd years, and I've played in some very bad conditions. Because I'm not a patient person, my scores in bad weather have been high. If I got a few strokes over par early in my round, I would take too many chances during the rest of the round trying to make some birdies. I'd then boil as I watched my score rise with my blood pressure. A calm head and good management skills are just as important as hitting the ball solidly when you're trying to get through tough days in the wind and rain.

I remember playing the TPC Championship at Sawgrass in the late 1980s on one of the windiest days we'd ever seen. J. C. Snead hit a beautiful downwind approach to an elevated green. Somehow the ball stopped on the green with the wind blowing upwards of 50 mph. J. C. started walking toward the green when his Panama hat blew off and started to tumble toward the green. After minutes of scurrying along the ground, the hat blew onto the green and hit his golf ball! That's a 2-shot penalty, and an incredibly bad case of luck.

If the wind is blowing hard enough to be a nuisance, the following may help you deal with wind conditions:

- **Widen your stance to lower your center of gravity.** This automatically makes your swing shorter (for control) because turning your body is more difficult when your feet are set wider apart. (See Figure 12-5.)
- **Swing easier.** I always take a less-lofted club than normal and swing easier. This way, I have a better chance of hitting the ball squarely. By hitting the ball squarely, I can count on a consistent distance the ball will travel with every club, even in bad conditions.

Figure 12-5: Windy means wider.

- **Use the wind — don't abuse the wind.** Let the ball go where the wind wants it to go. Don't try to fight it, or it'll be a long day. If the wind is blowing left to right at 30 mph, aim your ball left and let the wind bring it back. Don't aim right and try to hook it back into the wind. Leave that up to the airline pilots and the guys on the PGA Tour!
- **Choke down on the club.** Choking down means that you don't have to keep your left hand (for right-handed golfers) all the way at the end of the grip. This gives you more control. I like to put my left hand about 1 inch from the top of the grip. I have more control over the club, but the ball doesn't go as far because I don't use the full length of the shaft.
- **Allow for more run downwind and for shorter flight against the wind.** This part of the game has to be experienced to be understood. The more you play in windy conditions, the more comfortable you become in them.

Waterworld: Swingin' in the Rain

I'm from Southern California. I never saw too much rain, let alone played in it all the time. The rain that would make us Californians stay inside and play Yahtzee would be nothing for my buddies from the Pacific Northwest. They learned how to play in the rain and expected to play in the rain.

The right equipment: Smooth sailing or choppy seas

The best advice I can give you for playing in the rain is to be prepared to play in it. Pack all the equipment you'll need to handle the wetness:

- **An umbrella:** Pack one of those big golf umbrellas. And never open it downwind, or you'll end up like Mary Poppins, and the umbrella will end up looking like modern art.
- **Good rain gear:** That means jackets, pants, and headwear designed to be worn in the rain. You can spend as much as you want on these items. If you play in wet weather all the time, get yourself some good stuff that will last a long time. I don't mean a garbage bag with holes cut out for your head and arms. I mean the stuff that you buy from a pro shop or see in a magazine ad. Good rain gear costs between $100 and $700. Gore-Tex, a fabric that repels water, is a very popular fabric for rain gear.
- **Dry gloves:** If you wear gloves, keep a few in plastic bags in your golf bag. They'll stay dry if you leave a pocket open and the rain comes pouring in.
- **Dry towels:** Keep several dry towels in your bag, because the one you have outside will get wet sooner or later. On the Champions Tour, I keep a dry towel hanging from the rib on the underside of my umbrella and another dry one inside my side pocket. When it gets really wet, I wipe my club off on the closest dry caddie.
- **Dry grips:** This is one of the most important things to have in wet-weather golf. I once had a club slip out of my hands on the driving range and fly through the snack-shop window. I blamed it on an alien spacecraft.
- **Waterproof shoes:** Keep an extra pair of socks in your bag, too, in case the advertiser lied about those "waterproof" shoes.

Wet course conditions

A golf course changes significantly in the rain. You need to adjust your game accordingly and keep the following in mind:

- On a rainy day, the greens will be slow. Hit your putts harder and remember that the ball won't curve as much.
- If you hit a ball in the bunker, the sand will be firmer, and you won't have to swing as hard to get the ball out.
- The golf course will play longer because it's so soft. The good news is that the fairways and greens get softer and more receptive. The fairways and greens become, in effect, wider and bigger, respectively, because your shots don't bounce into trouble as much.
- Try not to let the conditions affect your normal routines. The best rain players always take their time and stay patient.

- Playing in the rain is one thing — playing in lightning is another thing altogether. When lightning strikes, your metallic golf club (along with the fact that you tend to be the highest point on the golf course, unless there's a tree around) can make you a target. Don't take chances. Drop your club and take cover.

A Game for All Seasons: Weathering the Elements

If you live in Florida, California, or Arizona, you only notice the change of seasons when 40 bazillion golfers from colder climes flood the area trying to get the seven starting times that are still available. If you live in an all-season climate and prefer to enjoy the changing weather without giving up your golf game, this section offers some tips.

Swing into spring: Time to thaw out and get to work

The golfing populace anticipates spring like no other season. You've been indoors for most of the winter, and you've read every book pertaining to your golf game. You've watched endless hours of golf on TV and ingested everything the announcers have told you not to do. It's time to bloom!

One of the first things you need to do is decide your goals for the upcoming year. Is your goal to be a better putter? Or do you want to become a longer driver? Or do you simply want to get the ball off the ground with more regularity?

Establish what you want to do with your game, and then set out to accomplish that feat. Set simple and attainable goals and work to achieve them.

My other springtime advice:

- **Practice all phases of your game.** Don't neglect weak areas of your game, but stay on top of your strengths as well. Spring is a time of blossoming — let your game do the same.
- **Map out an exercise program.** You probably neglected exercise during the winter. Spring is a good time to map out a game plan for your physical needs. Are you strong enough in your legs? Does your rotator cuff need strength? Does your cardiovascular system short out later in the round? Address these problems and get on a treadmill or hit the weight room. Chapter 4 tells you how you can develop a golf-specific fitness program.
- **Dress for the weather.** Spring is the hardest time of year to figure out what to wear. It can be hot. It can be cold. It can rain. It can be blowing 40 mph. It can be doing all these things in the first three holes. If you're carrying your bag, it can get heavy with all the extra gear in it. Take along your rain gear. Take along a light jacket. Bring hand warmers and your umbrella. Put an extra towel in your bag. Take along some antihistamines — it's spring and the pollen is everywhere.
- **Learn about yourself and your golf game.** ***Remember:*** Spring is the time of year to be enlightened.

To be surprised, to wonder, is to begin to understand.

—Spanish philosopher Jose Ortega y Gasset

Summer golf: Fun in the sun

Summer is the time of year to go play the game. I hope that you've been practicing hard on your game, working toward those goals you set forth in the spring. But there's a big difference between practicing and playing. The more you practice, the easier you should find it to play the game well. Summer is the time to find out whether your game has improved.

The following suggestions will help you make the most of your days in the sun:

- **Work on your course management.** How can you best play this particular golf course? Sometimes, for one reason or another, you can't play a certain hole. Figure out how you can avoid the trouble you're having on that hole and devise a plan. Everyone has strengths and weaknesses. Do you have the discipline to carry out your plan? That's why summer is great for playing the game and understanding yourself. You can go out after work and play 18 holes before it gets dark. Summer is the time to stop thinking about your golf swing and become the ball.

- **Maintain your equipment.** During the summer, I get new grips on my clubs. The grips are called *half cord* because they have some cord blended into the underside of the grip. The new grips give me a better hold on the club during sweaty summers. I also use a driver with a little more loft to take advantage of summer's drier air (which causes the ball to fly farther).
- **Practice competing by playing in organized leagues.** You play a different game when your score counts and is published in the local paper.
- **Dress for fun in the sun.** Take along sunblock of at least SPF 15, and put it on twice a day. Not everyone wants to look like George Hamilton. And wear a hat that covers your ears. Mine burn off in the summer.
- **Play in the mornings.** The afternoons are often too darned hot.

- **Drink plenty of fluids during those hot days.** You don't want to dehydrate and shrivel up like a prune, so keep your liquid intake constant. I try to drink water on every tee during the heat of summer. One hint: Alcoholic beverages will knock you on your rear end if you drink them outdoors on a hot day. Stick with water and save the adult beverages for the 19th hole.

Have a ball in the fall

Without a doubt, fall is the best time of year to play golf: The golf courses are in good shape, the leaves are turning in much of the country, and the scenery is amazing. The weather is delightful, and all sorts of sports are on TV. Both you and your game should be in good shape.

If you have the time and the money, make travel plans to the Northeast and play golf there. The colors are astounding. I live in Vail, Colorado, which is also breathtaking in the fall. Many vacation plans can make the trip affordable. Get a bunch of friends you enjoy and start planning a trip now. My house is out, though — it's way too small.

Play as much golf as you can in the fall so that you'll be really tired of the game and won't miss it so much going into the winter — then you can take a legitimate golf break.

Here are three fall golf tips:

- **Dress for the fall much like you do for the spring.** Take a lot of stuff with you because the weather can do anything.
- **Assess everything you did with your game this year.** Did your techniques work? If not, were your goals unrealistic? Was your teacher helpful? Take a long, hard look and start to devise a game plan for next spring.

- **Look at new equipment as your game progresses.** Fall is a good time to buy equipment, because all the new stuff comes out in the spring. By fall, prices are lower for last year's clubs. I love a good buy, though I haven't had to buy clubs since I bought a putter eight years ago in San Diego.

Winterize your game

If you choose to get away from the fireplace, golf in the winter can be tolerable. For much of the country, anyone can play in the winter on a reasonable day with a light wind — especially when you don't have to mow the grass until April.

Prepare yourself for brisk weather

If you're brave enough to venture onto the frozen tundra, I have three musts for you:

- **Take a large Thermos with something warm to drink for the whole day.** You may think that bourbon chasers will make the day much more fun, but the golf deteriorates and you'll actually feel colder.
- **Dress warmly.** I've used silk long johns on cold days, and they work well. Women's seamless long johns work best, but if you're a guy, the salesperson looks at you funny when you ask for a women's size 14. That kind of request may lead to the wrong conclusions.
    - **Wear waterproof golf shoes and thick socks.** Some hunting socks have little heaters in them. I also wear wool pants over my silk long johns and then use my rain pants as the top layer when it's really cold. A turtleneck with a light, tightly knit sweater does well under a rain or wind jacket made of Gore-Tex or one of those other new miracle-fiber, space-age fabrics. A knit ski cap tops off this cozy ensemble.
    - **Among the great inventions of all time are those little hand warmers that come in plastic pouches.** You shake those things, and they stay warm for eight hours. I put them everywhere on cold days. Let your imagination run wild. Hand warmers can keep you toasty on a cold winter's day when you're three down to your worst enemy.
    - **Keep your hands warm by using cart gloves.** These oversize fingerless gloves have a soft, warm lining and fit right over your hand, even if you're already wearing a glove. I put a hand warmer in each one.
- **Your attitude is the best weapon for a harsh winter day.** ***Remember:*** you're out on the course for the exercise — walk instead of taking a cart. Besides, you really feel cold when your fresh face collides with an arctic blast of winter. If you must take a cart, make sure that it has a windshield. Some clubs have enclosed carts with heaters in them.

Adjust your swing for a cold day

When you swing a club with all these clothes on, you probably won't have as long a swing as normal. The clothes restrict your motion. I usually take my jacket off to swing the club and then put it right back on. Because of the restriction of the clothes, I make my swing a little slower than normal, which helps put my swing into a slow rhythm on a cold day. Don't get fast and furious to get done.

Keep in mind a couple of other points when you're playing in cold weather:

- **Lower your expectations as the weather worsens.** When you're dressed for the Iditarod, don't think that you can pull off the same shots that you normally do. Good short game skills and game management are the most important aspects of winter golf.
- **Get counseling if you play much in these extreme conditions.** Golf may be too much of a priority in your life.

Indoor golf: What you can do at home

Winter is the time to practice fixing all those faults that you accumulated during the preceding year. Here's how:

1. **Place a large mirror behind you.**
2. **Pretend that you're hitting away from the mirror, and check your swing when your shaft is parallel to the ground in your backswing.**

   Is your shaft on a line that's parallel to the line made by your toes? If it is, that's good.
3. **Continue to swing and go to the top.**

   Is your shaft on a line that's parallel to the line made by your heels? If it is, that's good.

These two positions are important to the golf swing. Repeat this exercise until you can do it in your sleep.

Winter is a good time to become one with your swing (say what?). Have someone make a videotape of your golf swing. Play the tape over and over until you have a really good picture of what it looks like. Feel your own swing. Then work on those areas that you need to attend to — an instructor can help determine those areas (see Chapter 3 for more on working with an instructor). Make your changes and do another tape of your swing. Not only should you be able to see the changes, but you should feel them as well. Videotaping helps you understand your movements and helps the body and brain get on the same page. Golf can be Zenlike.

If you really can't get golf off your mind (and it's too cold to go ice fishing!), stay safe and warm indoors and check out the online golf options that I discuss in Chapter 17.

Part IV
Taking Your Game Public

In this part . . .

You're finally out there among the flora and fauna, chasing your golf ball around the course. In this part, I show you how to warm up, how to play "smart golf," and how to impress your new friends. And in case the idea of betting strikes your fancy, Chapter 15 gives you the odds.

Chapter 13

Ready, Set, Play!

In This Chapter

- Warming up your mind and body
- Arriving early to work on your swing
- Developing your plan of attack
- Getting used to playing in front of an audience

You know the basics of the game. You've got the right equipment, you know how to access instruction from various sources, and you know your way around different sorts of courses. You've developed a swing that suits your body and soul. You're armed with simple fixes for common problems, and you know how to play in all sorts of weather. At this point, you could probably hit a terrific bunker shot from a buried lie during a tornado!

Well, maybe during a blustery day. I'll save tornado play for a future edition of this book. The point is, you're ready to get out there and put all your learning to the test.

Warming Up Your Body

After you've warmed up your mind, you need to do the same for your body. Warm-ups are important. Not only do a few simple exercises loosen your muscles and help your swing, but they also help you psychologically as well. I like to step onto the first tee knowing that I'm as ready as I can be. Feeling loose rather than tight is reassuring. Besides, golfers, along with the rest of the world, are a lot more aware of physical fitness and diet today than in days gone by. Lee Trevino, a two-time U.S. Open, British Open, and PGA champion and later one of the top players on the senior tour, calls the PGA Tour players "flat-bellies." Which they are, compared to some of the more rotund "round-bellies" on the senior tour. I think this is called progress!

Staying positive: It's never your fault

Okay, you're ready to hit the links. The first thing you need to be sure of is that you're at the right course. The second thing is that you know where each hole goes. Both may seem obvious and easy to achieve, but things can go wrong. I know. I've been there. Listen to this tale of woe from a few years ago.

I was trying to qualify for the U.S. Open. The sectional qualifying course I was assigned to was Carlton Oaks in Southern California. No problem. I'd played there many times and knew the course well. I'd have a good shot at qualifying on this course. Or so I thought.

I got to the 13th hole and still had a chance of making the U.S. Open. But I needed a good finish. The 13th is a dogleg to the left, par-4, some 400-plus yards: a good testing hole. But I needed a birdie, so I decided to hit my drive down the 12th fairway, the hole I had just played. That would leave me a better angle for my second shot to the 13th green and cut more than 50 yards from the hole. The only slight snag was that my ball would have to fly over some trees.

I drove the ball perfectly and then hit a long iron to the green over the trees, a good one, too. The only thing I recall thinking is that the hole was longer than I remembered; I had to hit a 4-iron to the green when I expected a 7-iron to be enough. Still, I hit it solidly, so all was well.

When I got to the green, I was alone. So I waited for the rest of my group. And waited. And waited. Eventually I lost patience, putted out, and then started to look for the others. I soon found them. They were waving to me from a green about 100 yards away. I had played to the wrong green! There was only one thing left to do. Two, actually. I fired my caddie and walked to the clubhouse. Luckily, I found the right clubhouse.

Firing my caddie may seem petty, but the caddie is actually an important part of being a professional golfer. Even if you aren't a pro, no matter what goes wrong on the course, it is never — I repeat, *never* — your fault. You must always find someone or something else to blame for any misfortune. In other words, you must be creative in the excuse department.

There have been some great excuses over the years. My own favorite came from Greg Norman. A few years ago, he blamed a miscued shot on a worm popping up out of the ground next to his ball as he swung. Poor Greg was so distracted that he couldn't hit the shot properly! Then there was Jack Nicklaus at the 1995 British Open at St. Andrews. In the first round, Jack hit his second shot on the 14th hole, a long par-5, into what is known as Hell Bunker. It's well named, being basically a large, deep, sand-filled hole in the ground. Anyway, seeing his ball down there came as a bit of a surprise to Jack. He apparently felt that his shot should have flown comfortably over said bunker. And his excuse? His ball must have been deflected by seed heads!

These two examples are extreme, of course. But you should apply the same principle to your game. You can often tell a good player from his reaction to misfortune. He'll blame his equipment, the wind, a bad yardage, whatever. On the other hand, less-secure golfers take all responsibility for bad shots. Whatever they do is awful. In fact, they really stink at this stupid game. That's what they tell themselves — usually to the point that it ruins their next shot. And the next. And the next. Whatever they perceive themselves to be, they become.

Again, that's the extreme example. Just be sure that you err toward the former rather than the latter. What the heck, be a little unrealistic. Try to fool yourself!

Johnny Bench, the great Cincinnati Reds catcher, showed me the following stretches. He used them when he played baseball, and he's in the Hall of Fame — so who am I to argue?

Holding a club by the head, place the grip end in your armpit so that the shaft runs the length of your arm (use a club that is the same length as your arm for this one, as shown in Figure 13-1). That action in itself stretches your arm and shoulders. Now bend forward until your arm is horizontal. The forward movement stretches your lower back, one of the most important areas in your body when it comes to playing golf. If your back is stiff, making a full turn on the backswing is tough. Hold this position for a few seconds; then switch arms and repeat. Keep doing this stretch until you feel ready to swing.

Another method of loosening up is more traditional. Instead of practicing your swing with one club in your hands, double the load (see Figure 13-2). Swing two clubs. Go slowly, trying to make as full a back-and-through swing as you can. The extra weight soon stretches away any tightness.

This next exercise is one that you'll see many players use on the first tee. Jack Nicklaus has always done it. All you have to do is place a club across your back and hold it in place with your hands or elbows. Then turn back and through as if making a golf swing, as shown in Figure 13-3. Again, this action really stretches your back muscles.

Holding the club like this, bend forward.

Then switch arms and do it again.

Figure 13-1: Stretch those muscles!

Figure 13-2: Double your swing weight and swing nice and easy.

Figure 13-3: Watch your back!

Warming Up Your Swing

If you go to any professional golf tournament, you'll see that most players show up on the practice range about an hour before they're due to tee off. Showing up early leaves them time to tune their swings and strokes before the game starts for real.

I'm one of those players who like to schedule about an hour for pre-round practice. But half that time is probably enough for you. You're only going to hit some balls so that you can build a feel and a rhythm for the upcoming round. You shouldn't make any last-minute changes to your swing.

Start your warm-up by hitting some short wedge shots (see Figure 13-4). Don't go straight to your driver and start blasting away. That's asking for trouble. You can easily pull a muscle if you swing too hard too soon. Plus, it's unlikely that you'll immediately begin to hit long, straight drives if you don't warm up first. More than likely, you'll hit short, crooked shots. And those aren't good for the psyche.

Before each round, hit a few wedge shots...

and then a few 6-irons...

and then a few drivers...

and finish up with a few long putts.

Figure 13-4: Warming up.

1. **Start with the wedge.**

   Focus on making contact with the ball. Nothing else. Try to turn your shoulders a little more with each shot. Hit about 20 balls without worrying about where they're going. Just swing the club smoothly.

2. **Move next to your midirons.**

   I like to hit my 6-iron at this point. I'm just about warmed up, and the 6-iron has just enough loft that I don't have to work too hard at getting the ball flying forward. Again, hit about 20 balls.

3. **Hit the big stick.**

   I recommend that you hit no more than a dozen drives. Getting carried away with this club is easy. And when you go overboard, your swing can get a little quick. ***Remember:*** You're only warming up. Focus on your rhythm and timing — not on the ball.

4. **Before you leave the range, hit a few more balls with your wedge.**

   You're not looking for distance with this club, only smoothness. That's a good thought to leave with.

5. **Finally, spend about ten minutes on the practice putting green.**

   You need to get a feel for the pace of the greens. Start with short uphill putts of 2 to 3 feet. Get your confidence and then proceed to longer putts of 20 to 30 feet. After that, practice putting to opposite fringes to get the feeling of speed. Focus on the pace rather than the direction. You're ready now — knock them all in!

First-Tee Strategies

The best players start every round with a plan for how they're going to approach the course. They know which holes they can attack and which holes are best to play safely. So should you.

Many people say that golf is 90 percent mental and 10 percent physical. You'll find a lot of truth in that statement. The fewer mental errors you make, the lower your score will be. And the *great* thing about bad thinking is that everyone at every level of play can work on eliminating it.

Think of golf as a game of chess. You have to think two or three moves ahead. Over every shot, you should be thinking, "Where do I need to put this ball in order to make my next shot as easy as possible?"

I could write a whole book on the countless number of strategic situations you can find yourself in on the course. Trouble is, I don't have the space for that in this book, and you don't need all that information yet. So what follows is a brief overview of "tactical golf." I've selected three common situations; you'll come across each one at least once in almost every round you play. You can apply the thinking and strategy behind each one to many other problems that you'll encounter. So don't get too wrapped up in the specifics of each scenario — think "big picture."

Strategy 1: Don't be a sucker

You're playing a 170-yard par-3 hole (see Figure 13-5). As you can see, the hole is cut toward the left side of the green, behind a large bunker. If your first inclination is to fire straight at the flag, think again. Ask yourself these questions:

- What are your chances of pulling off such a difficult shot?
- What happens if you miss?
- Is the shot too risky?

If the answers are (a) less than 50 percent, (b) you take 5 to get down from the bunker, or (c) yes, then play toward the safe part of the green.

Only if you happen to be an exceptional bunker player should you even try to go for the flag.

Think of it this way: Golf is a game of numbers. If you shoot at the pin here, you bring the number 2 into play. If you hit a great shot, you have a great opportunity for a deuce. That's the upside. The downside is that missing the green makes the numbers 5, 6, and maybe even 7 possibilities, especially if you aren't too strong from sand or if you're unlucky enough to find a really bad lie.

If, on the other hand, you play for the middle of the green, your numbers are reduced. Say you hit the putting surface with your first shot. In all likelihood, the most you can take for the hole is 4, and you can take that only if you 3-putt. You'll get a lot of 3s from that position, and once in a while you'll hole the long putt — so a 2 isn't impossible.

Even if you miss the green on that side, you'll probably be left with a relatively simple chip or pitch. So unless you mess up terribly, 4 is again your worst score for the hole. I like those numbers better, don't you?

Anyway, those are the specifics of this particular situation. In the broader scheme of things, you should follow this policy more often than not. If you decide to be a middle-of-the-green shooter, practice your long-putting a lot. You're going to have a lot of 30- to 40-foot putts, so be ready for them. In the long run, you'll come out ahead.

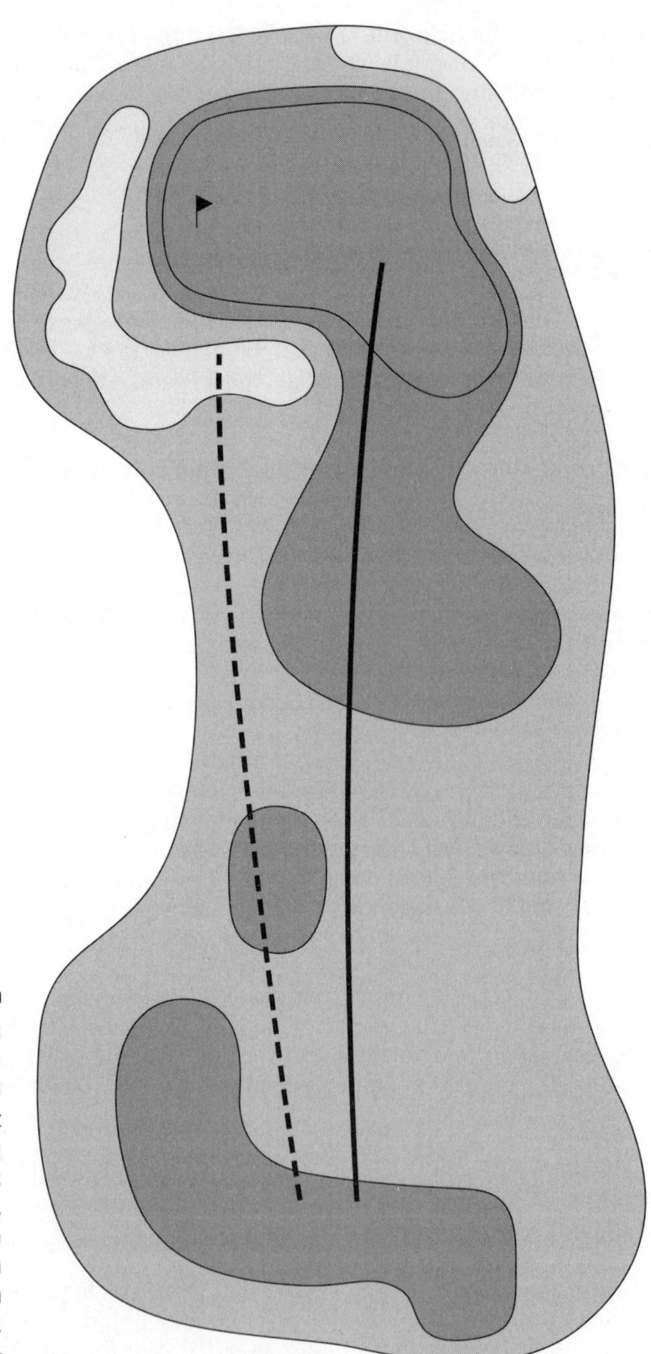

Figure 13-5: Don't be a sucker and aim straight for the flag (dotted line); instead, take the safer path away from the bunker.

Strategy 2: Think before you drive

You're on a par-4 hole of just over 400 yards (see Figure 13-6). But the actual yardage isn't that important. The key to this hole is the narrowing of the fairway at the point where your drive is most likely to finish. When this situation comes up, tee off with your 3-wood, 5-wood, or whatever club you can hit safely into the wide part of the fairway. Even if you can't quite reach the green in two shots, that's the best strategy. Again, it's a question of numbers. If you risk hitting your driver and miss the fairway, you're going to waste at least one shot getting the ball back into play — maybe more than one if you get a bad lie. Then you *still* have a longish shot to the green. If you miss the green, you're going to take at least 6 shots. Not good.

Now follow a better scenario. You hit your 3-wood from the tee safely down the fairway. Then you hit your 5-wood, leaving the ball about 25 yards from the green. All you have left is a simple little chip or pitch. Most times, you'll make no more than 5 on the hole. Indeed, you'll nearly always have a putt for a 4. I know most of you won't do this, but it makes sense, doesn't it?

All you have to do is pay attention to the layout of the hole and plan accordingly.

Strategy 3: Play three easy shots

The par-5 hole is long, just over 500 yards (see Figure 13-7). Your first inclination is again to reach for your driver. Most of the time, that's probably the correct play — but not always. Look at this hole. You can break it down into three relatively easy shots with the same club. Say you hit your 4-iron 170 yards. Three shots can put you on the green. To me, breaking down the hole is easier for the beginning player than trying to squeeze every possible yard out of the driver and getting into trouble. (I know you gorillas out there won't consider this. But I had to do this as a disclaimer.)

No law of golf says that you must use your driver from the tee. If you don't feel comfortable with your driver, go with your 3-wood. If your 3-wood doesn't feel right, go to the 5-wood. And if you still aren't happy, try your 3-iron or a hybrid club. Don't hit until you're confident that you can hit the ball into the fairway with the club that's in your hands. I'd rather be 200 yards from the tee and in the fairway than 250 yards out in the rough. If you don't believe me, try this test. Every time you miss a fairway from the tee, pick your ball up and drop it 15 yards farther back — but in the middle of the fairway. Then play from there. Bet you'll shoot anywhere from 5 to 10 shots fewer than normal for 18 holes. In other words, it's better to be in a spot where you can hit the ball cleanly than in a tough spot — even if the clean shot is longer.

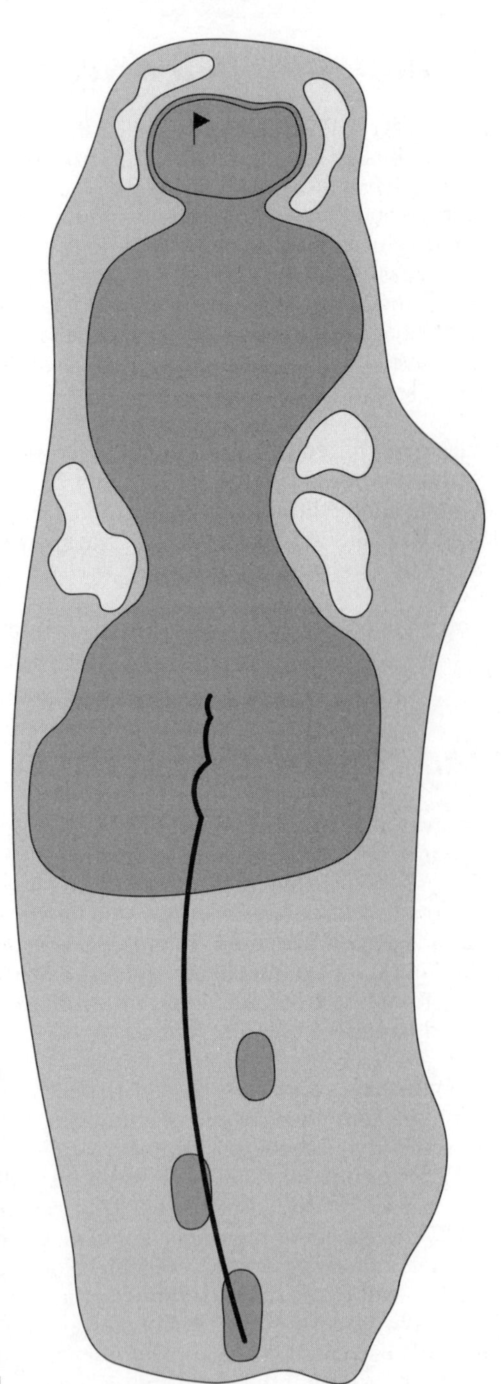

Figure 13-6: Go for the wide part of the fairway by using less club (a 3-wood or 5-wood, for example).

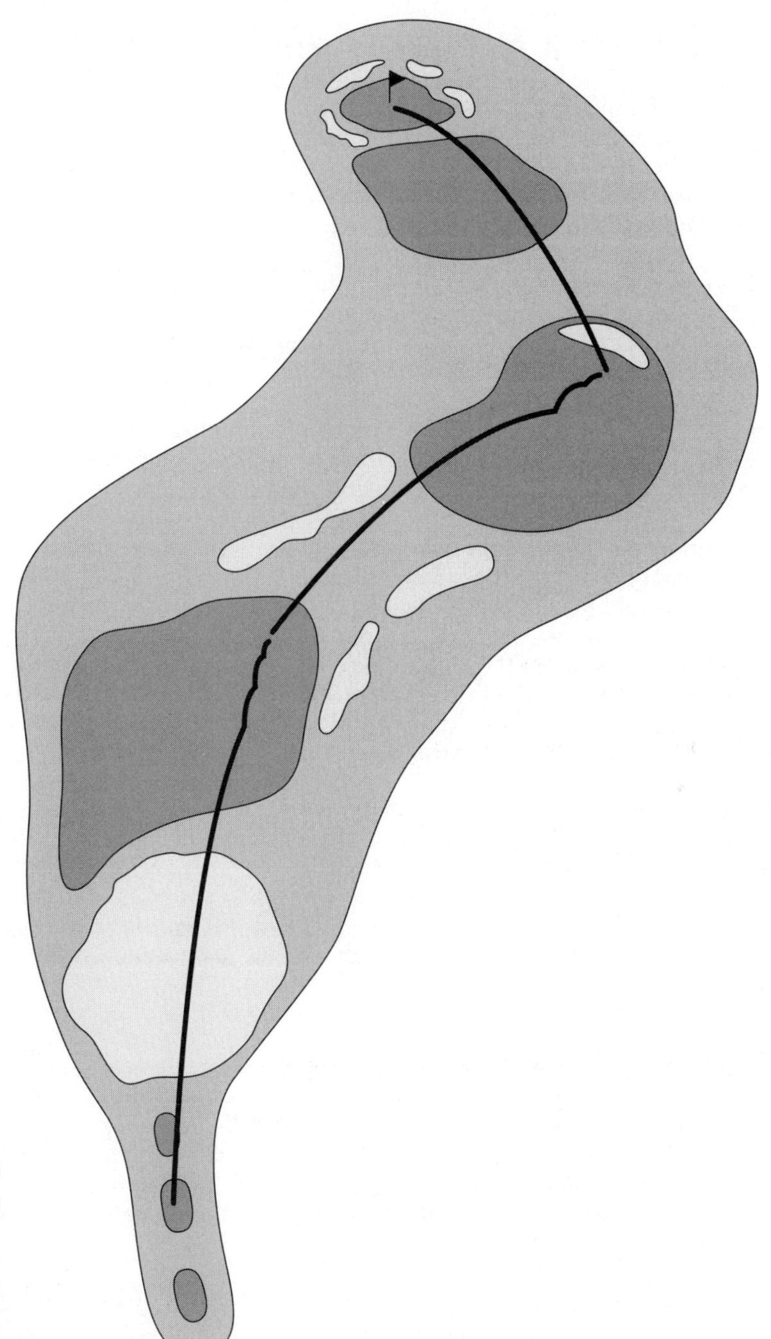

Figure 13-7: Turn long holes into three easy shots.

Know your strengths and weaknesses

To really employ good strategy on the golf course, you have to know your strengths and weaknesses. For example, on the par-4 hole described earlier in this chapter (see "Strategy 2: Think before you drive"), a really accurate driver of the ball could take the chance and try to hit the ball into the narrow gap. She's playing to her strength.

But how do you find out where your pluses and minuses are? Simple. All you have to do is keep a close record of your rounds over a period of time. By a close record, I don't simply mean your score on each hole. You have to break down the numbers a bit more than that.

Look at the score card in Figure 13-8, where John has marked his score in detail. You can see how many fairways he hit. How many times he hit the green. And how many putts he took on each green.

If John tracks these things over, say, ten rounds, trends soon appear. Assume that this round is typical for John. Clearly, John isn't a very good putter. Forty-two putts for 18 holes is poor by any standard, especially when he isn't hitting that many greens — only one in three. If John were hitting 12 or 13 greens, you'd expect more putts because he'd often be near the edge of the green. But this card tells another story. John's missing a lot of greens and taking a lot of putts. So either his chipping and pitching are very bad, or his putting is letting him down. Probably the latter.

On the other hand, John isn't a bad driver, at least in terms of accuracy. He's hitting more than half the fairways. So, at least in the short term, John needs to work on his short game and putting.

Keep a record of your scores that details various aspects of your game. You'll soon know which part (or parts) of your game need some work.

Beat the first-tee jitters

The opening shot of any round is often the most stressful. You're not into your round yet. Even the practice shots that you may have hit aren't the real thing. And people are nearly always around when you hit that first shot. If you're like most golfers, you'll be intimidated by even the thought of striking a ball in full view of the public.

How a player reacts to first-tee jitters is an individual thing. You just have to get out there and do it and see what happens. Common symptoms: Blurred vision. A desire to get this over and done with as soon as possible. Loss of reason.

Men's Course Rating/Slope Blue 73.1/137 White 71.0/130													Women's Course Rating/Slope Red 73.7/128		
Blue Tees	White Tees	Par	Hcp	JOHN				HOLE	HIT FAIRWAY	HIT GREEN		NO. PUTTS	Hcp	Par	Red Tees
377	361	4	11	4				1	✓	✓		2	13	4	310
514	467	5	13	8				2	✓	0		3	3	5	428
446	423	4	1	7				3	0	0		2	1	4	389
376	356	4	5	6				4	0	0		2	11	4	325
362	344	4	7	5				5	0	✓		3	7	4	316
376	360	4	9	6				6	✓	0		2	9	4	335
166	130	3	17	4				7	0	✓		3	17	3	108
429	407	4	3	5				8	✓	✓		3	5	4	368
161	145	3	15	5				9	0	0		2	15	3	122
3207	2993	35		50				Out	4	4		22		35	2701
		Initial											Initial		
366	348	4	18	5				10	0	0		2	14	4	320
570	537	5	10	7				11	✓	0		3	2	5	504
438	420	4	2	5				12	✓	0		2	6	4	389
197	182	3	12	4				13	0	0		2	16	3	145
507	475	5	14	5				14	✓	✓		2	4	5	425
398	380	4	4	5				15	0	✓		3	8	4	350
380	366	4	6	5				16	✓	0		2	10	4	339
165	151	3	16	4				17	0	0		2	18	3	133
397	375	4	8	5				18	0	0		2	12	4	341
3418	3234	36		45				In	3	2		20		36	2946
6625	6227	71		95				Tot	7	6		42		71	5647
	Handicap												Handicap		
	Net Score												Net Score		
	Adjust												Adjust		

Scorer Attested Date

Figure 13-8: Keep a close record of your rounds to track your strengths and weaknesses.

The most common mistake, however, is doing everything twice as fast as you normally would. By *everything,* I mean looking down the fairway, standing up to the ball, swinging — the lot. Your increased pace is due to the misguided notion that if you get this swing over with really quickly, no one will see it. It's the hit-it-and-go syndrome, and you should avoid it.

How to be cool on the course

When you show up at the course, it's okay to be a little late. If you've got a 9 a.m. tee time, get there at about 8:30. Then your partners are starting to panic a bit about where you are. Always change your shoes while sitting on the trunk of your car. That's cool. Always have a carry bag, never a pull cart. Pull carts aren't cool. Get one of those little bags with the prongs on to keep it upright when you set it down. Very cool.

Never tie your shoelaces until you get to the tee. On the tee, bend down to tie them while complaining about all the things that hurt. Bursitis in your right shoulder. That pesky tendonitis in your left knee. The sore elbow you sustained while carrying an old lady's groceries. Whatever. Elicit sympathy from your companions. Get up very slowly. Adjust yourself. Grab your back. Then get into stroke negotiations. . . .

What's also very cool is having your own turn of golfing phrase. Make up your own language. Don't say stuff like "wow" or "far out." Keep your talk underground. Use stuff that no one else can understand. For example, Fairway Louie refers to the local denizens of our golf course as "herds of grazing hack," because they're always looking for balls in the rough. If you come up with some good stuff, everyone will start using your language. It's a domino effect.

At first, though, I'd recommend that you do more listening than talking. It's like when you go to a foreign country. You have to listen before you start spouting off. Listen to how golfers express themselves during moments of elation, anger, and solitude. After you pick up the lingo, you can add your own touches to it. In golf terminology, there's no right or wrong as long as you don't act like a geek.

I remember when my golf swing wasn't where I wanted it to be. I had a bad grip, a bad takeaway, a bad position at the top. I was never comfortable with myself, so how could I be comfortable with others watching? I'd get up there, hit the ball as soon as I could, and get out of the way. After I understood the mechanics of my swing, I lost that dread. All of a sudden, I stood over the ball as long as I wanted to. I thought about what I was doing, not about what others were thinking. I wanted people to watch, to revel in the positions in my golf swing, because they were good positions. I didn't mind showing off.

Being overly concerned about your audience is really a social problem. Rather than taking refuge in your pre-shot routine and whatever swing thought you may be using, you're thinking about what other people may be thinking. The secret to overcoming this social problem is to immerse yourself in your routine. Forget all that outside stuff. Say, "Okay, I'm going to start behind the ball. Then I'm going to look at my line, take five steps to the ball, swing the club away to the inside and turn my shoulders." Whatever you say to yourself, just remember to focus *internally,* not externally.

Playing Games

The best format I know of for the beginning golfer is a *scramble.* In that format, you're usually part of a team of four. Everyone tees off. Then you pick the best of the four shots. Then everyone plays another shot from where that "best shot" lies. And so on. A scramble is great for beginners because you have less pressure to hit every shot well. You can lean on your partners a bit. Plus, you get to watch better players up close. And you get to experience some of the game's camaraderie. Scrambles are typically full of rooting, cheering, and high-fives. In short, they're a lot of fun.

You can also play in games where the format is *stableford.* In this game, the scoring is by points rather than strokes. You get one point for a *bogey* (score of one over par) on each hole; two points for a par; three for a *birdie* (one under par); and four points for an *eagle* (two under par). Thus, a round in which you par every hole reaps you 36 points. The great thing is that in a stableford, you don't have to complete every hole. You can take your 9s and 10s without irreparably damaging your score. You simply don't get any points for a hole in which you take more than a bogey. That's with your handicap strokes deducted, of course. (For more on golf handicapping, see the next chapter.)

After you've played for a while, however, you may find that you play most of your golf with three companions. That's known as a *foursome* in the United States (a *four-ball* elsewhere). The format is simple. You split into two teams of two and play what is known as a *best-ball* game. That is, the best score on each team on each hole counts as the score for that team. For example, if we're partners and you make a 5 on the first hole and I make a 4, then our team scores a 4 for the hole.

Keeping Score

Don't get too wrapped up in how many shots you're taking to play a round, at least at first. For many golfers, the score doesn't mean that much anyway. Most of the guys I grew up with never kept score. That's because they were always playing a match against another player or team. In a match like that, all that matters is how you compare with your opponents. It's never "me against the course." It's always "me against you." So if I'm having a really bad hole, I simply concede it to you and then move on to the next one.

Believe me, that's a totally different game from the one that you see the pros playing on TV every week. For them, every shot is vital — the difference between making the cut or not, or finishing in or out of the big money. That's why the pro game is better left to the pros.

Practicing

It's amazing, but nearly half of high-handicap golfers don't practice. Are you one of them? You can't expect to improve if you don't put some time in. Now, I can already hear you whining, "I don't have the time!" Well, stop your griping, because I made it easy for you. I put together a sample practice schedule that you can easily work into your weekly routine. You may want to tone it down at the office — it looks bad if your boss walks in while you're practicing your putting — although you may be able to make use of all the time you spend on those long conference calls.

Practice can be fun. You can modify the schedule to fit your goals and your playing level. Now, if you don't want to take strokes off your game, skip this part, but if you're a weekend warrior who wants to improve, follow this quick road map to success:

- **Practice your swing whenever possible.** You can practice most of the suggestions in Part II in your basement, living room, or backyard. Place old clubs in various locations around your house so that it's convenient to swing when the spirit (or schedule) moves you.
- **Make imaginary swings in front of a mirror or window** with your arms and hands in the proper position (see Part II). If you don't have a club handy, that's okay. Visualize and feel the correct position.
- **Grip a club when you watch television** — you're not doing anything else! Try swinging a club during a commercial — unless it's one of my commercials. In that case, put your club down and turn up the volume.
- **Build a practice area in your house or office where you can easily work on your short game.** Use those plastic practice balls. Set up a small obstacle course in your yard. (Your kids can help you with this part.)
- **Where and when possible, hit a bucket of balls during lunch.** If it's a hot day in July, you may want to hit the showers before you head back to the office.

Here's a sample practice schedule:

- **Monday:** Health-club workout (1 hour); putt on rug (15 minutes)
- **Tuesday:** Swing a club at home in front of a mirror or window (30 minutes)
- **Wednesday:** Health-club workout (1 hour); read a golf magazine or golf book or watch a golf video or DVD (30 minutes)

- **Thursday:** Swing a club or chip (1 hour)
- **Friday:** Health-club workout (1 hour); practice range, including golf drills (1 hour)
- **Saturday:** Practice range (1 hour); play 18 holes
- **Sunday:** Watch golf on TV; practice range (30 minutes); play 9 holes

Tips for seniors

Now that I'm on the senior tour, I get a chance to tee it up with some of the same guys who used to beat the pants off me on the PGA Tour. I still love to play, but I realize that, as I age, my game will change. I can deal with it. We all have to. If you've become a senior golfer since the last edition of this book came out, or if you're taking up the game for the first time, you need to know some things to keep your game young.

As you may be finding out already (or will find out soon enough), you just don't hit the ball as far as you used to. There are four basic reasons for this:

- **Poor posture:** Bad posture — often from wearing bifocals — stops you from turning properly. Be careful how you hold your head, and keep it off your chest. Maintain good posture by standing in front of a full-length mirror and holding a club out in front of you. Continue looking in the mirror as you lower the club into the hitting position. Don't let your head tilt or move forward. When you master this technique, you'll be able to make that turn and swing your arms.
- **Lack of rotation on your backswing:** You probably aren't turning your hips and shoulders enough on the backswing. You can increase your range of motion by increasing your flexibility. See Chapter 4 for stretching exercises that can help. Then review the elements of the swing in Chapters 6 and 7, get out to the range, and work out those kinks.
- **Decrease in strength:** As you grow older, you lose strength in your hands and forearms, which makes it harder to hold your wrists in the proper position on the downswing. This weakness reduces the speed at which the club strikes the ball. Simple drills to combat loss of strength include squeezing a tennis ball, doing forearm curls with light barbells, and Harvey Penick's drill: Swing a club back and forth like a scythe 20 or 30 times a day. I don't recommend doing this one anywhere near the old Ming vase.
- **Lack of rotation in the follow-through:** You may be so intent on hitting the ball that you're not swinging through to the other side. This causes the club to stop 3 or 4 feet beyond the ball and the arms to stop somewhere around your chest, with your belt buckle pointing to the right of your target. As you can imagine, this type of swing will not result in a pretty shot. The ball will fly to the right and be, well, weak. To correct such a problem, repeat this drill each day until it feels natural: While looking in a full-length mirror, go to the top of your backswing (see Chapter 6) and then mirror-image that position on the follow-through. Your belt buckle should always face to the left of your target. To make this happen, you must transfer 90 percent of your weight from your right foot to your left foot.

I can't stress this enough: If you're not on some kind of exercise program, get on one (see Chapter 4). Consult your local golf pro for suggestions, too. A good program coupled with a stretching routine will improve your flexibility and strength — and your golf game. It will benefit your life as well.

Chapter 14

Rules, Etiquette, and Scoring

In This Chapter

- Playing by the rules
- Respecting other golfers
- Keeping score
- Handling penalty shots

Golf is not a game lacking in structure. In fact, it is rife with rules of play, rules of etiquette, and rules of scoring. You may never master all the intricacies of these rules, but you should familiarize yourself with some of the more important ones.

Blimey, It's a Stymie: The Ancient Rules of Golf

The Honourable Company of Edinburgh Golfers devised the original 13Rules of Golf in 1744, over a *wee dram* (whisky) or 12, no doubt. Anyway, the Rules are worth recounting in this chapter, to show you how little the Rules of Golf have changed over the centuries.

1. You must tee your ball within a club's length of the hole.
2. Your tee must be upon the ground.
3. You are not to change the ball which you strike off the tee.
4. You are not to remove any stones, bones, or any break club, for the sake of playing your ball. Except upon the fair green, and that's only within a club's length of your ball.
5. If your ball comes among watter, or any watery filth, you are at liberty to take out your ball and bringing it behind the hazard and teeing it, you may play it with any club and allow your adversary a stroke, for so getting out your ball.

6. If your balls be found anywhere touching one another you are to lift the first ball, till you play the last.
7. At holling, you are to play honestly for the hole, and not to play upon your adversary's ball, not lying in your way to the hole.
8. If you should lose your ball, by its being taken up, or any other way you are to go back to the spot, where you struck last, and drop another ball, and allow your adversary a stroke for the misfortune.
9. No man at holling his ball, is to be allowed, to mark his way to the hole with his club or any thing else.
10. If a ball be stopp'd by any person, horse, dog, or any thing else, the ball so stopp'd must be played where it lyes.
11. If you draw your club, in order to strike and proceed so far in the stroke, as to be bringing down your club; if then, your club shall break, in any way, it is to be counted a stroke.
12. He whose ball lyes farthest from the hole is obliged to play first.
13. Neither trench, ditch or dyke, made for the preservation of the links, nor the scholar's holes or the soldier's lines, shall be counted a hazard. But the ball is to be taken out, teed and play'd with any iron club.

As you can tell from the language and terms used in 1744, these rules were designed for match play (see "Match play," later in this chapter). My particular favorite is Rule 6. It wasn't that long before the rule was redefined from "touching" to "within 6 inches" — which in turn led to the *stymie rule.* The stymie has long since passed into legend, but it was a lot of fun. Basically, *stymie* meant that whenever your opponent's ball lay between your ball and the hole, you couldn't ask him to mark his ball. You had to find some way around it. Usually, that meant chipping over his ball, which is great fun, especially if you're close to the hole.

Another rule I particularly like is the one stating that you could leave your opponent's ball where it lay if it was near the edge of the hole. As of the late 1960s, you could use such a situation to your advantage, with the other ball acting as a backstop of sorts. Nothing could hack off your opponent more than your ball going into the hole off his! Happy days!

The Rules Today

The Rules since those far-off early days have been refined countless times. Take a look at a rulebook today (you can pick one up from almost any professional's shop, or order one directly from the United States Golf Association), and you'll find a seemingly endless list of clauses and subclauses — all of which make the game sound very difficult and complicated.

In my opinion, the Rules are too complex. For a smart, enjoyable look at them, pick up a copy of *Golf Rules & Etiquette For Dummies,* by John Steinbreder. There's also an excellent book by Jeffrey S. Kuhn and Bryan A. Garner, *The Rules of Golf in Plain English.* And if you're not ready to memorize those two tomes, you can get by with about a dozen simple rules. In fact, common sense can help, too. You won't go too far wrong on the course if you:

- Play the course as you find it.
- Play the ball as it lies.
- If you can't do either of those things, do what's fair.

To demonstrate just how crazy the Rules of Golf can get and how easy it is to commit an infraction, look at the cases of Craig Stadler and Paul Azinger.

You may remember the Stadler case. Craig was playing the 14th hole at Torrey Pines in San Diego during a PGA Tour event. Because his ball was under a tree, he used a towel to kneel down as he hit the ball out because he didn't want to get his pants dirty.

That sounds harmless enough, doesn't it? Think again. Some smart guy out there in TV land was watching all this (the next day, no less) and thought he was part of a new game show: *You Make the Ruling.* He called the PGA Tour and said that Stadler was guilty of "building a stance." By kneeling on top of something, even a towel, Stadler was technically changing his shot, breaking Rule 13-3 (a player is entitled to place his feet firmly in taking his stance, but he shall not build his stance).

The officials had no option but to agree, so Craig was disqualified for signing the wrong score card — 24 hours after the fact. Technically, an event isn't over until the competitors have completed 72 holes. At the time that Craig's rules infraction came to light, he had played only 54 holes. Madness! Stadler clearly had no intent to gain advantage. But it was adios, Craig.

The same sort of thing happened with Paul Azinger. At the Doral tournament in Florida in 1996, Azinger played a shot from inside the edge of the lake on the final hole. Just before he started his swing, he flicked a rock out of the way while taking his stance. Cue the Rules police. Another phone call got Azinger thrown out for "moving loose impediments in a hazard." Common sense and the Rules parted company again.

Another incident occurred at the LPGA's Samsung World Championship in 2005, when Michelle Wie took a drop several inches closer to the hole than allowed. A *Sports Illustrated* writer noticed the infraction, and Michelle was disqualified — in her first event as a professional!

In all three cases, the Rules of Golf were violated. The players were not cheating, however; they broke the Rules accidentally. And what got them thrown out of those tournaments were not the original infractions, but signing incorrect score cards.

Anyway, the point is that although the Rules of Golf are designed to help you, they can be a minefield. Watch where you step!

Marking a score card

Score cards can be a little daunting when you first look at them (see Figure 14-1). All those numbers and little boxes. But fear not — first impressions can be misleading. Keeping score is actually simpler than it looks.

Ten rules you need to know

By Mike Shea, PGA Tour Rules Official

Rule 1: You must play the same ball from the teeing ground into the hole. Change only when the rules allow.

Rule 3-2: You must hole out on each hole. If you don't, you don't have a score and are thus disqualified.

Rule 6-5: You are responsible for playing your own ball. Put an identification mark on it.

Rule 13: You must play the ball as it lies.

Rule 13-4: When your ball is in a hazard, whether a bunker or a water hazard, you cannot touch the ground or water in the hazard with your club before impact.

Rule 16: You cannot improve the line of a putt before your stroke by repairing marks made by the spikes on players' shoes.

Rule 24: Obstructions are anything artificial. Some are moveable. Others are not, so you must drop your ball within one club length of your nearest point of relief — no penalty.

Rule 26: If your ball is lost in a water hazard, you can drop another behind the hazard, keeping the point where the ball last crossed the hazard between you and the hole — with a one-stroke penalty.

Rule 27: If you lose your ball anywhere other than in a hazard, return to where you hit your previous shot and hit another — with a one-stroke penalty.

Rule 28: If your ball is unplayable, you have three options (each carries a one-stroke penalty):

- Play from where you hit your last shot.
- Drop within two club lengths of where your ball is now, no closer to the hole.
- Keep the point where the ball is between you and the hole and drop your ball on that line. You can go back as far as you want.

Source: *The Rules of Golf* as approved by the United States Golf Association (USGA) and the Royal and Ancient Golf Club of St. Andrews, Scotland

Say your handicap is 9 and mine is 14. That means you're going to give me 5 strokes over the course of the round. I get those strokes at the holes rated the most difficult. That's logical. And equally logical is the fact that these holes are handicapped 1 through 5. So mark those stroke holes before you begin. (I discuss scoring and handicaps later in this chapter.)

Men's Course Rating/Slope
Blue 73.1/137
White 71.0/130

Women's Course Rating/Slope
Red 73.7/128

Blue Tees	White Tees	Par	Hcp	JOHN-8	PAUL-14+6		HOLE	Hcp	Par	Red Tees
377	361	4	11	4	4	E	1	13	4	310
514	467	5	13	4	5	J+1	2	3	5	428
446	423	4	1	4	4	E	3	1	4	389
376	356	4	5	5	5	P+1	4	11	4	325
362	344	4	7	4	6	E	5	7	4	316
376	360	4	9	5	5	E	6	9	4	335
166	130	3	17	2	4	J+1	7	17	3	108
429	407	4	3	5	5	E	8	5	4	368
161	145	3	15	4	3	P+1	9	15	3	122
3207	2993	35		37	41		Out		35	2701
			Initial					Initial		
366	348	4	18	4	5	E	10	14	4	320
570	537	5	10	5	6	J+1	11	2	5	504
438	420	4	2	4	4	E	12	6	4	389
197	182	3	12	3	4	J+1	13	16	3	145
507	475	5	14	5	6	J+2	14	4	5	425
398	380	4	4	5	5	J+1	15	8	4	350
380	366	4	6	4	4	E	16	10	4	339
165	151	3	16	4	3	P+1	17	18	3	133
397	375	4	8	4	3	P+2	18	12	4	341
3418	3234	36		38	40		In		36	2946
6625	6227	71		75	81		Tot		71	5647
			Handicap					Handicap		
			Net Score					Net Score		
			Adjust					Adjust		

Scorer Attested Date

Figure 14-1: Marking your card.

After the match has begun, keep track of the score with simple pluses or minuses in a spare row of boxes.

In stroke or medal play, you're expected to keep and score your playing companion's card. His name will be at the top, his handicap in the box at the bottom of the card. All you have to do is record his score for each hole in the box provided. You don't even have to add it up.

Teeing up

You must tee up between the markers, not in front of them, and no more than two club lengths behind them (see Figure 14-2). If you tee off outside this area, you get a two-shot penalty in *stroke play,* and in match play, you must replay your shot from the teeing area. (See the "Stroke play" and "Match play" sections, later in this chapter, for more differences between the two.)

You don't have to stand within the teeing area; your feet can be outside it. This is useful to know when the only piece of level ground is outside the teeing area or if the hole is a sharp dogleg. You can give yourself a better angle by *teeing up wide* (standing outside the teeing area).

Figure 14-2 The tee is bigger than you think.

Finding a lost ball

At this stage of your life, you're going to hit more than your fair share of errant shots. Some of those are going to finish in spots where finding the ball is a little tricky. And sometimes you won't find the ball at all.

If you can't find the ball in the five minutes you're allowed, you have to return to the tee or to the point where you last hit the ball and play another ball. With penalty, stroke, and distance, you'll be hitting 3 off the tee. One way to avoid having to walk all the way back to the tee after failing to find your ball is to hit a provisional ball as soon as you think that the first one may be lost. Then if you can't find the first ball, play the second ball. Be sure, however, to announce to your playing partners that you're playing a provisional ball. If you don't, you must play the second ball — with the penalty — even if you find the first ball.

How can you keep lost balls to a minimum? First, when your wild shot is in midair, watch it like a hawk. If you don't, you won't have any idea where it went. Now you're probably thinking that sounds pretty obvious, but not watching the shot is perhaps the number-one reason (after bad technique) why balls get lost. Temper gets the better of too many players. They're too busy slamming the club into the ground to watch where the ball goes. Don't make that mistake.

Pay attention when the ball lands, too. Give yourself a reference — like a tree — near the landing area. You should also put an identifying mark on your ball before you begin play so you can be sure that the ball you find is the one you hit.

Looking for a ball is a much-neglected art form. I see people wandering aimlessly, going over the same spot time after time. Be systematic. Walk back and forth without retracing your steps. Your chances of finding the ball are much greater that way.

You have five minutes to look for a lost ball from the moment you start to search. Time yourself. Even if you find the ball after five minutes have elapsed, you still have to go back to the spot you played from to hit another ball. Them's the rules.

Dropping a ball

There will be times when you have to pick up your ball and drop it. Every golf course has places that allow you to take a free drop. A cart path is one — you can move your ball away from the path with no penalty. Casual water (such as a puddle) is another. If you find yourself in this position, follow this routine:

1. **Lift and clean your ball.**
2. **Find the nearest spot where you have complete relief from the problem and mark that spot with a tee.**

   You not only have to get the ball away from the obstruction, but your feet as well. So find the spot where your feet are clear of the obstruction and then determine where the clubhead would be if you hit from there. This is the spot you want to mark. The spot you choose cannot be closer to the hole.
3. **Measure one club length from that mark.**
4. **Now drop the ball.**

   Stand tall, holding the ball at shoulder height and at arm's length, as shown in Figure 14-3. Let the ball drop vertically. You aren't allowed to "spin" the ball into a more favorable spot. Where you drop depends on what rule applies — just be sure that the ball doesn't end up nearer the hole than it was when you picked it up. If it does, you have to pick up the ball and drop it again.

How you drop the ball makes no difference; however, you always have to stand upright when dropping. I once had to drop my ball in a bunker where the sand was wet. The ball was obviously going to *plug* when it landed (that is, get buried in the sand), so I asked whether I could lie down to drop it. The answer was negative. Oh, well. . . .

Taking advice

Advice has two sides. First, you cannot either give advice to or receive advice from anyone other than your caddie. That means you can't ask your playing companion what club he or she hit. Neither can you say anything that may help in the playing of his or her next stroke.

This rule is a tough one, and even the best have been caught breaking it. In the 1971 Ryder Cup matches in St. Louis, Arnold Palmer was playing Bernard Gallacher of Scotland. Palmer hit a lovely shot onto a par-3, whereupon Gallacher's caddie said, "Great shot, Arnie. What club did you hit?" Arnold, being Arnold, told him. Gallacher was unaware of the exchange, but the referee heard it. Palmer, despite his own protestations, was awarded the hole. That was in match play; in stroke play, it's a 2-shot penalty. So take care!

First, find the spot where your feet are clear of the obstruction.

You get one more club length from there.

Now drop your ball.

Figure 14-3: Dropping your ball.

Second, you're going to find yourself playing with people, lots of people, who think of themselves as experts on every aspect of the golf swing. These know-it-alls usually mean well, but they're dangerous to your golfing health. Ignore them. Or, if that proves too difficult, listen, smile politely, and then go about your business as if they had never uttered a word.

Etiquette: How to Play the Right Way

In golf, unlike almost any of the trash-talking sports you can watch on TV, sportsmanship is paramount. Golf is an easy game to cheat at, so every player is on his or her honor. But there's more to it than that. Golf has its own code of etiquette: semiofficial "rules" of courtesy that every player is expected to follow. Here are the main things you need to know:

- **Don't talk while someone is playing a stroke.** Give your partners time and silence while they're analyzing the situation, making their practice swings, and actually making their swings for real. Don't stand near them or move about, either, especially when you're on the greens. Stay out of their peripheral vision while they're putting. Don't stand near the hole or walk between your partner's ball and the hole. Even be mindful of your shadow. The *line* of a putt — the path it must follow to the hole — is holy ground.

  The key is being aware of your companions' — and their golf balls' — whereabouts and temperament. Easygoing types may not mind if you gab away while they're choosing a club, but that isn't true for everyone. If in doubt, stand still and shut up. If you're a problem more than once, you'll be told about it.

- **Be ready to play when it's your turn — when your ball lies farthest from the hole.** Make your decisions while you're walking to your ball or while waiting for someone else to play. Be ready to play. And when it's your turn to hit, do so without delay. You don't have to rush; just get on with it.

- **The *honor* (that is, the first shot) on a given tee goes to the player with the lowest score on the previous hole.** If that hole was tied, the player with the lowest score on the hole before that is said to be up and retains the honor. In other words, you have the honor until you lose it.

- **Make sure everyone in your foursome is behind you when you hit.** You're not going to hit every shot where you're aiming it. If in doubt, wait for your playing partners to get out of your line of play. The same is true for the group in front; wait until they are well out of range before you hit. Even if it would take a career shot for you to reach them, wait. Lawyers love golfers who ignore this rule of thumb.

- **Pay attention to the group behind you, too.** Are they waiting for you on every shot? Is there a gap between you and the group ahead of you? If the answer to either or both is yes, step aside and invite the group behind you to play through. This is no reflection on your ability. All it means is that the group behind plays faster than you do.

  The best and most timesaving place to let a group behind play through is at a par-3 (it's the shortest hole and, therefore, the quickest way of playing through). After hitting your ball onto the green, mark it, and wave to them to play. Stand off to the side of the green as they hit. After they've all hit, replace your ball and putt out. Then let them go. Simple, isn't it?

Sadly, you're likely to see this piece of basic good manners abused time and again by players who don't know any better and have no place on a golf course. Ignore them. Do what's right. Stepping aside makes your round more enjoyable. Think about it. Who likes to ruin someone else's day? Give your ego a rest and let them through.

- **Help out the greenskeeper.** A busy golf course takes a lot of a pounding over a day's play — all those balls landing on greens, feet walking through bunkers, and divots of earth flying through the air. Do your bit for the golf course. Repair any ball marks you see on the greens. (You can use your tee or a special tool called a *divot fixer,* which costs about a dollar in the pro shop.)

Here's how to repair ball marks: Stick the repair tool in the green around the perimeter of the indentation. Start at the rear. Gently lift the compacted dirt. Replace any loose pieces of grass or turf in the center of the hole. Then take your putter and tap down the raised turf until it's level again (see Figure 14-4). You can repair ball marks either before or after you putt. It's a good habit to have.

Finally, smooth out or rake any footprints in bunkers, as shown in Figure 14-5 (but only after you play out). And replace any divots you find on the fairways and tees.

- **If you must play in a golf cart (take my advice and walk if you can), park it well away from greens, tees, and bunkers.** To speed up play, you should park on the side of the green nearest the next tee. The same is true if you're carrying your bag. Don't set it down near any of the aforementioned, but do leave it in a spot on the way to the next tee.
- **Leave the green as soon as everyone has finished putting.** You'll see this a lot, and after a while it'll drive you crazy. You're ready to play your approach shot to the green, and the people in front are crowding around the hole marking their cards. That's poor etiquette on two counts: It delays play, and the last thing the greenskeeper wants is a lot of footprints around the cup. Mark your card on the way to the next tee.

Ten things to say when you hit a bad shot

- I wasn't loose.
- I looked up.
- I just had a lesson, and the pro screwed me up.
- I borrowed these clubs.
- These new shoes are hurting my feet.
- This new glove doesn't fit.
- I had a bad lie.
- The club slipped.
- I can't play well when the dew point is this high.
- The sun was in my eyes.

When a ball lands on a soft green, it often leaves a *pitch mark*.

Lift the back edge of the hole...

and then flatten it out.

Figure 14-4: Take care of the green.

Figure 14-5: Use your rake.

The Handicap System

If you, as a beginner, are completing 18-hole rounds in less than 80 shots, you're either a cheat or the next Jack Nicklaus or Annika Sorenstam. In all probability, you are neither, which makes it likely that your scores are considerably higher than par. Enter the handicap system.

The United States Golf Association constructed the handicap system to level the playing field for everyone. The association has an esoteric system of "course rating" and something called "slope" to help them compute exactly how many strokes everyone should get. In all my years in golf, I have yet to meet anyone who either understands or can explain how the course rating and slope are computed, so I'm not going to try. Be like everyone else — accept both and go with the flow.

The handicap system is one reason I think that golf is the best of all games. Handicapping allows any two players, whatever their level of play, to go out and have an enjoyable — and competitive — game together. Try to compete on, say, a tennis court. I can't go out with Andre Agassi and have any fun at all. Neither can he. The disparity in our ability levels makes competitive play impossible. Not so with golf.

Getting a handicap

If you've never played golf before, you won't have a handicap yet. Don't worry — you've got plenty of time. When you can consistently hit the ball at least 150 yards with a driver, you're ready to play a full 18-hole round of golf.

When you reach the stage where you can hit the ball a decent distance on the range, you're ready to do the same on a real golf course. You want to test yourself and give your progress a number. Make that two numbers: your score and your handicap.

The first thing you need to do is keep score. Get a golfer friend to accompany you in a round of 18 holes. This person must keep score and sign your card at the end of the round. To be valid, a card needs two signatures — your own and that of the person you're playing with. That way, all scores are clearly valid, and corruption is kept to a minimum.

You need to play at least ten rounds before you're eligible for a handicap. Don't ask why; those are the rules. Before you complete ten rounds, you're in a kind of cocoon from which you emerge as a beautiful, full-fledged, handicap golfer.

At first, your handicap will probably drop quite quickly. Most new golfers improve by leaps and bounds at first. After that, improvement may continue, but at a much slower pace.

Of course, the handicap system is easy to abuse, and some people do. Interestingly, most abuse occurs when players want their handicaps to be higher. They either fabricate high scores, or they don't record their better rounds so that their handicaps rise. Thus, they get more strokes from other players in betting matches. A few golfers go the other way; they want a lower handicap than they can realistically play to so that their scores look better. Find these people with vanity handicaps and wager with them for everything they own!

Don't get too cynical, though. Any abuse of the system is thankfully confined to a tiny minority of players, which is another reason why golf is such a great game. Golfers can generally be trusted. The few cheats are soon identified and ostracized.

Calculating your handicap

Okay, you're wondering how you get a handicap, right? All you have to do is hand in your scores at the course where you normally play. Then you're off and running. Your handicap at any one time is the average of the best 10 of your previous 20 scores (see Figure 14-6). Technically it's 96 percent of that number, but let the math whizzes handle that wrinkle.

Your handicap fairly accurately reflects your current form because you must record your score every time you go out. Most clubs and public facilities make things easy for you. They have computers into which you feed your scores. The program does all the work and updates your handicap.

Name JOHN DOE 355 GHIN©

Golf Handicap and Information Network©

Club GOLF & GOLF CLUB
Club # 30-106-1 GHIN # 2437-213
Effective Date 09/08/99
Scores Posted 46

USGA HCP INDEX 12.1
HOME 14

SCORE HISTORY — MOST RECENT FIRST * IF USED

1	90*	92	92	90	87*
6	91	92	90	89 A	92
11	87*	88*	86*	79*T	93
16	87*	82*	84*	94	86*

Figure 14-6: Your handicap card.

You don't have to be a member of a club to get a handicap. Many public facilities have their own handicap computers. For a nominal fee, you can usually get yourself an identification number and access to the software.

Suppose that your ten scores average out at exactly 100. In other words, for your first ten rounds of golf, you hit 1,000 shots. If par for the 18-hole course you played is 72, your average score is 28 over par. That figure, 28, is your handicap.

Every time you play from then on, your handicap adjusts to account for your most recent score. Suppose that your 11th round is a 96. That's only 24 over the par of 72. So your net score — your actual score minus your handicap — is 68, 4 under that magic number of 72. That's good.

Remember: The lower your score is, the better you've played. When you feed that 96 into the handicap computer, you'll probably find that your handicap drops.

What your handicap means

In golf, the lower your handicap is, the better you are. Thus, if your handicap is 6 and mine is 10, you're a better player than I. On average, four strokes better, to be exact.

Assume that par for the 18-hole course we're going to play is 72. You, as someone with a handicap of 6, would be expected to play 18 holes in a total of 78 strokes, 6 more than par. I, on the other hand, being a 10-handicapper, would on a normal day hit the ball 82 times, 10 more than par. Thus, your handicap is the number of strokes over par you should take to play an 18-hole course.

When you're just starting out, you don't want to team up with three low-handicap players. Play with golfers of your own ability at first. When you get the hang of it, start playing with people who are better than you so that you can learn from them.

How to Keep Score

Scoring is another great thing about golf. You can easily see how you're doing because your score is in black and white on the score card. Every course you play has a score card. The score card tells you each hole's length, its par, and its rating relative to the other holes (see Figure 14-7).

Men's Course Rating/Slope
Blue 73.1/137
White 71.0/130

Women's Course Rating/Slope
Red 73.7/128

Blue Tees	White Tees	Par	Hcp	PAUL	JOHN	NICK	TERRY	HOLE					Hcp	Par	Red Tees
377	361	4	11	5	4	6	3	1					13	4	310
514	467	5	13	4	7	6	5	2					3	5	428
446	423	4	1	5	5	5	5	3					1	4	389
376	356	4	5	4	5	5	4	4					11	4	325
362	344	4	7	5	4	4	3	5					7	4	316
376	360	4	9	4	6	5	5	6					9	4	335
166	130	3	17	4	2	3	3	7					17	3	108
429	407	4	3	4	5	6	5	8					5	4	368
161	145	3	15	3	4	4	4	9					15	3	122
3207	2993	35		38	42	44	37	Out						35	2701
			Initial										Initial		
366	348	4	18	4	4	5	4	10					14	4	320
570	537	5	10	6	5	5	7	11					2	5	504
438	420	4	2	5	4	6	4	12					6	4	389
197	182	3	12	4	4	5	4	13					16	3	145
507	475	5	14	5	5	4	5	14					4	5	425
398	380	4	4	6	5	4	6	15					8	4	350
380	366	4	6	4	4	5	4	16					10	4	339
165	151	3	16	3	3	4	3	17					18	3	133
397	375	4	8	3	4	6	5	18					12	4	341
3418	3234	36		40	38	44	42	In						36	2946
6625	6227	71		78	80	88	79	Tot						71	5647
		Handicap		14	15	18	11						Handicap		
		Net Score		64	65	70	68						Net Score		
		Adjust											Adjust		

Scorer   Attested   6-15-99 Date

Figure 14-7: Keeping score.

The relationship of the holes is important when you're playing a head-to-head match. Say I have to give you 11 shots over 18 holes. In other words, on 11 holes during our round, you get to subtract one shot from your score. The obvious question is, "Which holes?" The card answers that question. You get your shots on the holes rated 1 through 11. These holes, in the opinion of the club committee, are the hardest 11 holes on the course. The number-one-rated hole is the toughest, and the number 18–rated hole is the easiest.

Although you have to report your score every time you set foot on the golf course (stroke play), most of your golf will typically be matches against others (match play), which is why each hole's rating is important.

Match play

Match play and stroke play have slightly different rules. In match play, you don't have to write down any score. The only thing that matters is the state of the game between you and your opponent.

The score is recorded as holes up or holes down. For example, say my score on the first hole was 4, and your score was 5 and you received no strokes on that hole. I'm now one up. Because each hole is a separate entity, you don't need to write down your actual score; you simply count the number of holes you've won or lost. In fact, if you're having a particularly bad time on a given hole, you can even pick up your ball and concede the hole. All you lose is that hole. Everything starts fresh on the next tee. Such a head-to-head match ends when one player is more holes up than the number of holes remaining. Thus, matches can be won by scores of "four and three." All that means is that one player was four holes ahead with only three left, the match finishing on the 15th green.

Stroke play

Stroke play is different. It's strictly card-and-pencil stuff. Now you're playing against everyone else in the field — or against that elusive standard, par — not just your playing companion. All you do is count one stroke each time you swing at the ball. If it takes you five strokes to play the first hole, you write 5 on your card for that hole. You don't record your own score, though. The card in your pocket has your playing companion's name on it. You keep his score, and he keeps yours. (You may keep your own score as well, but your playing partner keeps your official score.) At the end of the round, he signs his name to your card and gives it to you; you do the same with his card. After you've checked your score for each hole, you also sign your card. Then, if you're in an official tournament, you hand your card to the scorers. If you're playing a casual round, you record your score on the computer.

Take care when checking your card. One Rules of Golf quirk is that you're responsible for the accuracy of the score recorded under your name for each hole — your companion isn't. Any mistakes are deemed to have been made by you, not him. And you can't change a mistake later, even if you have witnesses. Take the case of Roberto DeVicenzo at the 1968 Masters. Millions of spectators and TV viewers saw him make a birdie 3 on the 17th hole in the final round. But the man marking his card, Tommy Aaron, mistakenly marked a 4. Checking his score after the round, DeVicenzo failed to notice the error and signed his card. The mistake cost him the chance of victory in a playoff with Bob Goalby. DeVicenzo had to accept a score one higher than he actually shot and lost by that one stroke. Tragic.

DeVicenzo's mistake illustrates what can happen when the score on your card is higher than the one you actually made on the hole. You're simply stuck with that score. If the opposite is the case and the score on the card is *lower* than it should be, the result is even worse: You're disqualified.

One last thing: Don't worry about the addition on your card. You aren't responsible for that part. As long as the numbers opposite each hole are correct, you're in the clear.

Penalty Shots

Penalty shots are an unfortunate part of every golfer's life. Sooner or later, you're going to incur a penalty shot or shots. I can't cover all the possible penalty situations in this book, but in the following sections I run you through the most common.

Out-of-bounds

Out-of-bounds is the term used when you hit your ball to a spot outside the confines of the golf course — over a boundary fence, for example. Out-of-bounds areas are usually marked with white stakes that are about 30 yards apart. If you're outside that line, you're out-of-bounds (often abbreviated with the dreaded initials "O.B.").

Okay, so it's happened; you've gone out-of-bounds. What are your options? Limited, I'm afraid. First, you're penalized stroke and distance. That means you must drop another ball (or tee up if the shot you hit out-of-bounds was from a tee) as near as possible to the spot you just played from. Say that shot was your first on that hole. Your next shot will count as your third on that hole. Count 'em:

- The shot you hit
- The stroke penalty
- The distance

So now you're "playing three" from the same spot.

Unplayable lies

Inevitably, you're going to hit a ball into a spot from which further progress is impossible. In a bush. Against a wall. Even buried in a bunker.

When the unplayable lie happens (and you are the sole judge of whether you can hit the ball), your situation dictates your options. In general, you have three escape routes.

- You can pick up the ball and drop it — no nearer the hole — within two club lengths (take your driver and place it end-to-end on the ground twice) of the original spot under penalty of one shot.
- You can pick up the ball, walk back as far as you want, keeping that original point between you and the hole, and then drop the ball. Again, it's a one-stroke penalty.
- You can return to the point where you hit the original shot. This option is the last resort because you lose distance, as well as adding the penalty shot. Believe me, there's nothing worse than a long walk burdened with a penalty stroke!

Water hazards

Water hazards are intimidating when you have to hit across one. You hear the dreaded splash before too long. "Watery graves," the English TV commentator Henry Longhurst used to call these things.

Anyway, whenever you see yellow stakes, you know the pond/creek/lake in question is a water hazard. If you hit into a water hazard, you may play the ball as it lies (no penalty), or if the ball is unplayable, choose from these options:

- Hit another ball from the spot you just hit from.
- Take the point where your ball crossed the water hazard and drop another ball (you can go back as far as you want, keeping that point between you and the hole).

You have a one-shot penalty in either case.

Lateral water hazards

If you're playing by the seaside, the beach is often termed a *lateral water hazard*. Red stakes mean lateral. Your options are either to play the ball as it lies (no penalty, but risky), or as follows, with a one-stroke penalty:

- Drop a ball at the point where the ball last crossed the boundary of the hazard — within two club lengths, no nearer the hole.
- Drop a ball as near as possible to the spot on the opposite margin of the water hazard, the same distance from the hole.
- Hit another ball from within two club lengths of the spot you just hit from.
- Take the point where the ball crossed the water hazard and drop another ball as far back as you want, keeping that point between you and the hole.

Airballs: The dreaded whiff

Airballs happen early in the life of a beginner. You make a mighty swing and miss the ball. The penalty? None, actually. But you must count that swing as a stroke.

If you swing at a ball with intent to hit it, that's a shot regardless of whether you make contact. You can't say, "That was a practice swing." If you meant to hit the ball, your swing counts as a stroke.

Airballs can be highly embarrassing, but they're part of the journey of golf.

Chapter 15

Gamesmanship and Sportsmanship

In This Chapter

- Avoiding hustles
- Doing the right thing on the course
- Playing with the pros

Betting is a touchy subject. Being the type of game that it is, golf lends itself to gambling. It probably won't be long before you find yourself playing for money. Oh, at first, the money won't be much — if you have any sense, that is. But after a while, the money games can get out of hand if you let them.

Fortunately, there are rules of thumb for gambling on the course — and for handling other tricky situations that every golfer is bound to face.

Wanna Bet?

In my experience, golfers come in two types: those who want a good, even match and those who don't. I recommend playing with the first group in your early days. Those folks won't take advantage of your inexperience. They want a good, close match, so they'll give you the shots you need to make a good showing. The winner will be the one who plays better that day. Nothing wrong with that, of course. If someone is to win, there has to be a loser — and sometimes, that loser will be you.

Unfortunately, the nice people I just described can be hard to find. That second group constitutes the vast majority of gambling golfers. They play golf for one reason: to bet and win. They don't play for the sunshine. They don't play for the exercise (unless getting in and out of a cart qualifies as exercise). And they surely don't play for relaxation. Most of them need clinical psychologists and straitjackets. They play to gamble with their buddies and beat them into bankruptcy.

The first tee

It's often said in golf that most matches are won on the first tee — the arena of negotiation, I call it. It's here that bets are fought over and agreed upon. The key is the number of strokes you'll give or receive over the course of a round.

Initially, you'll be playing with people whose handicaps are lower than yours. So you're going to get strokes from them. Say your handicap is 30 and your opponent's is 18. That's 12 strokes to you, right? Not if Mr. Cutthroat has his way. He'll argue that his wife just left him. Or that he hasn't played in two weeks because of his workload at the office. Or that his old football injury is acting up again. In any case, he'll try to cut your strokes down by at least three. That, he figures, is the edge he needs to beat you.

It goes without saying that you either (a) nod sympathetically; or (b) spin more tall tales than he just did. What you do *not* do is give up even a single stroke. Not one.

If you must give strokes to a player with a higher handicap, never *net* the strokes so that you're playing with zero. For example, if your handicap is 12 and your opponent's is 18, netting gives you 0 strokes and your opponent 6. Take all your strokes, because they'll be on the toughest holes.

Never play for more than you can afford to lose. Keep the bets small when you're a new golfer learning the gambling ropes in the big city. It's a great game to play and have fun with, but if you lose enough money that it starts to hurt, the recreational aspects pale. Be careful and proceed at your own risk.

There's a famous quote about pressure from Lee Trevino, in his early days one of golf's great hustlers. "Pressure," he said, "is $5 on the front nine, $5 on the back, and $5 for the 18 with $2 in your pocket."

Nassaus, skins, junk, and other wagers

A *nassau* is a three-part bet (like the one Trevino was talking about): A given amount is wagered on the front nine, the back nine and the total score. The bet was named for New York's Nassau Country Club, where it's said to have originated. It often leads to a *press.* That's when you're so far behind you concede the bet and double it for the holes that remain. There's even an *aloha press,* in which you press everything on the last hole.

Another popular format is *skins:* Each golfer puts up a certain fee per hole ($5 is common) that goes to the winner, but if two tie, all tie; the fee rolls over until somebody wins a hole outright.

Ten things to say when your partner or opponent hits a bad shot

- At least you're dressing better.
- Never up, never in.
- You'll get better on the back nine.
- At least we're not playing for much money.
- Well, it's a nice day, anyway.
- I never play well on the weekends, either.
- Does your spouse play?
- I have trouble with that shot, too.
- You should have warmed up more.
- That's a hard shot with the dew point this low.

Many golfers add bets for *greenies* (anyone hitting the green in one shot wins a predetermined sum from everyone else) or *sandies* (ditto for anyone who gets from a bunker into the hole in two shots). Such wagers are called *junk,* but everyone agrees they're fun. You can add *barkies* — you win if you hit a tree and still make par or better on a hole — or other bets of your own invention.

Giving putts

The green is one place where a little tactical planning can pay dividends. It's a fact of golf that no one, from a first-time beginner to the most famous pros, likes short putts, especially when they mean something. For that reason alone, you shouldn't be too generous in conceding short putts to your opponents. Always ask yourself if you would fancy hitting the putt. If the answer is "no" or even "not really," say nothing and watch.

That's the hard-nosed approach. If you're playing a friendly round or you're with your boss, be a bit more generous. The demarcation line has long been that anything "inside the leather" is "good." That means any putt closer than the length of the grip on your putter (or in some places, between the grip and the clubhead) is deemed to be a "gimme" or unmissable. Such a policy is still applicable today, although those long putters some players use have equally long grips — so watch out!

I've looked at the two extremes in conceding — or not conceding — short putts. But there's a middle ground also. The great Walter Hagen was the master of this, or so the story goes. "The Haig" was the best match player of his day. In the 1920s, he won four PGA championships in succession at match play. So he had to know a thing or two about psychology. One of his ploys was to concede a few shortish putts early in the match. That way, two things happened: His opponent got used to being given putts and, perhaps more important, the opponent was deprived of the "practice" of knocking a few in. Then, later in the round, old Walter wasn't so generous. The opponent would suddenly be faced with a knee-knocker, the sort of putt he hadn't hit all day.

I don't really recommend Walter's strategy. You can lose friends in a hurry if they miss that short one on the 17th. And your strategy may not work. ***Remember:*** A short putt missed on the 3rd green counts the same as one on the 17th or 18th.

Picking Partners

Again, you can make picking partners as cutthroat or as casual as you like. If you're just playing for fun or for a few dollars, who your partners are doesn't really matter. If you play with the same guys every time, everything will pretty much even out in the end, anyway.

But if things are a little more serious, you need to put some thought into your partners. Here are the rules I try to follow in "money" games:

- My partner always has a 1-iron in his bag.
- He has more than 37 tags hanging from his bag — preferably from Pebble Beach, PGA West, Harbour Town, and other famous, difficult courses.
- He has used the same putter since he was 5 years old.
- He's gone if he tells me about his marital problems on the practice range!

Match-Play Smarts

As you've probably guessed by now, match play generally involves a lot more strategy than stroke play. Strict card-and-pencil golf has a simple premise: Score the best you can. Match play is equally simple: Beat the other golfer. But doing so requires more thought. Here are my match-play rules:

- **Don't go for too much early.** Handing a couple of early holes to your opponent only hurts your confidence and boosts the confidence of the competition. So do risk it making a big number. Play conservatively at first.
- **Never lose your temper.** Nothing gives your opponent more heart than watching and listening as you lose your cool.

- **Pay attention to where your opponent's ball is at all times.** Your opponent's situation dictates your tactics on any given shot. For example, if he's deep in the woods, you may want to be less aggressive.
- **Figure that your opponent will hole every putt he looks at.** Then you won't be disappointed if he does make it. Of course, if he misses, you get a boost.
- **Watch your opponent.** Watch how fast he walks, for example. If he's slow, go fast; if he's fast, go slowly. Anything to break his natural rhythm.
- **Try never to hit two bad shots in a row.** Easier said than done, of course!
- **Never second-guess yourself.** If you're playing it safe, don't suddenly get aggressive halfway into your downswing. And if you're going for it, really do it. Even if you miss, you'll feel better. Take it from me — someone who has missed more than once!
- **Only concede a hole when the situation is hopeless.** Make your opponent win holes instead of losing them yourself. The more shots he has to hit under pressure, the more likely he is to make a mistake.

Never Give Up

In the 1972 British Open at Muirfield, Lee Trevino and Tony Jacklin were tied standing on the 17th tee in the final round. Distracted by a spectator, Trevino hooked his drive on the par-5 into a deep bunker. Jacklin drove perfectly. After splashing out only a few yards, Lee then hooked his third shot into heavy rough to the left and short of the green. Jacklin hit his fairway wood into the perfect spot, about 50 yards from the hole.

At that point, Trevino gave up. He quit. He told Jacklin that the championship was all his and did everything but shake his hand right there. Trevino's fourth shot flew right over the green halfway up a grass bank. Jacklin hit a so-so pitch to about 15 feet.

Barely glancing at the shot, Trevino then hit a lazy, give-up chip that rolled right into the cup! Par! Jacklin then three-putted for a 6. Trevino won.

I relate this story to you because it is so unusual — quitters never win. Don't be a quitter. Be a *grinder* — that's what golfers call a player who gives his all on every shot.

How to avoid a hustle

As a relatively new golfer, you're going to be a prime target for hustlers. They'll figure you're neither talented nor savvy enough to beat them. And they'll be right — at least until you've played a while. So avoid them. Here's what to look for:

- **Does he have a 1-iron in his bag? If so, don't play him.** Only good players can hit those things. (And in these days when even good players have traded long irons for hybrid clubs, be suspicious of anyone with a 2-iron, too.)
- **Never bet with a stranger.**
- **If you do bet, make it a straightforward nassau (front, back, 18 bet).** Don't get bamboozled with lots of side bets.
- **If he uses a ball that isn't new, say goodbye.** Bad players don't have old balls; they lose them too quickly.
- **As legendary teacher Harvey Penick used to say, "Beware of the golfer with a bad grip."** Why? Because he's found a way to make it work.
- **Another thing about the grip — look at your opponent's left hand.** If he has calluses, he's either played or practiced a lot. Adios.
- **If that left hand is less tan than the right, the same applies.** He's spent a lot of time wearing a golf glove.

Playing with Your Boss

When playing with your boss (or with anybody), you want to do your best. If you're just starting to play this game, you don't have to worry about beating the boss and feeling bad. He or she has probably played golf a lot longer than you have and just wants to get to know you on the course. The golf course is a great place to find out a person's true personality. The game leaves you psychologically naked in front of your peers.

If your game develops and you become a very good player, you're an asset to your company, and your boss should recognize your potential as a representative of the company. Millions of dollars in business deals have been negotiated on the golf course.

Play your best at all times and be helpful to people who don't play as well as you do. You'll reap the benefits for many years to come.

When golf is all business

Sure, golf is a game, but sometimes it's also serious business. Corporate golf outings have become an industry in themselves. And for every official company event, countless informal foursomes are getting together to schmooze outside the office.

If you play golf, sooner or later a business round is bound to happen to you. Maybe the chance to do a little networking is why you took up golf in the first place. So you need to know some basic rules when you mix business banter with the back nine; it's not all fun and games. Protocol is part of the puzzle.

- **Don't show off.** ***Remember:*** Golf is business — an extension of the workplace. You wouldn't yell and punch the air, showing up your boss and co-workers in the office, so don't do it on the fairway either. By all means play your best, but save the showboating for casual rounds with your friends.
- **Watch the raunchy humor.** Sure, you want everyone to have a good time. But unless you know your partners' attitudes and outlooks well, you risk not only offending them but losing their business, too.
- **Don't try to squeeze profit out of every minute.** At the very least, keep up the pretense that you're all out for good fun and good company — even if your companions couldn't sink a putt to save their mother's mortgage.
- **Let your group get settled into its game before talking business.** Never talk about business before the 5th hole — or better yet, the back nine.
- **Be prepared to drop the topic or risk losing the business.** No matter how seriously businesspeople take their line of work, they may be even more fanatical about their game of golf — especially on that one difficult shot. Let your feel of the individual dictate when to lay off business conversation.
- **Watch the wagers.** You may choose to accept bets in the interest of being a good sport, but suggesting them is not wise. If you lose the bet, be sure to do it gracefully — and to pay up pronto. If you win, don't gloat.
- **Never, ever cheat or fudge your score in any way.** However tempting cheating may be, it sends the wrong message. Do you want potential business partners to see you as dishonest — a corner-cutter or worse?

Hitting the links on a sunny day sure beats working in an office, and it's a great way to get to know the folks in your industry — and sometimes that means some high-level folks, not just the ones you run into at the water cooler. Believe me, I've been to enough corporate outings to know what a major business schmoozefest the links can be. (Just to give you an idea, my smiling face was at 41 business outings last year. Whew!) The bottom line is, get out on the links and mingle with the boss — it can do your career good. Just remember what you're there for. You're not at qualifying school for the PGA Tour.

Surviving a Pro-Am

I was sent off to war, a young man still slobbering from the fright. There were going to be people wearing camouflaged plaid, shooting at me, toward whom I had no ill will; would I be man enough to fight back? I was going to learn a lesson about life; the cruel nature of this odyssey was upon me. I was going to play in my first pro-am.

—Gary McCord, circa 1974, as he embarked without hesitation toward the first tee and certain death

There is a rite of passage in pro golf called a *pro-am*. This is the cornerstone of our being. If you're armed with a sizable amount of cash (around $5,000), you can tee it up with Tiger Woods, Phil Mickelson, or Ernie Els and tell your friends for the next 300 business lunches how you enthralled these guys with your prowess on the links and your witty banter between shots. In no other sport can a layman go on the playing field and get this close to the action — except by streaking at a nationally televised game. The shortcomings of the latter are obvious.

Pro-ams are played every Wednesday, or on the Champions Tour on Wednesdays and Thursdays. Each team consists of four amateurs and a pro. Corporations pay handsomely for the opportunity to put their names on tournaments and entertain their clients. This setup is unique in sports, and it's the pros' duty to see that corporate clients have a good time and want to come back for more.

Since 1998, there has been a pro-am for the budget-minded. Called the Saturday Series, it pairs amateurs with pros who have missed the cut in the current week's PGA Tour event, on a course near that week's tour venue. Entry fees are often less than half that at traditional pro-ams. To find out more about the Saturday Series, check out `www.saturdayseries.com`.

Much has been written about the attitudes of the tour players in these ubiquitous Wednesday pro-ams. The difficulties in concentrating on the day before a tournament while playing with nervous amateurs are many. However, no one seems to offer the quivering victims any advice. I always try to imagine what it would be like for me if I were plucked out of my comfort zone and thrust into the spotlight — say, on the hardwood with Shaquille O'Neal or in the boardroom with Bill Gates — and told not to make an idiot of myself. The truth is that neither Shaq nor Bill would expect me to be any good. I, on the other hand, would still like to give a decent account of myself, or at least limit the damage.

The first thing to keep in mind is that your pro requires one thing from you: that you enjoy yourself. The reason we play for so much money these days is

that you do enjoy the game, you do buy the equipment that you don't need, and you do love to watch us on television. So don't be overawed: Chances are you do something for a living that we would be completely useless at doing. A good pro will always do his or her best to put you at ease on the 1st tee, so when you make your first swing that makes contact with the planet 9 inches behind the ball and induces significant seismographic readings, you can at least have a laugh at it, too.

Here are my "Eight Steps to Pro-Am Heaven" — for pros and amateurs alike. A few do's and don'ts of playing with a pro — a road map through the purgatory of the pro-am. I hope that these few guidelines help both you and your pro enjoy the day.

Get a caddie

Having a caddie is the only way to play the pro-am game. You can walk free of hindrance and have clubs handed to you clean and dry. If possible, get one of the tour caddies whose player isn't in the pro-am. For $50 to $100, you can have someone who is used to being screamed at and blamed for the weather, the rate of inflation, and some of those hard-to-explain skin rashes.

Mind you, the caddie won't be able to club you because you don't know which part of the club the ball is about to bounce off of. However, he or she will be able to regale you with bizarre stories of "looper legends" in their quest for immortality on the fairways of life. These tales are worth the price of admission, and parental guidance is suggested.

Be ready to hit

You need to be ready to swing, even if it isn't your turn. Discuss with your partners the concept of *ready golf* before you tee off. This means forgetting whose honor it is — if you're ready, just go. Pro-am play is hideously slow at the best of times, and your pro will really appreciate it if you make the effort to keep things going.

Toss the cell phone

At the very least, turn it off. The surgical removal of a cellular phone from certain regions of the anatomy is painful and, to the best of my knowledge, is not covered under most health-insurance plans.

Get a yardage book

And ask a tour caddie how to use a yardage book. Doing so will make the pro very happy. Contribute to your pro's mental health by being the first "ammy" in the history of his or her pro-am career not to ask the question: "How far have I got from here?" There are only a certain number of times in your adult life that you can be asked this question before your spleen bursts. I am a better person without mine.

If you're out of the hole, pick up!

If you're out of the hole, pick it up, ball in pocket. Rest the ammo. Holster the bad boy. And be sure to tell your pro that you've done so. Not only will you contribute to the pace of play, but you'll also avoid the awkward situation of having the pro wait, expecting you to hit, while you rummage around in your bag looking for the source of that smell that has been emanating from there since you let the kids play with your rain gear.

This tip doesn't contradict the one earlier in this chapter, telling you to never give up. You should *not* pick up your ball if there's still a chance to help your team. But the moment that chance disappears, pocket that ball. In a pro-am, the only one thing worse than waiting around for no apparent reason is waiting around for a very bad apparent reason — for example, somebody who's holing out for a 9, net 8.

Don't sweat your score

And don't be upset if your pro doesn't know how your team stands. ***Remember:*** It's a Wednesday. He probably doesn't even know his own score, and, quite honestly, after the 26th pro-am of the year, he may not remember what his gender is.

Watch your step

I know, you're wearing soft spikes and it shouldn't matter, but the tradition of wandering on somebody's line, regardless of what's on the bottom of your soles, is a slow dance with a hot temper. Be very, very mindful of the line of your pro's putt. Look at TV coverage of a golf tournament and see how respectful the pros are of each other's lines. Stepping on another pro's line is close to religious desecration in our sport. I've pulled a groin muscle trying to mark my ball without stepping on the sacred line. But I think that, in my career, I've excelled at acrobatic markings of the ball because I was exceptional at the game Twister during my formative years.

Simply ask the pro where his line is, and he'll show you. If my ball is not in another player's line, I'll leave it right next to the coin the entire time we're on the green so that my amateur partners know where my line is and (I hope) avoid stepping on it.

Don't coach the pro

Finally, if you're still interested in playing this game with anybody ever again, do *not* give the pro any advice on how to play the course, even if your family has owned the property since the planet started to warm and you can wander it in the dark without hitting anything. Trust me, he thinks he knows more about it than you do just because he has his name on his bag.

It's a question of knowing what to look for. Even giving the occasional line off the tee can be dangerous because you don't normally play two club lengths from the back edge of the back tee. I can't tell you how many times I've heard, "Oops, I could have sworn you could carry that bunker!"

Part V

Golf: It's Electric!

"What exactly do the rules say about giving and receiving advice?"

In this part . . .

I've worked as a golf commentator for CBS sports since 1986. In this part of the book, I use my expertise to show you how to watch your favorite pro (even if it's not me) play this puzzling game. This part also explores some of the great golfing wonders that the Internet has to offer — all my favorite cyber-haunts — as well as the latest golf video games.

Chapter 16

Golf on TV

In This Chapter

- How I became a talking head
- Understanding TV golf
- Checking out the top players
- Finding a role model
- Learning by watching the top players

It is a medium that reaches the far corners of humanity; its video displays teach and formulate a way of life. No singular invention has influenced our lives and dictated our roles in society, whether good or bad, as much as television. That is way too much pressure for me; please turn me off.

—Gary McCord's acceptance speech to his audio-visual class at Lincoln Elementary School in 1959 after he was voted "Most Likely to Do the Weather Report Someday"

The year was 1986, and my professional goals and aspirations were in need of Dr. Kevorkian. "Limited success" was a nice way of describing my playing career. The tour was a vast, empty wasteland of setbacks and spent money. I was serving out the rest of my sentence with no chance of parole. Golf sucks.

As I boarded my airplane for Columbus, Ohio, nothing really was on my mind other than the two fat vacuum-cleaner salesmen I was going to be sitting between in the coach section. I was in my customary hesitant gaze when I was awakened by harsh criticism coming from the first-class section. It was the CBS crew that does golf, already enjoying the amenities of first class (although in a plastic cup) before takeoff.

Frank Chirkinian, the executive producer and director for CBS at the time, Pat Summerall, Ben Wright (the evil swine): All of them were basking in the knowledge that I was to be forever lost in the coach section wedged between two obese and slightly pungent salesmen who got their wardrobes from the Salvation Army. They said I could come up and use their restroom if I could peel myself from between the two guys. I hoped that the front of the airplane would fall off.

We were all going to Jack Nicklaus's golf tournament, the Memorial, in Columbus. We had just left Fort Worth, Texas, where I had played and CBS had televised the Colonial Invitational. I had just been elected to the policy board of the PGA Tour — the players elect three members of the tour, and along with three officers of the PGA of America and three independent business leaders, we make up the tour policy board, which basically runs the PGA Tour. It's a very important job for an idiot like me to have, but the players thought that my life wasn't miserable enough, so they staked me to this tree.

I was going to Columbus not to play in Nicklaus's tournament — it was an invitational, and I wasn't high enough on the money list to buy a Big Mac — but to go to policy-board meetings for the first three days of the week. They were closed-door meetings in which I could catch up on my sleep. The next tournament, the Kemper, was in Washington, D.C., but I wouldn't have to leave until the end of the week.

I was fighting for position on the armrest of seat 28B when the flight attendant came by and presented me with a bottle of champagne, compliments of the royal family in first class. These guys really know how to have a good time when the bubbly is free.

I started hesitantly toward the front of the plane to thank my benefactors and get away from the sumo-sized bookends I was seated between. As I scurried to first class, I fell on an idea that could help solve my problem of having nowhere to go after the policy-board meetings ended on Wednesday. I couldn't afford to go to Washington early, and I had no money to fly home for the four days in between. I was a golfer caught in the headlights of bankruptcy.

After some quick banter, I told Frank that I had nothing to do from Thursday to Sunday, and because I was on the policy board making decisions about TV contracts, I should watch how a televised event is produced. "Show up Friday for rehearsal at 11 and check into the Stouffer's on Thursday; we'll have a room for you," Frank said. "Now get back to the screaming kids in coach before I have you thrown off the plane for being up here." He had the bedside manner of Attila the Hun sporting a bad case of hemorrhoids, but at that moment I loved him.

I showed up promptly at 11, well fed from gorging on room service and weary-eyed from the menu of movies that I signed to the room. I was a pig, and I enjoyed the wallow.

I opened the door to Frank's office, and he bellowed from the confines of his trailer for me to go out to the 16th hole. He didn't sound like he wanted to engage in light conversation, so I broke into a slight trot out toward the 16th. I couldn't help but wonder why I wasn't going to sit in the trucks with Frank while he did the telecast to gain some insight into how a telecast is produced, every once in a while getting Frank some snacks or engaging him in casual conversation. Why was I going to the 16th hole?

As I started to walk toward the tee, a voice came serenading down from high atop the tower, beckoning me to come up. It was Verne Lundquist, the veteran announcer. I managed to make my way up the tower and exchanged idle conversation with Verne's spotter. Verne then handed me a headset and told me to grab a chair. I asked what the headset was for, and he said, "Didn't Frank tell you that he wanted to try you as an announcer this week?" As I weighed the decision between doing some spotting with caddies who missed the cut and being on national television, the conversation with myself was, as usual, very short.

"Where do I sit, Verne, and what do I do?" I said.

It looks like this in the tower: A little enclosure is surrounded with clear plastic, much like the front seat of a car, with the windshield surrounding the front and you looking out at the green. Two monitors in front of the announcer show the action taking place and a current leader board. The spotter is next to you, giving you the scores and the clubs the players are hitting. In this case, spotter Carl took up most of the room. Carl, who weighs 385 pounds, looks like he just ate a sumo wrestler. There was not much room left in the front seat of this car.

My seat was outside this cubicle, next to the cameraman. Looking down at the action for the first time was really interesting. Golf looks incredibly easy from way up there. How can those guys screw up so many shots?!? I was above the tension, up in the clouds. My, how this view changes your perspective on the game.

But there were voices everywhere. The voice in my left ear was the director, Frank, and the other voices were all the announcers from their towers. Occasionally, I would hear a rogue voice, and I had no idea who it was. I found out later that a guy operating a CB unit in the neighborhood had come through on our headsets. Welcome to network TV.

The rehearsal went pretty smoothly. I found out two things:

- **Your conversation must be short.** The action jumps all over the place, and you can't get stuck in the middle of a story.
- **Never answer anything Frank says directly.** The viewers can't hear Frank.

Those are the rules; obey at all costs.

The next day, my first on national television, was going smoothly. Verne and I were clicking like a car counter on a Los Angeles freeway. He would ask a question; I would answer. I never said, "What did you say, Frank?" I was rolling.

Due to a starter's time that spreads the field, there was a large gap between the group that had just walked off the 16th green and the next group that was approaching the 14th green. I had some free time, so I kicked back in the chair and read some interesting tidbits on the personal lives of the golf pros.

I was awakened from my near-catatonic state by a combination of Frank throwing the action to Verne and Verne asking me what this putt was going to do. I looked down real fast and saw nobody on the 16th green. The next group walking up the 15th fairway. What was going on?

Verne had that Nordic look of desperation as he asked me again, and Frank was starting to annoy me with, "Answer him, you culturally lost golf derelict." I looked down at the green again, and there still wasn't anybody around. Were they seeing ghosts, or was this just a ruse to excite the poor rookie caught lost in thought? After several more verbal harassments from Frank and the look of a desperate sheepdog on the face of Verne, I decided to play along with their game. I said, "Verne, this putt should be fairly fast, because it's going down the hill toward the water." Verne met my response by saying, "Boy, you were right, Gary; that putt cruised by the hole and, if he'd hit it a little harder, it would have gone down in the water."

Wait a minute!

The 16th green at Muirfield Village golf course has no water anywhere near it, except for the drinking fountain on the tee. I made the water stuff up because the boys were trying to get the rookie and I was trying to throw them a curve. It was a wild pitch.

I heard Frank say, "Throw it to 18, Verne." Then Verne looked at me with those screeching Scandinavian eyes and asked if I could respond a little quicker next time. Frank hit his button and began to verbally blast me for my "funereal response," which I took as less than congratulatory.

At this point, I realized that they weren't kidding, and we really were on the air. Oh, no! "Verne," I said, "Could you help me in my moment of conjecture and look down on the 16th green and tell me if you see anybody, or do I have to call a ghostbuster?

"Of course there's nobody there," said Verne. Now I really was confused. "Verne, if there's nobody there, why did you say the ball rolled 7 feet by the hole when I made up the thing about the water being there in the first place?" I asked, dumbfounded.

"There is water there," Verne said, with a stern look of what-in-the-heck-are-you-talking-about? on his face.

"There's no water on the 16th hole," I said.

"I know that, you idiot, but we were doing the 12th hole!"

"Wait a minute, we're doing the 12th hole also? I was told to go out to the 16th hole with you."

What had happened was that, during rehearsal, we hadn't used a camera for our *other* hole, the 12th, because the camera was broken. I had no way of knowing that I was supposed to be looking at the 12th hole as well as the 16th, unless I had called the Psychic Friends hotline. Confusing business, huh?

As life weaves its reckless mysteries, the par-3 12th hole at Muirfield Village has water surrounding the green. The putt had come from the top tier really fast toward the water and had gone 7 feet past the hole. I totally made something up, and it just happened to be a perfect call in this less-than-perfect business.

This is my legacy; I am bound by its structure. I cannot deny its existence. It has made me rich. I hope that I can bring you insight on how this medium works so that you can understand our chaos.

The growth in the popularity of golf over the last 40 years has been reflected in the amount of coverage the game gets on television. Christmas week may be the only time of year when you can't watch the pros teeing it up in some exotic locale. Television has embraced golf to the extent that the top players today are as well known as their counterparts in baseball, basketball, and football. In this chapter, I show you why.

Why Golf Is So Popular

Golf is a sport that's played all year long, from the first week in January through the second week in December. Golf on the tube has grown proportionately, from a few shows in the 1950s to nonstop golf on TV today. We get that with the Golf Channel, which covers golf 24 hours a day.

The places that TV takes you during the golf year are a vacationer's dream. Every Saturday and Sunday, you can do the couch thing and watch the various tours play from every corner of the globe. The golf is good, but the pictures are stunning. The viewing audience and the PGA Tour start to prepare themselves in the Florida swing for the first major tournament of the year in early April, when Augusta and the Masters Tournament are in full bloom. Then the PGA Tour settles into normalcy for a while, as players start to prepare for the heat and the long rough of the U.S. Open in mid-June. The month of July is for the British Open and its storied past; plenty of plaid and windblown golf balls decorate the landscape. The last of the four majors, the PGA Championship, is played in August. These are the tournaments that all professional golfers gear up to play well in. They're the measure of a player's worth and his quest — and they make for great viewing.

During the first part of the year, many celebrities play in the AT&T tournament at Pebble Beach and the Bob Hope Chrysler Classic. If viewing the stars is your thing, you can see these would-be golfers hacking away at all their inhibitions during these pro-am tournaments.

If Hollywood stars are not your idea of role models, maybe professional golfers can fill the void. You don't see much trash talk or foul play on the golf course. In fact, golf may be the only game in which the players police themselves. Almost weekly, there's an example of a player on the PGA Tour penalizing himself for some inadvertent Rules transgression. Can you imagine a basketball player turning down two points because he pushed someone out of the way en route to the basket? Probably not!

Golf and Television

Sports and TV have become inextricably linked through the years. As recently as 1946, fans were still providing their own images to the dramatic radio broadcast of the 1946 World Series.

Baseball proved to be perfect for a new tube technology that beamed rays of hypnotic light into everyone's home. But golf presented many unique challenges to television coverage. Aside from playing on 150 acres as opposed to being surrounded by fences at a distance of 400 feet from home plate, there was constant, ongoing action with many athletes competing independently at any given moment. What's a broadcaster to do?

Keep it simple — and they did. The first broadcast of a golf event was the renowned Tam O'Shanter Classic from Chicago on Sunday, August 22, 1953. One camera fixed on the 18th hole. Perhaps as an indication of the excitement that golf would eventually bring to the tube, the moment for this particular coverage was opportune. Lew Worsham, a modestly successful pro, approached the 18th not unlike many finishing holes that year, but the difference this time was that this shot would yield an often sought, but not often produced, result: a hole-in-one. If you're interested, the videotape of that monumental moment is available in the game's video archives.

It was the unbridled charisma of one man that turned the nation's attention to the sport of captains and kings. Arnold Palmer, of the hitch-and-smile, go-for-broke style and unwavering charm, turned the viewing world on its ear and kept viewers glued to their sets. In 1960, Palmer began carrying an industry on his back as golf and television developed together to provide a foundation for a sport that would ultimately reap immense rewards in the great sports and television-rights derby.

Behind the scenes

Many people believe that golf is the most difficult sport to cover. Think about it: The playing field is anything but standard. No precisely measured court or white lines of delineation. The playing field is a park, a wide-open expanse covering acres of competitive challenges. There are no timeouts and no clock. Play begins at ten-minute intervals, and players embark upon the playing field for their bid at the color red. (For the uninitiated, scores below par are noted on the scoreboard with red numbers.) At any one time, 100 or more competitors may be playing on the same course, all on different holes. No orchestrated playing time here. So how does it get covered?

First, golf courses have to be technically prepped. That's just a fancy way of saying that you must run cable, and lots of it, in order to broadcast signals from the golf course to the television truck. A small army of engineers and cable-pullers usually invades on the Sunday or Monday preceding broadcast week. Tractor-trailers filled with several million dollars worth of cameras and technical equipment are deployed. The average telecast requires miles of cable, often two dozen or more cameras mobilized in a variety of ways, videotape machines, digital disc recorders, character generators, spotters, high-tech graphics gizmos (for those great images of super-slo-mo swings and golf balls squished against clubfaces at impact), and a control room staffed with some of the best producers and directors in the industry.

The staff is divided into two groups, known as *above the line* and *below the line.* Those with above-the-line duties are the folks who make the production and story-line decisions. I'll start at the top:

- **Producer:** The producer is responsible for creating the story line of the event. Remember how different golf is from basketball, football, and most other sports. It may be the only sport in which the participant hits a stationary ball, but often at great distances. The better producers and directors are able to provide a variety of replays and isolated coverage of the action. It requires them to be intimately conversant with the game itself and to know all the key players. Although the story line is dictated by who is playing well, the viewer must be mindful that a dozen contestants or more may be newsworthy. The producer's task is to capture the players' shot-making efforts and to make the drama coherent to the viewer.

- **Director:** The director is responsible for placing cameras at strategic spots around the course to capture the best possible angles of coverage. The director communicates with the camera personnel, the audio crew, and other technical people to provide insightful coverage of the action on the course. While the producer may say, "Let's go to Vijay Singh next on the ninth green," the director is responsible for readying those cameras and operators and for framing the shots that will most dramatically convey the action to viewers. The director also oversees the complex array of audio tracks, graphics, and limitless special effects.
- **Associate directors:** One associate director supports the producer and director. Although titles may change from network to network, standard coverage usually involves an "iso" truck in which an associate director records coverage of shots that are central to the story line but not shown live. You might hear an announcer say, "Moments ago. . . ." Taped coverage assures the viewer of seeing as many shots as possible in a sensible sequence to show and tell the whole story. Some producers favor using more taped shots than others.

  A second associate director is known as the *sundial,* or timer. (Sundial is an inside joke, a nickname for one A.D. whose countdowns in and out of commercials were less than accurate.) Approximately 12 times in a telecast, the network breaks for at least 2 minutes of commercials or promotional announcements. Someone is responsible for giving a count out of the program action into the commercial time to make the transition appear seamless to the viewer. The same is true coming out of a commercial back to the center of activity, the remote truck.
- **Talent:** The remaining critical element of the above-the-line team is the talent. That's us, the talking heads you hear on the air. The producers and directors provide the blueprint of the telecast, but the talent delivers it. We are the artisans who sell the vision. The National Football League might employ as many as four announcers per broadcast, and baseball maybe three, but the multiple broadcast booths in a golf telecast necessitate a team of announcers in this decidedly individual sport. Networks use up to eight on-air personalities to recite the golf action. Chemistry is key. Do you love Johnny Miller and Roger Maltbie? Jim Nantz? Mike Tirico? Lanny Wadkins? Paul Azinger? Maybe even me? Each network's team has a unique personality.

The 18th tower is the focal point where the host and key analyst hold forth. From there, networks differ. Some choose the analyst-per-green format á la CBS, erecting towers adjacent to the final few greens on the course. From these vantage points, the announcers have clear, above-the-gallery views and can call the action of a particular hole or report on a neighboring hole within view of the tower. ABC uses a secondary studio in which the talent view the monitor and report each shot played. All networks employ on-course personnel who walk with designated players and report on the action from the ground.

- **Technical personnel:** The below-the-line folks are the technical people — camera and audio operators, engineers, and tech gurus. Of course, everyone involved in this tightly knit, interlocking puzzle is important, but one key individual brings it all together, being in charge of pressing the buttons that effectively determine which pictures and sounds go on the air. That person is the technical director. The burden of the end product falls to the technical director, who sits in the production truck next to the director. If you ever notice a glitch in moving from one shot to another or a graphic appearing and then disappearing hastily, chances are that the technical director made a mistake or got some bad information from the field.

All in all, when you add up all the above-the-line and below-the-line folks, the spotters, the runners, and the *craft-services personnel* (which is a fancy, entertainment-industry way of saying *caterers*), a network may roll into town with a production crew of more than 100 people — not to mention the satellite truck that beams signals from the remote broadcast site off a satellite, to the studio, and eventually to your TV set.

Let's make a deal

Of course, none of this would happen if there weren't a demand for telecasts of well over 1,000 hours of professional golf every year. Golf continues to grow in popularity for a variety of reasons, not the least of which is the support of corporate America. Why? Well, first by golf's very position in the world as a game played by the captains and kings of industry. It's a game of tradition, honor, and integrity. The image of the game presented by the players is essential to the sponsors and magnified in importance by what has become an increasingly cluttered world of athletes whose mugs — and sometimes mug shots — are apt to be found on the front page of the newspaper rather than in the back.

Golf forged its way to prominence as a major player in television sports in a rather innovative fashion. It began meekly in an effort to gain exposure on TV. Time buys, rights, and production deals are the principal forces that drive network coverage.

Time buys

A network places an hourly value on its airtime — no different from a supermarket stocking shelves. Each hour of airtime represents a quantifiable asset for the network. In this case, a program buyer negotiates a date and airtime for a program. The program buyer purchases the time from the network, arranges to sell the time to advertisers, and then receives all the revenue produced in the allotted airtime.

Here's an example: The McCord Challenge buys two hours of time from GHI Network. McCord pays the network, say around $1 million. Network rules allow the producer to sell 18 commercial units within the hour. So, for its million dollars, the McCord group receives 36 commercial units (18 × 2) to allocate to its list of sponsors or to sell.

The formula is fairly basic, and not inexpensive because the packager bears the production cost, and costs can easily top $500,000 for reasonable golf coverage. With professional talent added, there's well over a $1.5-million investment from the outset. That's before the cost of a tournament purse, and on-site event amenities from range balls to security to cookies in the players' locker room.

Rights and production

Here's where networks take a risk. The escalation in sports rights fees in recent decades has resulted in billion-dollar TV contracts for the NFL, NBA, Major League Baseball, and NASCAR as well as golf. Network executives decide that they're willing to pay an upfront fee to the rights holders and provide production in exchange for the opportunity to maximize their investment in the advertising marketplace.

Ten things a golf announcer should *never* do

- **Never talk to your director on the air.** No one else can hear the director, and people will think you have an imaginary friend.
- **Don't get the sound guy mad at you.** He'll cut you off when you're making a witty comment and keep you on the air while you're mumbling.
- **Never tell the TV audience how good a player you used to be.**
- **Never say that a shot is impossible.** You'll quickly be proven wrong.
- **Never talk down to the audience.**
- **Don't get into long stories.** You'll be cut off as the director switches to another hole.
- **Never use clichés.** It shows that you're lazy.
- **Never tell the audience what viewers can clearly see on the TV screen.**
- **Never assume that the audience knows anything about the game of golf.**
- **Never, ever assume that what you do for a living has any role in the elevation of humankind.**

Golf, through its increasing popularity, its broadening appeal, and the valuable image it provides for sponsors — the quality and virtually unmatched demographics delivered — has taken its place among the major TV sports. The PGA Tour signed a contract worth nearly $1 billion with the three broadcast networks plus ESPN, USA, and the Golf Channel for 2003 to 2006, a pot of gold that keeps on overflowing.

What to Watch for on TV

By all means, enjoy the physical beauty of golf on television. But pay attention to the players, too. You can learn a lot from watching not only their swings but also their whole demeanor on the course. Listen to the language, the jargon, the parlance being used. If you read this book — or any golf book — I'm sure that you'll notice the complexity of the game's terms. There's a lot of room for confusion. Watching the game on TV can help. This is especially true when a commentator analyzes a player's swing: He'll use terminology that you need to understand to become part of the golfing world. (See Appendix A for more help with golf terminology.)

Watch the players carefully. Pay attention to the rhythm of their swings. Pay attention to their mannerisms — the way they waggle the club, the triggers that set their swings in motion, the way they putt, the way they set their feet in the sand before they play from bunkers, the way they stand on uphill and downhill lies. In other words, watch everything! Soak it all in. Immerse yourself in the atmosphere and ambience of golf. You'll soon be walking the walk and talking the talk.

That's the big picture. That's what everyone should watch. But what about you specifically?

Watching Ernie Els or Annika Sorenstam on television is a good idea for everyone. But there's a limit to what most people can learn from most players. Pay particular attention to someone like Ernie if you happen to be tall and slim. But if you happen to be shorter and more heavyset, you need to look elsewhere. Make Lee Trevino, Craig Stadler, or Karrie Webb your role model. In other words, find someone whose body type approximates your own.

Then watch how that person stands to the ball at address. See how his arms hang. See how much she flexes her knees. Golfers who are taller have much more flex in their knees than their shorter counterparts.

Watch how "your pro" swings the club. Do his arms move away from his body as the club moves back? How much does she turn her shoulders? How good is his balance? Does she have a lot of wrist action in her swing? Or does he use his arms to create width? Watch the pros every chance you get. Emulating their swings and the way they conduct themselves will help your game.

What to Look for in the Top Pros

The players who get the most airtime are, of course, the more successful ones. No network is going to waste valuable minutes on someone who's out of contention. Viewers want to watch the tournament being won and lost, so those players shooting the lowest scores are the ones you'll see most on TV.

Here's what to look for in some of the most prominent players.

- **Tiger Woods:** Look at his virtuosity in every aspect of the game. He has left no stone unturned in his pursuit of perfection. His stalking of Jack Nicklaus's record of 18 major wins is his driving force, providing his will to succeed.
- **Phil Mickelson:** With two major victories under his belt (as of this writing), look for Phil to take advantage of his precise short game and really focus on the majors for the rest of his career. He gives golf fans all over the country a role model they love to root for.
- **Vijay Singh:** The golf motor that never stops, his aggressive, tireless pursuit of a repeatable golf swing is legendary on the practice tee, and has him playing better than ever in his 40s.
- **Ernie Els:** The Big Easy has a golf swing that brings glimpses of the legendary Sam Snead, with a demeanor that is made for greatness in major championships. He'll be a great player for a long time.
- **Annika Sorenstam:** The lady supreme of the LPGA Tour, her record in terms of victories and winning percentage is better than anyone else's on any tour, man or woman. She has set the standard that the new blood of the next generation will aspire to.
- **John Daly:** The PGA Tour's science project — always evolving. Sometimes imagining what John is thinking on the golf course is hard. But John is still one of the biggest draws in the game. Why? Because he hits the ball the farthest. Deep down inside, that's what everyone wants to do.
- **Sergio Garcia:** He has an electric golf game that should produce a step up to the next level — victories in major championships. He drives the ball long and straight and has a wonderful short game. If he putts better when it counts, he'll move up in class.
- **Michelle Wie:** This young lady has the potential to do what Tiger Woods did on the PGA Tour. Michelle turned pro late in 2005. When her time comes — as I think it will, sooner or later — she could dominate on the LPGA Tour. She has more talent than anyone I've seen come up in a long time. It should be fun to watch her find her way to the top.

Tigermania!

Millions of golfers and golf fans owe their allegiance to one player. Thanks in large part to Tiger Woods, the game is now in its latest golden age.

A new phenomenon was born when Woods arrived. In the 1990s, he slew courses with his length, made every putt he needed to make, trademarked a fist pump, and for several years could do no wrong. His first three wins came against Davis Love III, Payne Stewart, and Tom Lehman — and he ran through those men as if they were players in the U.S. Amateur. He turned Augusta National into the proverbial pitch-and-putt course, reaching the par-5s with wedges. He was golf's highlight tape. *Newsweek* put him on the cover. *Sports Illustrated* made him its Sportsman of the Year. Jack Nicklaus predicted that Tiger would win as many Masters titles as Nicklaus and Arnold Palmer — combined.

Because he is of mixed heritage — his father is black and his mother is Thai — Tiger was more than just a golfer with the skills to excel. He was also a golfer of the people, a young man who represented the breaking down of ethnic barriers. People said that he transcended the game, that he was a crossover star who brought people to golf who had never considered golf a sport. Kids began turning up at golf tournaments — in droves. They were white and black, Asian and Hispanic, boys and girls. Golf had a new crowd, and it was hungry for this kid from Cypress, California, who turned golf into a video game. When Tiger smiles, it seems that the whole golf world smiles with him. It is a powerful thing.

What we relearned as Tiger Woods "slumped" in 2003 and 2004 is that golf is not like basketball. One player cannot dominate it the way Michael Jordan did in the NBA. Golf is a game of cycles, and not even Tiger can dominate all the time. For one thing, he has more great players to beat than Arnold Palmer did. He also has to deal with more than Palmer did — pressures that can turn a young man old in a hurry. Tiger plays almost every tournament under a death threat, surrounded by a phalanx of security personnel. He cannot go to dinner or a movie without being mobbed.

Potentially, he still could be the greatest golfer who ever lived. He has the talent and the will, as he proved by retooling his swing and roaring again in 2005, when he won his ninth and tenth majors. Time is on his side, and he certainly has all the tools. But there's more to golf than warp clubhead speed and a burning competitive edge. Tiger must keep refining those tools as he continues to live with the highest set of expectations placed on any golfer who has put a peg in the ground.

Take Your Punishment

You can learn the most from the players on TV by watching how they handle problems. Professional players make most of their decisions with their heads, not their hearts. So pay close attention to rules, situations, and the times when a player has to manufacture a weird and wonderful shot to extricate the ball from trouble. And don't forget to watch the more-frequent occasions when a player accepts that a mistake has been made, takes the punishment, and moves on. That's when you know you've been watching a real golfer, one who understands that everyone makes mistakes, and that he or she just made one.

That last point reminds me of a time when I let my heart — or my ego — rule my decision-making process. I was playing in Memphis, I think. Anyway, I had to birdie the last three holes during my second round in order to make the cut. After my drive at the 16th, I had 223 yards to the hole, which was cut dangerously close to a large lake. I chose a 4-iron, convinced that I had enough club. I didn't. Splash!

I turned to my caddie and told him to give me another ball. He did. I hit the next shot perfectly. Splash!

"Give me another ball." Splash!

"Give me another ball." Splash!

"Give me another ball." Splash!

By this time, I knew that I clearly was using the wrong club. I knew it. My caddie knew it. The local police knew it. But I wasn't going to give up. This was my manhood we were testing here.

Eventually, my caddie handed me another ball with a 3-iron, one more club. I said, "What's this?" He told me that I had only one ball left. So I took the 3-iron and hit my last ball onto the green. I holed the putt for, I think, a 15.

The moral of the story? If you do stuff this stupid, they might make a movie of it. In this case they did — the movie was *Tin Cup,* and Kevin Costner was my alter ego in my pursuit of disaster.

The Masters and me

The entire CBS production crew, including Frank Chirkinian (my producer at the time) and I, were dining at the Tournament Players Championship two weeks before the 1987 Masters. The conversation turned quickly to who would be assigned to which holes during the telecast in Augusta. Everyone had his assignments except for me. I was left holding air.

I had been working with CBS on a part-time basis for only a few months, but the announcing crew was excited that I would be going to Augusta. When Frank excluded me from the fracas, anarchy prevailed. Pat Summerall led the charge for my inclusion, and the others followed, but to no avail. It was late in the day on the Saturday telecast when Frank, between commercial breaks, announced to everyone that I was going to the hallowed grounds of Augusta National after all.

I was told to be at Augusta by Tuesday for a meeting with Hord Hardin, the tournament director. Frank was waiting for me when I arrived. We proceeded to Hardin's office; I felt like I was going to the principal's office. There was a look of concern on Frank's face as we went into the catacombs of the clubhouse at Augusta.

Jim Nantz joined us as we walked down the narrow corridor toward the door at the end of the hall. I was dressed rather spectacularly in white Calvin Klein jeans and a bulky DKNY sweater ablaze in yellow, the whole outfit topped with a Panama straw hat. I was a walking rebuke to tradition.

As we approached the darkened door at the end of the hall, it creaked open as if willed by a higher power. A shadowy figure appeared backlit against a ray of sun filtered through the lone window. Hord Hardin greeted us like Lurch of *The Addams Family.* Frank and Jim sat in the corner, and I proceeded to take residence on the big couch in front of Hardin's desk. I was the plot.

After introductions and small talk about my work on television, Hardin proceeded to make a passionate speech about the flavor of this tournament. "We must maintain tradition; it is the cornerstone of the tournament," he said with conviction. The speech was beautiful and actually kept my attention, which is hard to do. But I couldn't help looking around and seeing the dimly lit pictures of Bobby Jones and the 13th hole that filled the room. It dawned on me that this was Augusta National, home of the Masters, and that this was a big deal. At moments like these, when I'm truly moved, I do stupid things. I think I do them because it relieves tension. I waited until Hardin had made his closing remarks, and then abruptly stood up and asked him if he thought the clown outfit I had planned to wear on Saturday was out of the question. Frank immediately put his head in his hands, and Jim started to whistle.

Hardin looked at Frank, who was not about to look up, and then addressed me. "Probably a good idea," he said.

"Darn, I'm gonna lose the deposit," I said with my Panama hat pulled down over my eyes. It was a retort that would have made Bill Murray proud.

As Hardin closed the aging oak door of his office behind us, Frank reached up, grabbed the back of my neck, and applied a pressure hold that would have choked a Burmese python. "Don't you ever just shut up and listen, you moron?" he asked. I couldn't respond because of the restriction of air in my esophagus, but Jim was faintly heard to say, "Maybe this is a bad idea bringing him here." Frank affirmed the notion with more pressure on my neck. But I was on the broadcast.

The honeymoon didn't last long. In 1994, while trying to be articulate about a shot to the 17th green, I explained that Jose Maria Olazabal had better not hit it over the green because there were "body bags" down there, and no one ever recovers. That was the first strike. I paddled on down this river of no return and decided to describe the next putt by Tom Lehman, also on the 17th green, as being so fast that I didn't think they mowed those greens, "I think they bikini wax 'em." Strike two, three, four — and don't come back again.

The rest is history, which is what my colorful Masters commentary became: history!

Chapter 17

Golf on the Web

In This Chapter

- Where to find the coolest golf Web sites
- How to "tour" great courses from your home or office
- How to buy golf gear online

You'll be amazed at the world of golf you can explore without leaving your desk. You can travel to exotic locales, visit great courses, and buy golf clubs, golf balls, golf clothes, and golf books (including *For Dummies* books!). These days, it's all on the Internet.

Cool Cyber-Golf Sites

The Internet offers a nearly infinite array of golf stuff. Google the word *golf* and you get 91,500,000 sites. But if you surf the Net aimlessly, you'll only drown in a digital deluge. So here's a quick look at some of my favorite cyber-golf hangouts. Together, these sites offer 99 percent of what you need on the information superhighway. You can thank me later.

The PGA Tour

Millions of golf fans turn to the PGA Tour's site for news, statistics, player profiles, and, perhaps most important of all, up-to-the-minute tournament coverage (see Figure 17-1). At `www.pgatour.com`, you can follow your favorite players as they compete, drill down into their stats, and even look at their score cards. You can check out audio and video clips, too. And to the delight of hardcore fans, there's now ShotLink, an interactive feature that allows users to get an inside look at every shot by every player only nanoseconds after it happens.

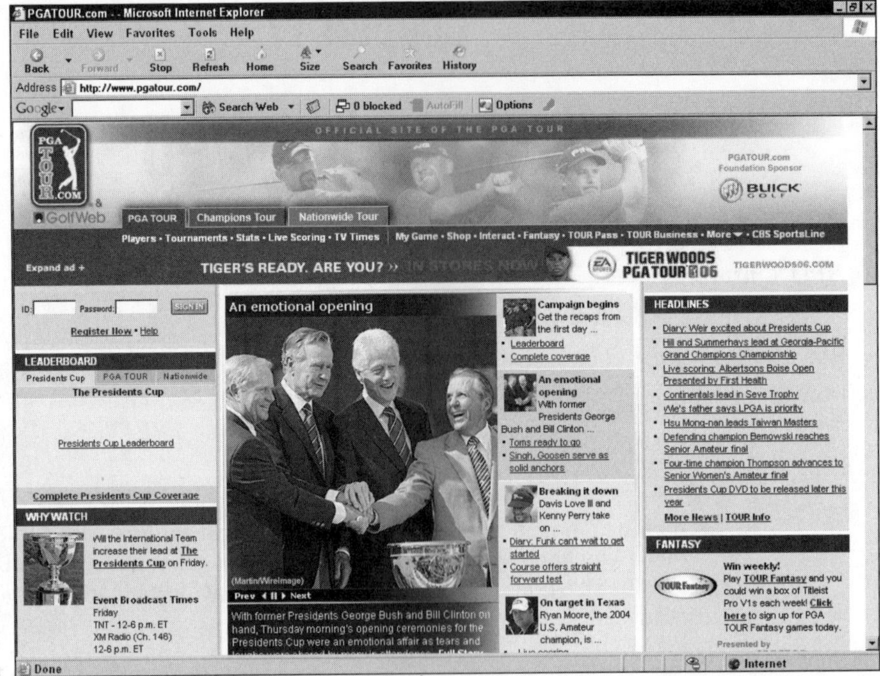

Figure 17-1: The home page of the PGA Tour. Don't forget to click on that Champions Tour tab.

You can follow more than Tiger, Phil, and friends at this site. This is also the home site of the Champions Tour — the one I play on — and the Nationwide Tour, golf's highest "minor league," where you'll find the stars of tomorrow.

There's fantasy here, too. PGATour.com is home to the Tour's official fantasy golf game, in which you get to spend a million virtual dollars to assemble a dream team of five PGA Tour stars who'll play for *you* every week. TOUR Fantasy is free to play, and you can win golf goodies.

The LPGA

This site is similar to `www.pgatour.com` (see the preceding section), if not nearly as lavish. Here's where you'll find stats, profiles, and live tournament updates from the Ladies Professional Golf Association (see Figure 17-2). Want to follow Annika Sorenstam's latest quest to make LPGA history? Want to read a blog by one of the young stars who are making women's golf one of the fastest-growing attractions of all? Here's your chance — just go to `www.lpga.com`.

Figure 17-2: You go, ladies! The home page of the LPGA.

GOLFonline

GOLFonline (www.golfonline.com) is an interactive magazine. This cyber-phenomenon combines the interactive nature of networking with the informational content of a golf magazine (see Figure 17-3). GOLFonline includes original, up-to-date contributions from well-known golf writers and personalities, including columnist David Feherty, my fellow CBS golf commentator and one of the funniest writers around. It also offers plenty of instruction. GOLFonline is all about insight and interactivity on subjects ranging from tournaments and travel to equipment and swing tips, all presented using some of the best text and multimedia capabilities available. It's one of the best resources I've seen at the intersection of two of society's most popular bodies: golfers and online users.

GolfObserver.com

One of the sport's best sites features an amazing amount of information every day, updated faster than you can say "Fore!" (See Figure 17-4.) At GolfObserver.com you'll find headlines, stats, smart columnists, tournament previews and reviews, and the invaluable Golf Notebook. I check this site all the time to make sure I haven't missed anything.

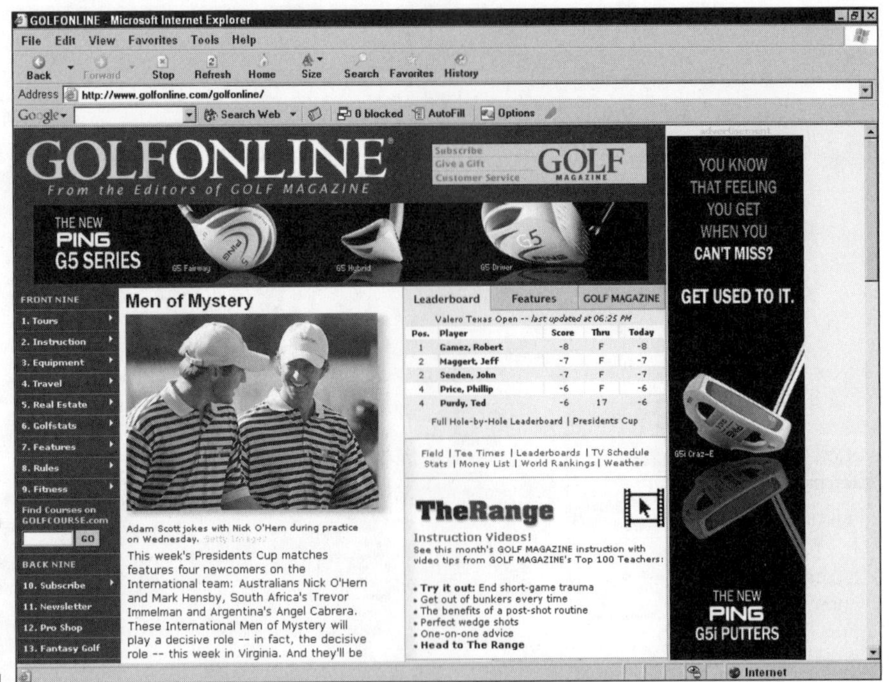

Figure 17-3: The GOLFonline home page.

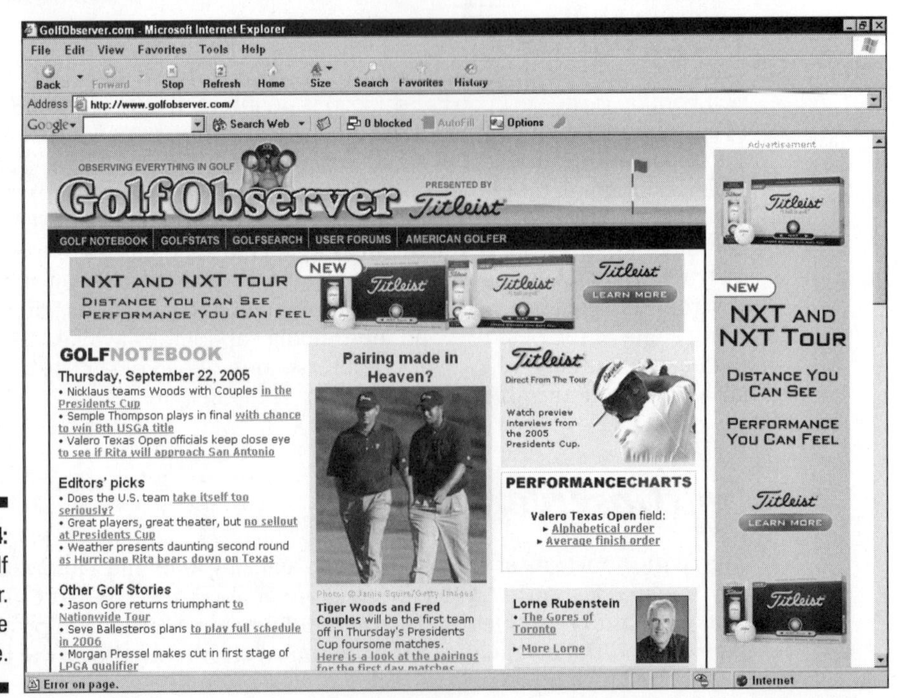

Figure 17-4: The Golf Observer.com home page.

ESPN

What list of golf-related Web sites would be complete without something from our friends at ESPN (`www.espn.go.com/golf/index`)? Check out schedules, statistics, and player rankings for the PGA, LPGA, Champions, Nationwide, and European tours, along with the day's top golf headlines. And if that's not enough to keep you occupied, you'll find additional features, including cool contests, polls, and weekly columns that make this golf site one of the hottest on the Web (see Figure 17-5).

Sports Illustrated

Get inside golf with coverage from one of the media's heaviest hitters. *Sports Illustrated* brings you the top news stories, tournament schedules, leader boards, statistics, and player information, with columns from *SI* insiders and bonus material from the magazine's special "Golf Plus" section (`www.sportsillustrated.cnn.com/golf/`). Beyond being a great sports-news site, SI.com often makes its editorial staff and even pro golfers available to address your questions and comments. There's plenty to see on this informative site (see Figure 17-6).

Figure 17-5: The golf home at ESPN.com.

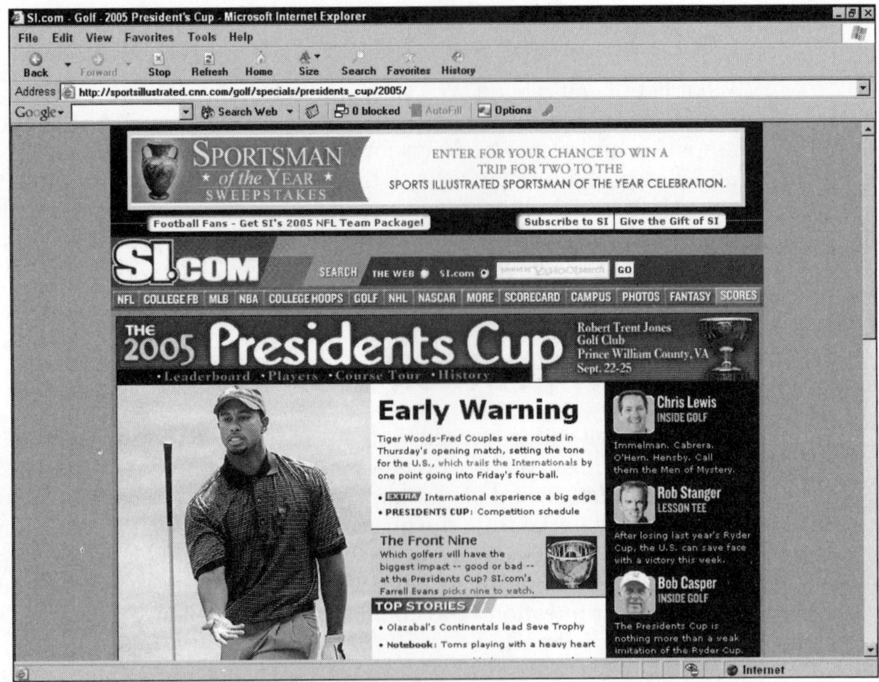

Figure 17-6: No football phones, just golf — the SI.com golf page.

The Golf Channel Online

From the only TV network devoted to golf 24 hours a day comes a well-organized, interactive Web site (`www.thegolfchannel.com`; see Figure 17-7). Check live leader boards, Golf Channel schedules, and photo and video galleries; play trivia games; and read up-to-date news features from Golf Channel personalities. You can also e-mail your questions and opinions to the staff during some of their live television shows to get instant professional advice. With these great free features, there's almost no need to pay for lessons!

The PGA of America

The official site of the Professional Golfer's Association of America (not the PGA Tour) features the latest golf headlines and industry news, as well as current tour schedules and standings (`www.pga.com`; see Figure 17-8). Plan a golf vacation, enter to win cool golf stuff, or check out other PGA-recommended golf links. This is definitely the place to be during the annual PGA Championship.

Figure 17-7: Golf on the cyber-tube — the Golf Channel's home on the Internet.

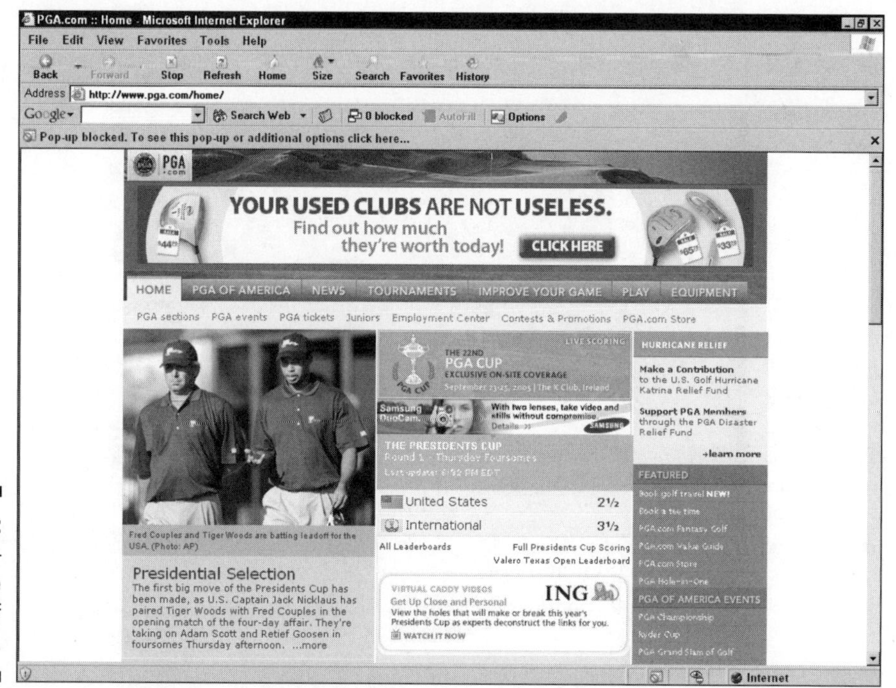

Figure 17-8: PGA.com — home of the PGA of America.

While I'm at it, this is the place to mention three other sites you'll want to visit during the majors. There's great coverage of the Masters every spring at `www.masters.org` (see Figure 17-9), and wall-to-wall U.S. Open stuff at the United States Golf Association's Web site, `www.usga.org`. And you can follow each year's British Open at two related sites, `www.opengolf.com` and `www.randa.org`. The latter is worth a visit any time of year — it's the home cyber-turf of the Royal and Ancient Golf Club of St. Andrews (the mecca of the golf world).

Golf.com

Wouldn't you like to have reserved that domain name about 15 years ago? One of the better golf sites on the Web, Golf.com (`www.golf.com`; see Figure 17-10) boasts a great mix of information, including excellent coverage of golf-travel destinations, tour commentary, and the latest equipment, plus plenty of games, contests, and links to other golf sites. You can also click your way to an official USGA handicap.

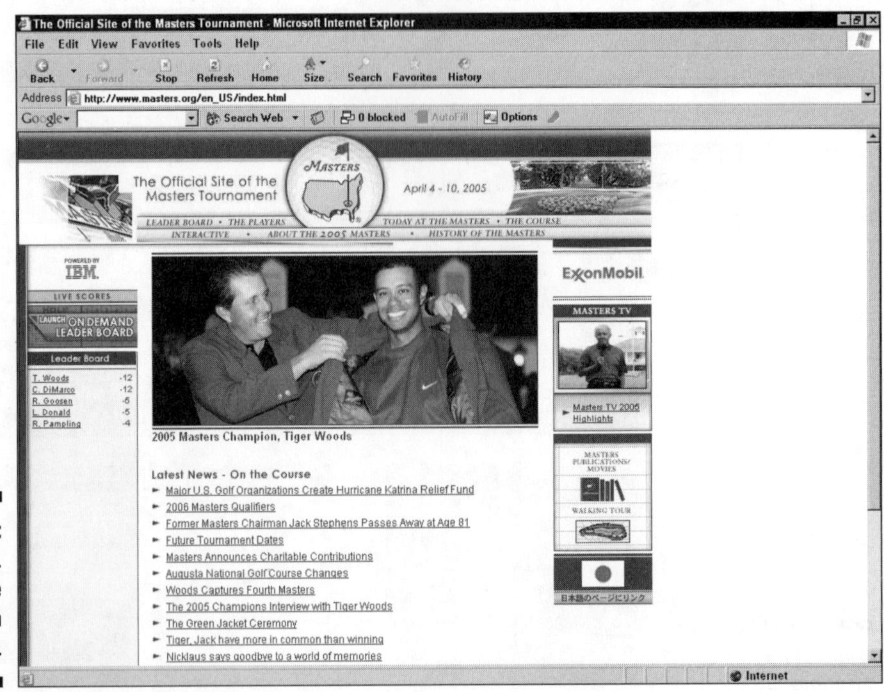

Figure 17-9: Masters.org — home of the green jacket.

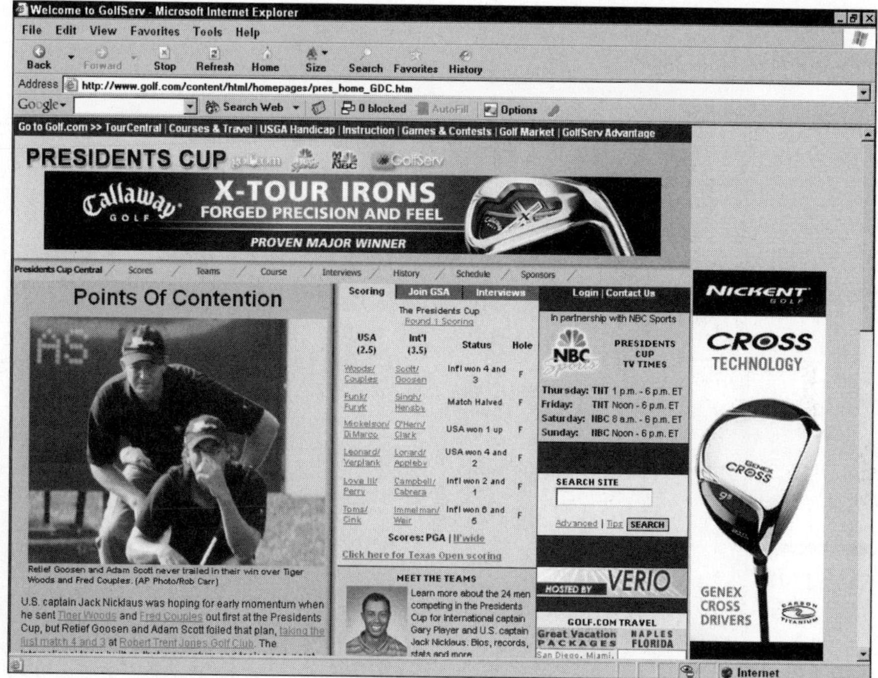

Figure 17-10: Golf.com remains one of the better golf sites on the Web.

Golf Digest

In collaboration with ESPN, America's premier golf magazine has created one of the best sites on the Web (`www.golfdigest.com`). GolfDigest.com is chock-full of insightful commentary, interesting stories, and professional instruction (see Figure 17-11). You'll find inside stuff from the magazine, opinions from notable writers, and reports from the tours. You can also find an equipment hotline, get info about *Golf Digest* golf schools, view swing sequences of great players, search for specific tips, and browse through back issues of the magazine.

World Golf

Whenever I feel like exploring the wide world of golf, I tootle on over to World Golf (`www.worldgolf.com`). This site is an online international golf and travel guide. It features numerous links that let you bounce easily from one area of the golfing world to another. You can make reservations at St. Andrews in Scotland and then view pictures of desert courses in Palm Springs. World Golf is easy to navigate and offers dozens of departments (see Figure 17-12). You can check worldwide weather and even use the site's currency converter to see how far your dollar will go in, say, Andorra.

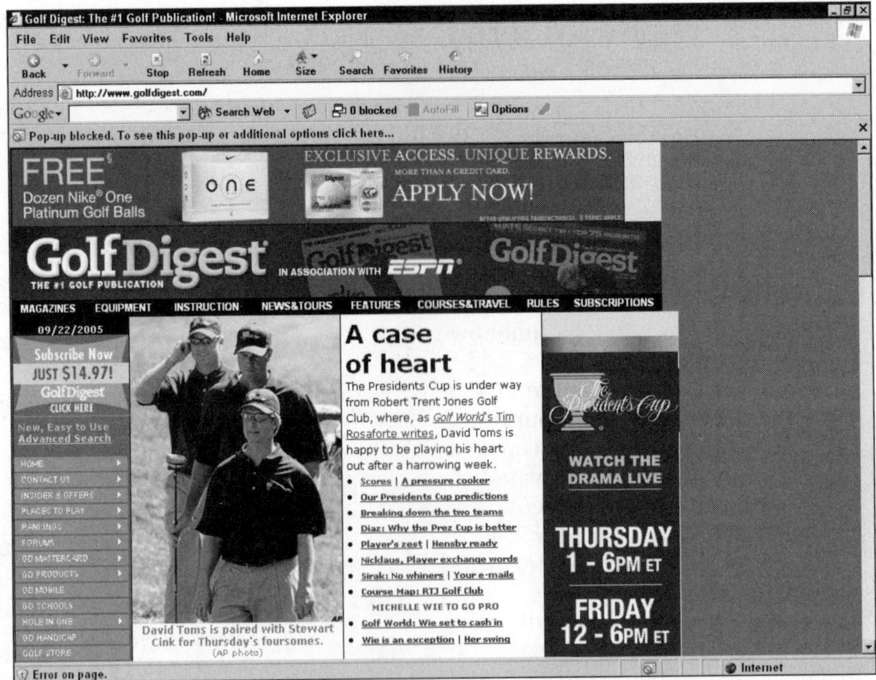

Figure 17-11: *Golf Digest* online.

Figure 17-12: Welcome to my world — WorldGolf.com.

Online Course Guides

Are you having fun yet? Sure you are. As you can see, there's a whole virtual world out there, just waiting to be discovered. Don't be shy. Now it's time for a virtual tour of about a zillion golf courses.

If you don't have enough time or money to play all the world's great courses, don't fret. The Net can take you to them for free. Web sites carry descriptions, layouts, and score cards for countless golf courses around the world. From the comfort of your own desk chair, you can explore championship layouts from Alabama to Zimbabwe.

For example, Figure 17-13 shows the home page for golf's oldest and greatest course: the Old Course at St Andrews, Scotland (`www.standrews.org.uk`). From this site, you can view historical information about the course, make hotel and tee-time reservations, and even play a virtual round. Similar pages cover other famous golf courses and resorts — often with gorgeous photos — from Pebble Beach (`www.pebble-beach.com`) to PGA West (`www.pgawest.com`) to Shadow Creek (`www.shadowcreek.com`).

Many of the sites I discuss earlier, in the "Cool Cyber-Golf Sites" section, feature guides to golf courses. You can also find sites that specialize in giving golfers an up-close-and-virtual look at courses nation- and worldwide. Here's a look at some of the best.

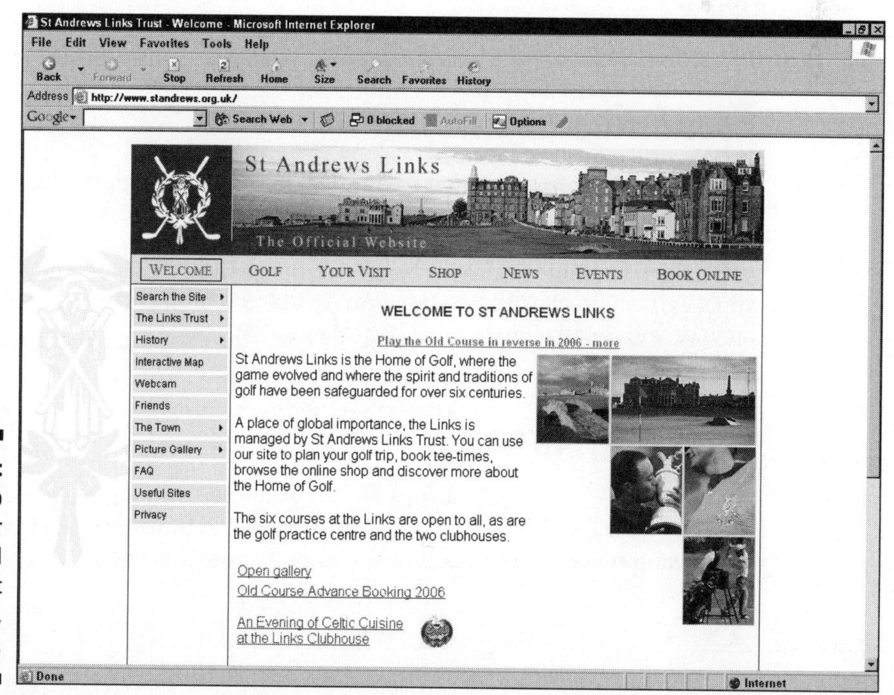

Figure 17-13: The Web site for the Old Course at St. Andrews, Scotland.

About.com: The course-guide helper

This handy site provides links to several prominent Web sites devoted to courses. Start by visiting `http://golf.about.com/od/findagolfcourse`. From there, you can find your way to just about any tee or green on earth.

The Golf Magazine Golf Course Guide

The *Golf Magazine* Golf Course Guide (`www.golfcourse.com`), part of the GolfOnline.com empire, boasts one of the largest golf-course databases. You can easily find what you need, even if you don't quite know what you're looking for. Beyond its course listings, the *Golf Magazine* Golf Course Guide can easily bounce you back to the main site for golf tips, classified ads, news, rules, online golf games, and its very own chat room. You're bound to find something useful while you call your travel agent!

GolfCourses.com

No, this isn't a repeat of the preceding item. At GolfCourses(plural!).com (`www.golfcourses.com`), you can check out tee-time availability at thousands of courses. One special feature is a slide show of the current week's PGA Tour venue. You'll also find featured resorts, deals, links, reviews, and more (see Figure 17-14).

Fore! Reservations

Getting tee times just got a lot easier. The information superhighway has an on-ramp called Fore! Reservations (`www.teeitup.com`). This nationwide reservation system provides you with direct access to thousands of courses at the click of a button. Just choose a state, and a list of available courses appears. Double-click the course you're interested in, and — voila! — you're on your way. I can almost smell the fresh-cut grass.

PlayGolfNow.com

PlayGolfNow.com (`www.playgolfnow.com`) gives you quick access to more than 24,000 courses around the world. The site features a golf-course locator, a hotel and resort locator, golf tips, and golf news (see Figure 17-15).

Figure 17-14: GolfCourses.com offers slide shows and more.

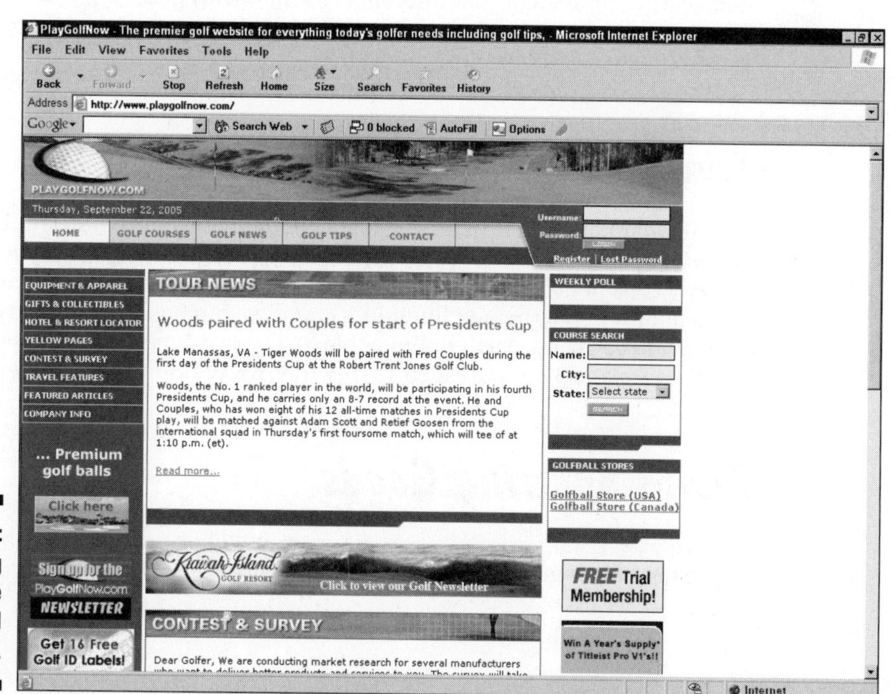

Figure 17-15: Reserving your place in the world of golf.

GolfClubAtlas.com

You won't find course discounts or a tee-time locator here — just the smartest, most passionate discussion of the merits of the world's golf courses you're likely to find anywhere. The brainchild of founder Ran Morrissett, GolfClubAtlas.com (`www.golfclubatlas.com`) is dedicated to all things having to do with golf-course design. You can find out about famous architects and their work, see photos of noteworthy holes, and spend hours online, kicking opinions around with some highly knowledgeable folks — including some of the architects themselves.

But be warned: When you click on "Discussion Group," you may find it addictive.

Virtual Pro Shops: Buying Golf Gear Online

I can't let you get away from my tour of the Net without trying to sell you something. In addition to golfing hangouts and course guides, cyberspace offers a plethora of great pro shops selling golf-related gear. Every major manufacturer (and even some unusual minor ones) has a presence on the Web, so don't hesitate to check out such sites as CallawayGolf.com, NikeGolf.com, Ping.com, TaylorMadeGolf.com, and Titleist.com. Many of the cyber hangouts listed earlier in this chapter offer links to their own pro shops as well. The sites mentioned in this section specialize in bringing you good prices on brand-name new and used products.

eBay

The 500-pound gorilla of Web sales has become one of the hubs of the golf market. At eBay's golf section (`http://buy.ebay.com/golf`), you'll find not only tons of golf equipment but clothing, carts, games, and memorabilia, not to mention golf-themed humidors, candles, hip flasks, and plenty of other stuff you never knew existed. But act fast: The last time I looked, there were only 6 hours and 17 minutes left to buy that Betty Boop putter cover.

Dick's Sporting Goods

Head to `www.dickssportinggoods.com` and click on "Golf Pro Shop" for a vast array of golf gear, much of it at bargain prices, at the Web HQ of Dick's

Sporting Goods. A full-service chain with stores throughout the East and Midwest as well as Texas, Colorado, Utah, and Nevada, Dick's is where you might find a hot new driver for $100 less than you'd pay elsewhere, or a dozen premium balls for half the sticker price.

GolfDiscount.com

For more than 25 years, GolfDiscount.com (`www.golfdiscount.com`) has helped golfers around the world buy equipment at low prices. The site even dedicates a page to feedback from loyal customers. With great prices on all the top brands and an online golf expert for recommendations, questions, and prices, GolfDiscount.com is hard to beat. The site also provides links to the Web sites of every manufacturer it carries.

Golf Galaxy

One of the biggest online marketers offers a simple guarantee: "Never undersold. Period." This is a site (`www.golfgalaxy.com`) that's got more than low prices. Golf Galaxy offers competitions on the Golf Galaxy Tour ("open to all golfers who normally score 95 or less on 18 holes") and even has its own Director of Golf, a PGA professional.

Edwin Watts Golf

The site for the popular Edwin Watts stores in the southeastern United States offers deals on all sorts of gear, plus a newsletter and a golf-club leasing program (`www.edwinwatts.com`).

Nevada Bob's Golf

With more than 100 stores worldwide, Nevada Bob's is a colossus of golf equipment. The site (`www.nevadabobs.com`) offers leading brands plus products designed by major vendors exclusively for Nevada Bob's. There's also a terrific program for junior players: When juniors purchase a set of clubs, Nevada Bob's gives them half the money back when they grow out of those clubs and buy a new set.

Planet Golf

Planet Golf was founded on the notion that golfers don't have to wear "golf" clothing. It's a unique site (www.planetgolf.com; see Figure 17-16), where you can even watch the company's cool TV commercials. Planet Golf sells hip links apparel for golf dudes and dudettes surfing the Web. Heck, it sure beats knickers.

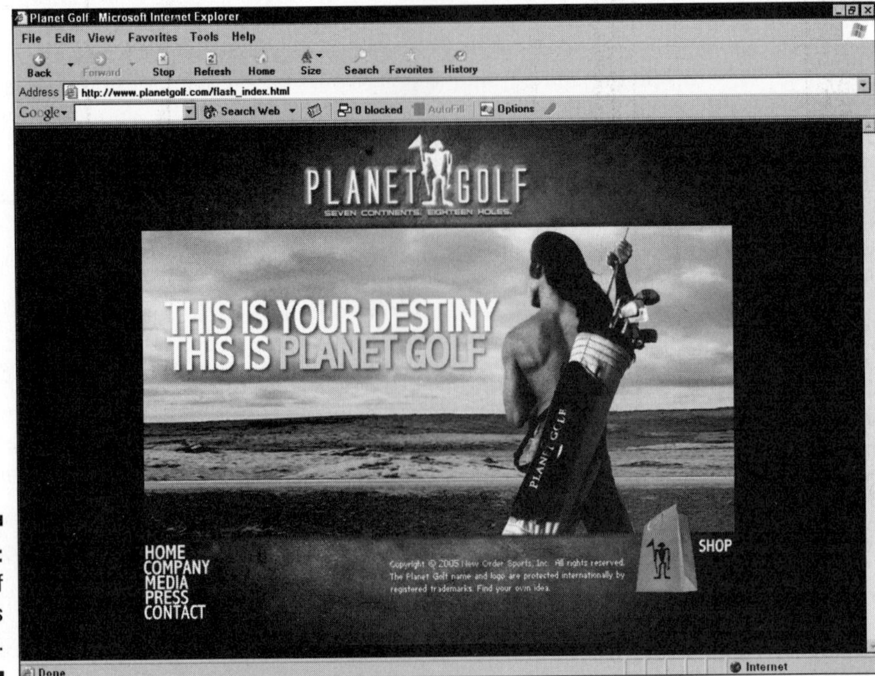

Figure 17-16: Planet Golf is out of this world.

Chapter 18

Tiger versus Golden Tee: The Best of Virtual Golf

In This Chapter

- Finding out why Tiger Woods PGA Tour is the top video game
- Looking at golf simulators: Almost the real thing?
- Understanding the Golden Tee phenomenon

It's amazing but true: Video games are a bigger business than Hollywood. All those beeps and boings coming out of arcades, PCs, and consoles like PlayStation, Xbox, and GameCube rake in more money than all the movies made in any given year. Millions of consumers are introduced to golf through virtual versions of the game. That must be why so many teenagers think of me as the guy from Tiger's video game, not the guy on TV.

There's one possible downside to all this: Electronic golf games tend to make the game seem pretty easy. You press a button or roll a trackball and — boom! — the ball flies 300 yards. As you probably know by now, real golf is much harder. In real life, the ball has an annoying tendency to dribble sideways and stop.

But there's an upside, too: Video golf is fun! And the competition can be fierce.

The Leader: Tiger Woods PGA Tour

Tiger Woods PGA Tour is the dominant game, an ever-evolving cornucopia of wizardry from the folks at EA Sports. Since its debut almost ten years ago, Tiger's product has led the field, thanks to realistic action and more features than you can shake a driver at.

Through the magic of *mo-cappin'* (cybertalk for a process called motion capture), Woods's real swing is replicated muscle-by-muscle in the video version, which is played on countless Sony PlayStations, Microsoft Xboxes, and Nintendo GameCubes worldwide.

In the newest edition, Tiger Woods PGA Tour 2006, tour pros Chris DiMarco, Mike Weir, Luke Donald, and wacky dresser Ian Poulter join 17 other pros and 27 fictional players to challenge Tiger. You can use one of them or build your own golfer, Frankenstein-style, by mixing and matching with EA Sports's Game Face technology. The action unfolds on dazzling digitized versions of more than a dozen famous courses.

In the game's Rivals Mode, you must beat great golfers of the past — using old equipment and wearing vintage clothes — from Ben Hogan to Arnold Palmer to Jack Nicklaus. Conquer them all and you go head-to-head against Tiger for the all-time title.

I'm in there, too — not as a player, but as one of the announcers you hear during play. My specialty is taunting players who hit bad shots. My announcing partner is David Feherty, my CBS colleague. To record our commentary, we had to hole up in a sound booth for three days, eight hours a day. Now, being stuck in a room with Feherty all day is not unlike spending eight hours in a phone booth with 30 adolescent baboons. But it was worth the ordeal — I did the game to reach more young people, and it sure has worked. Now kids come up to me and say, "Hey, you're the dude who taunts me in the game!"

But the young get the last laugh. When the grandkids come over to my house, my granddaughter Terra, who's 10, beats the tar out of me and then *she* taunts *me.*

Other golf video games

Although the Tiger Woods game has lapped most of the field, there's no shortage of video diversions for you to try. Most of the others tend to be more cartoonish than the EA Sports product, but that can be a plus — particularly for younger gamers.

Here's a list of games you may want to have a look at:

- **Mario Golf: Toadstool Tour** from Nintendo stars the mustachioed character from Donkey Kong and his friends. There are several courses, from an easy par-3 circuit to some holes that could challenge any tour pro.
- **Disney Golf** brings Mickey Mouse, Goofy, and other favorites from the Magic Kingdom onto the links in various settings and formats. Kids under 10 might like this one most of all.
- **Hot Shots Golf FORE!** from Sony can get too off-the-wall for some folks, but others find its irreverence refreshing. There's minigolf here, too.

Golf Simulators: Almost Reality?

Electronic golf simulators have gotten so good that they're almost as much fun as the real thing — and you can play Pebble Beach all by yourself in 45 minutes. The one thing that sets them apart from all other virtual versions of the game is that you really get to swing a club. The graphics in such games may not quite match those of PC and console entertainments, but it's nice to use more muscles than just the ones in your thumbs.

Many great golf simulators are available, from the huge (and hugely expensive) to new, inexpensive models that would fit in a briefcase. Here's a sampling:

- **AboutGolf** simulators (www.aboutgolf.com) feature excellent graphics, great courses, and heavy-duty science to produce the next generation of indoor golf. Introduced in 2003, these machines are too expensive for home use (unless you're Bill Gates); you'll find them in the growing chain of PGA Tour Superstores.
- **DeadSolid** simulators (www.deadsolidgolf.com) let you swing full-out at a screen. The company's Ballflight Trajectory Sensor projects where your shot will go, and you putt right into the screen. The machines rent for $2,000 to $2,500 a day; you'll see them at conventions as well as at a few golf shops and sports bars. There are home models available, too, though they can cost as much as a small car.
- **High Definition Golf** from Interactive Sports Technologies (www.istgolf.com), another full-swing simulator, boasts photo-realistic courses and optional swing analysis. Like the AboutGolf and DeadSolid simulators, this one may be too expensive for most golfers to own, but it's great fun to play if you find one in your town.
- **Launchpad** from Electric~Spin Coporation (www.electricspin.com) is a different story — a compact device that sells for a reasonable $249. This is a cut-down version of the much larger full-swing simulators. Using a short club and a ball on a tether, you can "play" Pebble Beach, St. Andrews, Bethpage Black, and other courses. Launchpad can also work in conjunction with Tiger Woods PGA Tour.
- **PC Tour Personal Golf Simulator** from Club Champ (www.thepctour.com) is another small device that works with a laptop and sells for less than $300. Hitting a ball on a stand over a strip of artificial turf, you can play alone or in a foursome and use every club in your bag.

Some of these golf simulators are so good that you'll never get any work done. But that's okay — after all, that's what golf is for!

The Golden Tee Phenomenon

If you've been in a sports bar in the last few years, you've surely seen the arcade-style game called Golden Tee Golf. Back in 1989, the game was developed by a couple of tech whizzes at Incredible Technologies, a small firm in Arlington Heights, Illinois. They packed almost as much info into the programming as NASA used to put a man on the moon, and paired it with a trackball that let players wham the pixilated ball vast distances, with hooks, slices, and backspin. Veteran tour star Peter Jacobsen provided the voiceover — "He's on the dance floor!" — which soon sounded as familiar as "What'll it be?" in taverns everywhere.

Golden Tee was no overnight sensation, but over the next decade it surprised everyone by becoming what the company calls "the most popular coin-op video game in history." Most of today's play, however, is with five- and ten-dollar bills, as well as with credit cards. There are more than 100,000 Golden Tee machines in use around the world. Most may still be in bars and pool halls, but some players put them in their homes. The last time I checked on eBay, you could buy a full-size arcade-style console for anywhere from $700 up to $2,995, with a brand-new Home Edition selling for $3,975. You can buy Golden Tee visors, shirts, and even golden golf tees — all for a game that requires no tees!

Golden Tee is fun, addictive, and fairly realistic when you get used to the trackball. My caddie, Matt Sanders, is terrific at it. To score well, you need to play like Matt — hurl yourself at that trackball for 400-yard drives, and figure out the shortcuts that are programmed into the game. Sometimes, for instance, you can drive the green on a par-4 hole by slicing the ball around a mountain. Get to where you can average 10 or more under par for an 18-hole round and you might be ready for tournament play.

But beware: There are players out there who routinely break 50 for a par-72 round. Many have more than 1,000 virtual holes in one, and some earn more than $75,000 a year playing Golden Tee tournaments. No matter how many beers you've had, do *not* bet with one of those guys.

Part VI
The Part of Tens

In this part . . .

This is my favorite section of the book. I give you ten timeless tips so that you can avoid the common faults I see repeated on golf courses all over the world. I tell you about some of my favorite golf courses, some of my favorite public golf courses, and who I think are the best players of all time. I even give you my top golf disaster stories.

This Part of Tens was my therapy. I needed to write this stuff to keep my sanity. I hope you enjoy this section and remember: In golf, we all speak the same language — utterances of the insane!

Chapter 19

Golf's Ten Commandments

In This Chapter

- Using the right club for the right shot
- Moving your head just a little
- Keeping your sense of humor
- Betting sensibly
- Adjusting your shot to deal with the wind
- Taking golf lessons
- Teeing the ball up
- Giving yourself a break when you mess up

Having been around golf for a while, I've noticed certain bad habits that my friends constantly repeat on the course. Just knowing not to make these mistakes will help you live a long and peaceful life on the links.

I've racked my feeble brain and jotted down ten tips so that you won't suffer the same cataclysms that I see on golf courses all over the world.

Take Enough Club to Get to Your Target

I'm constantly playing with amateurs who consistently come up short with their approach shots to the green. For whatever reason, they always choose a club that would get their shot only to the front of the green — even if they were to hit the most solid shot of their lives. Instead, take a club that you can swing at 80 percent and still get to the hole. Conserve your energy; you have a long life ahead of you!

If You Can Putt the Ball, Do It

Don't always use a lofted club around the greens. I have a friend at home called "Flop-Shot Fred" who is always playing high sand-wedge shots around the green, regardless of what the shot calls for. I think his idol is Phil Mickelson, who can hit these shots straight up in the air. Leave this kind of shot to guys like Phil, who can handle them. My best advice is to use a club that can hit this shot with the lowest trajectory possible. If you can putt the ball, do it.

Keep Your Head Fairly Steady

You're going to move your head a little during the swing, especially with the longer clubs. But try not to move it too much. Moving your head too much leads to all sorts of serious swing flaws that make this game very difficult. Have someone watch you to see whether you move your head, or watch yourself in the mirror while you take practice swings.

Keep Your Sense of Humor

If everything else fails, you can keep your sense of humor and still survive, or at least die laughing.

Bet Only What You Can Afford to Lose

You can cause some serious problems among friends by betting for more money than you have. Never bet what you can't afford to lose. My theory was to bet everything in my pocket except for $10, and that was to pay for the gas home.

Keep the Ball Low in the Wind

When the wind starts to kick up, I see golfers play their normal shots and fail to hit the ball lower to allow for the conditions. Play the ball back in your stance, put your hands ahead of the ball, and keep them ahead of the ball at impact. Keep the ball as low as you can, and you can manage your game much more efficiently. You probably won't lose as many golf balls, either.

Take Some Golf Lessons

If you really want to have fun playing this game, start off with a few lessons to get you on the right track. And, of course, read this book in its entirety. It's amazing what you can do with a clear concept in your mind of how to make a golf swing.

Do Not Give Lessons to Your Spouse

Giving golf lessons to your spouse should be a federal offense. Don't do it! Doing so can only lead to disaster. Invest some money in lessons instead. Get good instruction and reap the benefit: peace of mind.

Always Tee It Up at the Tee Boxes

Whenever it's legal (in the teeing area), tee the ball up. This game is more fun when the ball's in the air. As Jack Nicklaus once said, "Through years of experience I have learned that air offers less resistance than dirt."

Never Blame Yourself for a Bad Shot

Give yourself a break. This game is hard enough without blaming everything on yourself. Find creative ways to blame something else. I like to blame my bad shots on magnetic force fields from alien spacecraft. Let your mind go, and see how crazy your excuses can be. Save your sanity!

Chapter 20

Gary's Ten Favorite Courses

In This Chapter

- Getting a feel for some of the best courses in the world
- Looking at the courses your favorite golfers play

The longer you play golf, the more courses you visit. Some courses are along the ocean, and others are in the desert. Many have trees that frame your every shot. Others are devoid of trees, with a horizon that seems to stretch on forever.

Some golf courses are fastened onto flat land, and others are borne by the hills and valleys of rural America. Limitless features attach themselves to each golf course — that's what makes each course a separate journey. One of the reasons this game is so much fun is that the playing field is always changing.

Many golf architects have put their fingerprints on the map of American golf. These architects employ different design philosophies, which keeps the look of every golf course different. Robert Trent Jones incorporates large, undulating greens with enormous bunkers guarding the landing areas. Pete Dye uses railroad ties to reinforce the greens, giving his courses the "Dye" look. Jack Nicklaus uses wildly undulating greens and expansive fairways as his trademark. Tom Fazio works wonders with all sorts of land — he's a guy who could build you a terrific course on the moon. And Tom Doak is a minimalist, using natural terrain as much as he can. You'll see a wide variety of golf courses in your golfing life.

I based my choices for the all-time great courses on their challenge and beauty. Royal Melbourne is one that I haven't even played. Greg Norman told me that Royal Melbourne is in his top three, so who am I to argue?

These ten courses are my favorites. Half of them are private, and an act of Congress would not get you through the gates. (I list my favorite public courses in Chapter 21.) But half the courses on my list offer public access: Pebble Beach, Pinehurst No. 2, Harbour Town, the Straits course at Whistling Straits, and Bandon Dunes. They're not cheap, but you don't have to know the right people to play there.

Pebble Beach (Monterey, California)

Pebble Beach is an extraordinary place to do anything. Golf has made it popular, and the land has made it legendary. Robert Louis Stevenson called this stretch of land "the greatest meeting of land and sea in the world." Pebble Beach is truly one of the most beautiful spots on earth, and it's blessed with two of my favorite courses in the world: Pebble Beach and Cypress Point.

I've been playing Pebble Beach Golf Links since I was 15 years old. We used to play the California state amateur on these storied links. We would round up ten guys and rent a motel room together. We based the sleeping arrangements on how well we'd played that day: Low round would get his pick of the two beds. High round would get the other bed — we figured he needed some sleep with all the swinging he did that day. Everybody else grabbed some floor. Those were the fun days, when golf was a twinkle in your eye, and innocence made the game appear easy.

Pine Valley (Clementon, New Jersey)

Pine Valley is the greatest course without an ocean view. If you have a week to hang with your friends and play golf, Pine Valley is the place. The grounds are spectacular. Cottages house the overnight guests, and a great dining room is full of golf memorabilia. The walls are saturated with tall tales of Pine Valley's golf history. Best of all, most of the tall tales are true.

The course is one of the great designs in the world. Builder George Crump bought this stretch of New Jersey land in 1912, and got input on the course design from great architects including C. B. Macdonald, Harry Colt, Alister Mackenzie, Donald Ross and A. W. Tillinghast. You measure a golf course by how many holes you can remember after playing one round on it, and this course is instantly etched in your mind — every hole, every tree, and every bunker. I'm in total fascination when I walk through Pine Valley's corridor of perfectly maintained grass. This course is a place that breathes with exuberance.

Cypress Point (Monterey, California)

Cypress Point is a golf course of such beauty and solitude you'd think that it has holy qualities. From the quaint pro shop to the confining locker room and dusty rooms that perch atop the clubhouse, Cypress Point is the place for your final round.

The course winds from the pines into the sand dunes. Deer are everywhere, often dodging your errant tee shots. You can see the turbulent Pacific on a few holes going out and then again on most of the back nine, including the famous 16th — a gorgeous and scary par-3 that must be seen to be believed.

I'll never forget Cypress Point, which was the site of my first tour event in 1974. I birdied seven holes in a row (holes 7 through 13) and posted an opening round of 65. My career tapered off after that initial explosion.

Shinnecock Hills (Southampton, New York)

America's premier Scottish-style links course, Shinnecock Hills is a treasure. At this course, you play the game as it was designed to be played — along the ground when the wind blows. The world's best players saw how tough that could be during the 2004 U.S. Open at Shinnecock.

From the porch of the nation's oldest clubhouse all the way out to the Atlantic Ocean, Shinnecock Hills is an American-bred beauty. Wind and golf course are meshed into your being as you stroll through this artwork.

Pinehurst No. 2 (Pinehurst, North Carolina)

Pinehurst No. 2 is a masterpiece of design. Perhaps the most famous course designed by the great Donald Ross, it hosted the U.S. Open in 1999 and 2005. Hidden in the pines of Pinehurst, the course combines every facet of the game and boasts some of the best-designed greens in the world.

This entire complex at Pinehurst takes you back half a century with its rustic, Southern motif. Golf courses are everywhere — there are eight at the Pinehurst Resort and many others nearby — and golf is the central theme of the town.

We used to play a tour event at Pinehurst No. 2 every year, and we would get into a golf frenzy weeks before our arrival. Pinehurst No. 2 is second to none in the Southeast, a challenge to be revered and enjoyed.

Whistling Straits — Straits Course (Kohler, Wisconsin)

Whistling Straits opened in 1998 but really grabbed everyone's attention when it hosted the 2004 PGA Championship. Pete Dye took a flat wasteland on Wisconsin's lakefront and turned it into a rugged roller coaster of a course that evoked Scotland at every turn. You'll find grassy dunes and deep pot bunkers on the Straits Course, as well as stone bridges and even Scottish sheep standing almost sideways on hillsides.

When the wind whistles off Lake Michigan, this can be a terror track. But the greens are large enough that if you play from the set of tees that matches your skill level, you'll have a chance to score. We'll be playing the 2007 U.S. Senior Open here, and in 2010 the PGA Championship returns to Whistling Straits.

Bandon Dunes (Bandon, Oregon)

In 1999, an exciting new golf course opened on a remote stretch of Oregon coastline. The architect was David McLay Kidd, a Scotsman who put a remarkable, seemingly all-natural layout on a bluff above the Pacific. Kidd's large greens help give amateurs a chance, but the wind can play havoc with all kinds of shots. Bandon Dunes is a purist's delight — golf carts aren't allowed, and Kidd let this gorgeous stretch of land help dictate the routing of the course.

Bandon Dunes quickly became one of America's premier golf resorts. In 2001, a new course designed by Tom Doak, Pacific Dunes, earned rave reviews, and 2005 brought a third natural beauty, Bandon Trails, designed by Ben Crenshaw and Bill Coore. Mentioning them here is my way of applauding all three courses. Still, it was Kidd's creation that got the ball rolling. Bandon Dunes is one of the best and most important new golf courses we've seen in a long time.

Royal Melbourne (Melbourne, Australia)

My information about Royal Melbourne comes from the Aussies I know on tour. Greg Norman and Steve Elkington rave about the greens, which are said to be some of the fastest in the world. The tournament course dates back to

1891, when the club hired Alister Mackenzie to sail down from Scotland to oversee the design. The modern course is made up of 18 holes out of the 36 they have on site. I walked Royal Melbourne during the 2002 Presidents Cup and found that the Aussies were right: The course is beautiful, with large eucalyptus trees standing sentinel over the scene.

Harbour Town Links (Hilton Head Island, South Carolina)

An intensely beautiful and intriguing golf course, Harbour Town is set in the old oaks and then flirts with the Calibogue Sound for the finishing holes. Harbour Town is a great spot to vacation and enjoy world-class golf.

The PGA Tour's Heritage Classic — now called the MCI Heritage — was first played on this golf course in 1969. Harbour Town meanders through the pines, leaving tight alleys where there's not much room to drive your golf ball. This course has some of the smallest greens on tour, which drives the pros mad trying to figure out which club to hit to these elusive surfaces.

My memories of this golf course are many. One of the funniest was back in the '80s, when Bill Mallon (who was on the tour then — he's now a doctor) and I were the first guys off the tee on Sunday's round in the tournament. We weren't playing that well, so we decided we'd try to see how fast we could play the round. I was the last to putt on the 18th and holed a 6-footer for 75, which tied Bill, in the time of 1 hour, 37 minutes, and 15 seconds. We finished the 18th hole when the group behind us was walking down the 9th fairway. And they say PGA Tour players are slow. . . .

Long Cove Golf Club (Hilton Head Island, South Carolina)

Long Cove is a great course that I get to play when we go to Hilton Head Island to broadcast the MCI Heritage for CBS. A wonderful blend of water and trees that soothes and scares you at the same time, this venue will kick your rear end if you're not playing well — but it always does so in a dignified manner.

There's something so relaxing about the place that I slow down when I pass through the gates. Large yachts and alligators keep your interest as you wander through this Pete Dye masterpiece.

If you're ever lucky enough to be invited to this frolic in the forest, cast your eyes toward the water off the 17th tee. If you squint hard enough, you may see the iron that I threw in the lake one day — it's sitting on the bottom along with my golf ball. I never could hit the green with that 1-iron. Let it rest.

Chapter 21

Gary's Ten Favorite Public Courses

In This Chapter

- Seeing some of the best public courses around
- Finding courses you may want to play someday

Great courses anyone can play? In addition to Pebble Beach, Pinehurst No. 2, and the other public-access courses in Chapter 20, I've found superb public golf all over the country — from north to south and coast to coast, from tee to shining tee.

Alvamar Golf Course (Lawrence, Kansas)

I won the Kansas Open at Alvamar Golf Course when I was a mere lad, and I remember it as one of the finest-conditioned golf courses I had ever seen in my life. Alvamar is set on rolling hills, and my putter was on fire. I really like places where I've won, because they're few and far between.

Go to Kansas and look up this course. Maybe they've got my name on a plaque or something. Tell the employees that I sent you — I don't believe you'll regret your trek.

Bethpage State Park, the Black Course (Farmingdale, New York)

Bethpage State Park on Long Island, just east of New York City, has two of the best state-park courses in the United States. But the Black Course is the crown jewel. The course is a treat to play — it's a real challenge, and the greens fees won't bust your credit line. For decades there were rumblings that this place could hold a golf event of major proportions one day. It finally happened in 2002, when the U.S. Open came to the Black Course. That so-called "People's Open" was such a success that the Open will return to Bethpage in 2009.

This municipal layout by A. W. Tillinghast, rejuvenated by Rees Jones before the '02 Open, is a grand design that catches the attention of well-seasoned players and offers novices a place to grow and learn the game.

Cog Hill No. 4 (Lemont, Illinois)

Cog Hill is one of the great golf complexes in the United States. The Western Open was held here for years. Now it's the Cialis Western Open, but tour pros still flock to this place with nothing but nice things to say about it. That's a rarity on the PGA Tour nowadays.

Cog Hill has a great layout and could host a major event without doing much to the course. If you want to really find out how your game is, try Cog Hill No. 4 from the back trees. Bring along some provisions — you're going to be out there a while. They don't call the course "Dub's Dread" for nothing.

Grayhawk Golf Club, Talon and Raptor (Scottsdale, Arizona)

Grayhawk opened in 1995. Situated in the higher desert of north Scottsdale, this beautiful public facility has it all: a great clubhouse, two championship golf courses, a great practice facility, and me. That's right: Peter Kostis and I run a golf school at Grayhawk Golf Club. Phil Mickelson and Howard Twitty also represent Grayhawk on tour. You can see why I'm a little prejudiced about our place.

The service at this place has to be seen to be believed. You'll be treated like you just won the Masters. The golf courses are also superb, with Phoenix and the McDowell Mountains making for a spectacular setting.

If you ever get out to Phoenix, come up the hill and join us at Grayhawk for fun in the sun. You never know, Phil Mickelson may be around, and we can get him to buy us a beer!

The Homestead, Cascades Course (Hot Springs, Virginia)

The Homestead is one of the most peaceful settings you'll ever experience. This old golf facility — the first course was built in 1892 — has a certain civility about it. Grandeur is everywhere, and the course is fantastic. Settle in and enjoy the lifestyle.

I recommend seeing this beauty in October or early November, when the scenery is unbelievable. Take a few friends with you and spend at least three or four days at the Homestead.

Ocean Course (Kiawah Island, South Carolina)

This Pete Dye gem was the setting of the famed "War by the Shore" Ryder Cup matches in 1991, and later provided scenes for the movie *The Legend of Bagger Vance.* The Ocean Course at Kiawah winds through dunes and marshes, with views of the Atlantic from all 18 holes.

I'll be testing my swing and my nerves here in 2007, when the Ocean Course hosts the Senior PGA Championship. Five years later, the course gets a PGA Tour major: the 2012 PGA Championship.

Pinon Hills Golf Course (Farmington, New Mexico)

Finding Farmington, New Mexico, takes some doing, but once there, you'll see the outstanding Pinon Hills Golf Course laid out in the high mesas of New Mexico. The views from anywhere on the course are spectacular.

Pinon Hills is probably the best bargain on earth. The last report we got of the greens fee was $38 on the weekend, $33 on weekdays, and you can walk anytime. For $445.50 — about what it costs to play Pebble Beach once — you can buy a pass and play all year! So grab a friend and get to Farmington; they're waiting for you, and you don't need a lot of pesos to have fun.

San Luis Rey Downs (Bonsall, California)

San Luis Rey Downs is not the prettiest course in the world. It's not the best maintained either. But it is the place where I sharpened my clubs and my wit for the PGA Tour. Just up the road from Hellhole Canyon (no kidding), San Luis Rey Downs was full of scoundrels who would make any kind of bet, as long as they had an edge. Jimmy the Greek would've loved the place.

San Luis Rey Downs sits in a river bottom that fills up whenever Southern California has one of its rare wet spells. The bar is a melting pot of horse owners, trainers, and jockeys from the thoroughbred training facility located across the street. Mix them with public-fee golfers, and you get a rodeo of fun.

This course is the place where I plagiarized most of my weird TV lines. Everybody had a nickname, and a few golfers had served time. San Luis Rey Downs was the place where my friends hung out, and I enjoyed every minute of their company. After you play this game long enough, you learn that you can play the best-looking, most immaculately conditioned golf course in the world, but if you don't enjoy the company, the course's condition doesn't matter. I enjoy San Luis Rey Downs.

Torrey Pines Golf Course, South Course (San Diego, California)

Torrey Pines is the site of the PGA Tour's Buick Invitational. Since 2000, the winners there include Phil Mickelson (twice), Tiger Woods (twice), and John Daly. Nice pedigree, huh? A great public golf course, Torrey is well maintained and offers a challenge for any golfer. The South Course serves up many long and demanding holes that are tougher than the winds kicked up by the Pacific Ocean.

You can see the ocean from all over the course, and you get a really good look as you walk along the cliff on No. 4. Colorful hang gliders fill the sky. During the fall, you may see whales migrating to Mexico. You have to do a lot to concentrate on the golf at Torrey.

The city of San Diego has a real gem in Torrey Pines. At almost any time of year, you can enjoy the golf and sunshine.

Tournament Players Club (TPC) at Sawgrass, Stadium Course (Ponte Vedra Beach, Florida)

Our flagship golf course — the most famous of the chain of fine Tournament Players Clubs — is a beauty. Pete Dye conjured up this course from his cauldron. Carved out of the trees and swamps in north Florida, near Jacksonville, this course plays host to one of the biggest PGA Tour events of the year — the Players Championship. This event has the best field of any tournament we play on tour, and the course provides a wonderful challenge.

Public golf goes big-time

Good news: The largest area of growth in golf in recent years has been in public, not private, courses. Lots of those courses come to you courtesy of your state, county, or city government — proof that your tax dollars are hard at work. Actually, golf courses can be a big source of revenue, which is one reason governments build them.

The courses are better built these days. Forget the old image of worn and tattered municipal links. Chances are, a quality public course offering bargain rates is within an easy drive from your home. Fees are low, and most facilities offer a range of amenities from clubhouses to carts (not that you'd want to use a cart, would you?).

Public golf isn't just for homebodies, either. If you're interested in traveling, you can enjoy a fun, inexpensive vacation by touring the courses at America's best open-to-everyone facilities. One good example is the Robert Trent Jones Golf Trail in Alabama. Built by — guess who? — Robert Trent Jones, that grandmaster of greens design, this string of courses offers the same brilliant planning and layout features of Jones's most famous sites. The idea was such a hit that it was widely imitated. There's now an Audubon Golf Trail in Louisiana, a Magnolia Golf Trail in Mississippi, and even a Lewis and Clark Golf Trail in North Dakota.

The Trent Jones Trail in Alabama runs the length of the state and offers classic 54-hole spreads as well as a selection of par-3 courses for golfers looking for the chance to develop their skills on layouts that offer real character. Each course is different and reflects the distinctive topography of its location. And last I heard, each course charges between $37 and $75. How's that for a deal too good for a cash-conscious golf traveler to pass up?

Great-value public courses throughout the country offer charm and challenge to spare — and I'm not just talking about the golf trails or my personal favorites. Maybe you'll discover one or two favorites of your own.

To find out more about public courses across the United States and in your own hometown, check out Chapter 17. That's where you'll find Web sites chockablock with golf-course descriptions, details, directions, and more.

I remember that, when I first saw this place, I couldn't believe the difficulty of the golf course. I went home to San Luis Rey Downs and told the boys about the fright that possessed me on every hole. Through the years, the staff has made many refinements to the course, and in 1995, Greg Norman shot 24 under par to clobber the field. So the course can be had, and if you get a chance to play it, you'll be had, too. The TPC at Sawgrass is a marvelous facility with one of the most famous holes on earth — the par-3 17th with its island green. You can watch for yourself when the best players in the world test their nerves there every spring.

Chapter 22

Gary's Ten All-Time Favorite Male Players

In This Chapter

- Walter Hagen
- Fairway Louie
- Phil Mickelson
- Jack Nicklaus
- Mac O'Grady
- Arnold Palmer
- Sam Snead
- Titanic Thompson
- Lee Trevino
- Tiger Woods

These individuals play the game of golf at a different level. The course turns into their canvas as they display a certain panache in going about their work. To watch people of this caliber is to gaze upon the brightest of stars. They play the game as it was meant to be played. I have played with some of them and have heard stories about the others. They all wrote their own scripts and have set themselves apart from the norm. They've got game.

Walter Hagen

"Sir Walter" won the PGA Championship five times, the British Open four times, and the U.S. Open twice. While doing so, he redefined the role of the professional golfer in society. Before Hagen, the golf pro was low on the food chain. He was never allowed to walk through the front door of the clubhouse and was certainly never seen socializing with members.

Hagen changed all that with his game and his flamboyant personality. The public took him to heart. He would arrive at the course in a limousine, park next to the clubhouse he was barred from entering, and then have his chauffeur serve lunch in the back of the car. Not just any lunch: Full complements of wine and silver settings were the norm.

Hagen played golf with kings and queens, dukes and duchesses. On one famous occasion, he asked King Edward VIII to tend the flag for him: "Hey, Eddie, get the stick, will you?"

Hagen elevated himself to full celebrity, and the golfing world never looked the same again. Sir Walter really could play the game, and he was the first to make his living doing only that.

Fairway Louie

I went to school with this brilliant sage. He took seven years to get out of Riverside City College, a two-year college, but he eventually got it right. Fairway Louie got his master's from some faraway college and is now managing an avocado orchard in the hills of Bonsall, California. He lives in a mobile home and wears a lot of flannel, but he's still my friend. He took me to my first rock concert, showed me how to cheat on tests, and came to my first wedding. I've known Fairway a long time.

He is the on-again, off-again president of a course where I grew up. That's the only way he can play for nothing. He advised me to quit the tour many years ago — a wiser man I do not know. We see each other rarely nowadays, and I miss his dialogue. He is a voice of reason in days of madness.

Phil Mickelson

For years, fans loved him for his go-for-broke style. They loved him even more after he worked like crazy to improve, learning to play the percentages under pressure, and won the 2004 Masters. That victory, Phil's first in a major, was one of the most popular in recent history. He grabbed another major at the 2005 PGA Championship and looks poised to keep galleries rooting for him for years to come.

Jack Nicklaus

He simply was the one I grew up watching as he won and won and won.

Mac O'Grady

A paragraph cannot do our relationship justice. Mac showed me how to really understand this game. He knows more about the golf swing than anyone else I have ever met. He is a man of many complexities and much conjecture. He has a passion for the game and for life. My own existence has been immeasurably enhanced by his friendship.

Arnold Palmer

No one man has been more responsible for making golf the huge success that it is today than Arnold Palmer. He came to the tour swinging hard at every shot, never laying up, and always (it seemed) getting his golf ball out of trouble when it appeared that he was doomed to fail. He was flamboyant and charismatic, with a swagger that galleries flocked to see. And he happened along in the early days of golf on television. The nation had a new hero.

Arnie was responsible for all the attention that golf got in those early cathode-ray moments. He held our banner and set us on a new course for marketing. Golf — or any sport, for that matter — could not have had a better spokesman. He is, and always will be, the king.

Sam Snead

Sam started playing golf by carving up an old stick to resemble a club and then whacking away at rocks on the West Virginia farm where he grew up. What came of that youthful folly was the most natural-looking golf swing man has ever devised. Sam's swing is still the gold standard today.

Samuel Jackson Snead won 81 tournaments on the PGA Tour (though he told everyone that he'd won more). His flair for telling jokes and leaping up to kick the tops of doorjambs around the world's clubhouses are legendary. I had the opportunity to play and practice with Sam in his last years on tour. I will never forget those moments.

Titanic Thompson

Golf has a way of attracting gamblers of all kinds. There's none more legendary than Titanic Thompson. I have encountered very few of my peers who have not heard of or played a long-ago round of golf with this famous odds maker. As I understand it, Titanic would make bets that he had no way of losing, no matter how ridiculous they seemed. He roamed with the rich and famous during the middle of the 20th century and supplied us with stories we will tell deep into the 21st. He lived by his wits and imagination and added to the lore of golf.

Lee Trevino

In 1967, a 27-year-old Mexican American came out of nowhere to finish fifth in the U.S. Open. He didn't go back to El Paso, where he lived, but stayed to play a few more tournaments. He won enough money to stay on tour. "How long has this been going on?" he asked in jest.

He has been on and around the tour ever since. Our lives have been richer for Lee Trevino's presence. A nonstop conversationalist, Lee talked his way through 27 tour victories, stopped off at NBC for a while to do some announcing, and then went on to the Champions Tour, where he still competes.

The man has an unequalled flair for words and shot making. He takes this sometimes staid game and makes it fun. I hope we see another golfer like him in the future; he is a pleasure to watch and listen to.

Tiger Woods

Sure, he's the game's biggest star. But there's more than star power behind the phenomenon that is Tiger Woods. There's the competitive fire that makes him one of the hardest workers in the game, a golfer who *never* gives up. There's the brilliant short game that often escapes the notice of casual fans. And there's the will that makes him believe he can win every time out. Most pro golfers are in their primes during their 30s — that's almost scary, given that Tiger, with 10 majors to his credit, turned 30 on December 30, 2005.

Chapter 23

Gary's Ten All-Time Favorite Female Players

In This Chapter

- JoAnne Carner
- Laura Davies
- Juli Inkster
- Nancy Lopez
- Meg Mallon
- Annika Sorenstam
- Kathy Whitworth
- Michelle Wie
- Mickey Wright
- Babe Zaharias

Women are embracing the sport of golf in growing numbers. In fact, more than 20 percent of today's golfers are women, and they play an average of 16 rounds of golf a year.

The dominance of some of these fine athletes has secured women's golf in the pantheon of sports. Babe Zaharias is considered by some to be the greatest athlete — male or female — who ever lived. Kathy Whitworth has won more tournaments than anybody else who has ever picked up a golf club. These women have shown the world that they can play this game, and they have done it with dignity and élan. They're the ones who blazed a trail for Michelle Wie and millions of others to follow. Now millions of even younger girls can follow Michelle into the game.

JoAnne Carner

This outgoing Hall of Famer is one of the reasons the LPGA became a popular major sport. “Big Mama,” as she is called, is one of the greatest personalities the women’s tour has ever known. She has won 42 events and was the tour’s leading money winner 3 separate times. The LPGA has long been enriched by her performance as one of the game’s true ambassadors.

Laura Davies

Laura was one of the dominant figures on the women’s tour for years. Her enormous power reduced championship courses to mere pitch-and-putt status. She has an engaging way about her and is still a blast to watch as she destroys golf courses. She has won 20 times through 2005, including 4 majors, and she lights up the faces of galleries worldwide.

Juli Inkster

A Californian with an infectious smile, Juli was inducted into the LPGA Hall of Fame in 1999. In 1982, she became the first golfer, male or female, to win three consecutive U.S. amateur titles. The 1984 Rookie of the Year went on to win 30 times on tour, with 7 majors to her credit, including the U.S. Women’s Open in 1999 and 2002 and back-to-back victories in the 1999–2000 McDonald’s LPGA Championships.

Nancy Lopez

Nancy constantly has a smile on her face and plays the game with youthful zest. An outstanding representative of the LPGA, she is one of the great putters in golf history. She won 48 times including 3 majors, and while she isn’t playing as much these days, Nancy still adds life to everyone around her.

Meg Mallon

Meg joined the LPGA in 1987. She flirts with the golf course as she plays it, always trying something new to see if it will help her play better. Viewers can see the fun she has playing the game; that's why I like to watch Meg. Her most productive year was 1991, when she won two major titles. She has 18 wins in total, including the 2004 U.S. Women's Open.

Annika Sorenstam

This highly disciplined individual is one of the hardest workers in our sport. A native of Stockholm, Sweden, Annika has won 68 times with 9 majors — and counting — through 2005. In 2001, she shot a historic 59 in an LPGA event. The perennial player of the year is a perfectionist whose work ethic is esteemed by her peers. She is the first woman to have an annual scoring average under 70. She has inspired millions of girls to take up the game, and is widely regarded as the finest female player of her time, if not all time.

Kathy Whitworth

Of all the people who have played this game — male or female — Kathy Whitworth has won more times than anybody else. In her glorious career, she won 88 times, including 6 major championships. She dominated the tour from 1965 to 1973, finishing first on the money list eight times and second once. She was named player of the year seven times.

Michelle Wie

Like Tiger Woods, Michelle started playing at an early age — she was 4 years old — and excelled in a hurry. The pride of Hawaiian golf shot a 64 at age 10 and grew into a slender 6-footer who can bomb a drive more than 300 yards without visible effort. After turning pro just before her 16th birthday in October 2005, she set her sights on the game's highest level. If she continues to hone her game, Michelle might well become one of golf's biggest stars.

Mickey Wright

In the late 1950s and early 1960s, Mickey Wright was responsible for raising women's professional golf to a new level and placing it in the public eye. I was fortunate enough to see her play an exhibition match many years ago. I had heard so much about her golf swing — and I was not disappointed. She may have the best swing of anybody who's ever played this game. An 82-time winter, Mickey Wright ranks with Annika Sorenstam, Babe Zaharias, and a few others as one of the greatest players the LPGA has ever known. In her prime, she might have been the very best.

Babe Zaharias

Perhaps the most talented athlete of all time, Babe Didrikson Zaharias won two gold medals and one silver medal in track and field in the 1932 Olympics. Earlier that year, she won eight of ten events in the AAU's National Women's Track and Field Championship and won the meet as a one-woman team for Employer's Casualty. She then decided to take up golf. Among her achievements was being one of 13 founders of the LPGA. In a very brief LPGA career— lasting 8 years — she won 31 events and 10 major titles. She became a legend beyond the sport of golf, but she died of cancer at the early age of 45.

Chapter 24

The (More Than) Ten Worst Golf Disasters

In This Chapter

- From blown leads . . .
- . . . to missed putts

In golf, there's no place to hide. And that's the honor of it. The quarterback who's having a disgraceful day can retire to the bench. The batter who fears Randy Johnson can fake an injury. But the golfer who's brave enough to reach the lead has an extra kind of courage; he knows that, having gotten to center stage, there's no limit to how much he can disgrace himself.

—Thomas Boswell

Oops!

—Jean Van de Velde

Golf has to be the easiest sport in which to snatch defeat from the jaws of victory. The game can be positively diabolical — the worst always seems to happen, and complacency is severely punished. Ultimately, it's not whether the wheels come off, but when. Why do we delight in these debacles? I think there's a strong element of schadenfreude, a sort of perverse consolation, when the greats occasionally suffer the humiliation and heartbreak that we regular mortals deal with every day. And that's the key, I think: Awful as they are, these meltdowns happen to the best players on the planet.

A word on terminology: I prefer *disaster* to *collapse.* A collapse is your fault, but a disaster is something beyond your control, like a flood or an earthquake. Also, there's a fine line between "choking" and being the victim of a disaster. Choking is somehow culpable: Miss a 3-footer to win a major, and it's your fault. In any case, it's devastating when disasters happen, and nobody is immune — not even the best players in the world at the top of their game.

Jean Van de Velde, 1999 British Open at Carnoustie

France's best golfer had it made. With a 3-stroke lead as he stood on the final tee, Van de Velde knew that a double-bogey 6 was all he needed to win the Claret Jug — and change his life forever. Instead, he would need to change his pants. After his second shot bounced off a grandstand, he dunked a tricky pitch shot into Barry Burn — the stream near the 18th green at Carnoustie. Then the real comedy began.

Removing his shoes and socks, he waded into the water, planning to hit his ball out (see Figure 24-1). But thought better of it. He took a penalty drop, knocked his next shot into a greenside bunker, blasted out and finally made a tough putt for a 7. For a moment he was thrilled — at least he'd made a playoff!

Of course he lost the playoff. Paul Lawrie won, and Van de Velde could only shake his head. "Can I go out and play it again?" he asked.

Figure 24-1: *Sacre bleu!* Jean Van de Velde got the blues at Carnoustie.

Greg Norman, 1996 Masters

The greatest disaster in golf history happened to the reigning number-one player in the world. With more than 70 tournament victories worldwide, Greg Norman is certainly the best player never to win a green jacket (the symbol of a Masters victory), although he came close twice: In 1986, he bogied the 18th to lose by a stroke to Jack Nicklaus, and the following year he lost in a playoff when Larry Mize chipped in from 50 yards. But his opening three rounds at Augusta in 1996, including a record-tying 63 the first day, gave him a seemingly invincible six-shot lead. (No one with such a lead going into the final round had ever lost before.)

But on Sunday, he couldn't do anything right. Norman bogied the 9th, 10th, and 11th. He hit into the water on both 12 and 16 for double-bogey 5s. All told, he missed 10 of 18 greens on his way to a 6-over-par 78. He lost to Nick Faldo's 5-under 67 by 5 shots, an incredible 11-shot turnaround.

Norman somehow managed to smile during the excruciating post-round press conference. "God, I'd love to be up there putting that green jacket on, but it's not the end of the world," he told reporters. "I'm disappointed, I'm sad about it. I'm going to regret it, because I know I let it slip away. It's not the end of my life." He exhibited such dignity in the face of crushing disappointment that he received thousands of cards and letters praising his sportsmanship. He later described the outpouring of support as a transforming experience, claiming that he took more from the loss than he would have gained from a win.

Gil Morgan, 1992 U.S. Open at Pebble Beach

After opening rounds of 66 and 69, the 45-year-old former optometrist had a seven-shot lead when the wind started to gust off the Pacific. He double-bogied the 8th, bogied the 9th, double-bogied the 10th, bogied the 11th and 12th, and double-bogied the 14th. Though he managed to birdie 16 and 18, his lead was reduced to one shot. He shot 81 on Sunday for a tie for 13th. He never came as close to winning a PGA Tour major. "I kind of fell out of the sky," he said later. "It felt like my parachute had a hole in it."

Mark Calcavecchia, 1991 Ryder Cup at Kiawah Island

Calcavecchia was four up with four holes to play in his singles match against Colin Montgomerie. He lost the 15th and 16th, and then, at the par-3 17th, after Montgomerie hit his tee shot into the water and all he had to do was put his ball somewhere on dry land, Calcavecchia topped his tee ball into the water. He then missed a 2-foot putt, which would still have given him the win. All told, he made two triples and two bogies to lose the final four holes and halve (tie) the match, when a win would have clinched a victory for the United States. Fortunately for Calcavecchia's subsequent mental health, the United States won the Ryder Cup anyway.

Patty Sheehan, 1990 U.S. Women's Open at Atlanta Athletic Club

With the last two rounds being played on Sunday, Sheehan took a nine-shot lead into the final 27 holes but lost to Betsy King by one stroke. Most collapses are mental, but in Sheehan's case, the breakdown was physical. "I had no fuel on board when I went out [Sunday morning]," she said. "I started losing it. I was dehydrated. My body couldn't work. I couldn't think properly and I had no strength."

Sheehan redeemed herself with victories in the 1993 and 1994 U.S. Opens. "It doesn't hurt anymore," she said. "Thank God I was able to win and get rid of all the demons."

Scott Hoch, 1989 Masters

You're never safe — certainly not when you're nervous, and apparently not even when you're calm: On the 10th green of a playoff with Nick Faldo, Hoch missed a 2-footer to win the Masters, and lost the playoff on the following hole.

Later, Hoch expounded on the nightmare: "I was so at ease. I just knew the way things had transpired all week, especially that day, that the tournament was mine. I took it for granted. Standing over that putt, I didn't feel a thing. Nothing. It was like I was out there during a practice round. Why, I don't know. And I've never felt like that since. That's why, when the putt missed, it was more like, wait a minute — destiny doesn't happen like this. . . . I wasn't thinking. My mind was doing things it shouldn't have been. It should've been strictly on that putt, nothing else. Then it was like, 'Who am I going to go on with, Bryant Gumbel or the other guy tomorrow morning?' That kind of stuff. Then it was the biggest surprise in the world to me when it didn't go in. I'd been saying to myself, 'This is what it all comes down to — all the hardship and heartache all comes to this moment. Finally.' Then it crashed down on me."

Jeff Sluman, 1987 Tournament Players Championship at Sawgrass

Sluman and Sandy Lyle were in a sudden-death playoff, with Sluman facing a 5-footer on the 17th to win. Just as he was about to strike the putt, a spectator dove into the lake surrounding the island green, causing the gallery to break into cheers and catcalls. Sluman stepped back to compose himself and then stepped up . . . and missed the cup completely. He bogied the next hole to lose the playoff.

T. C. Chen, 1985 U.S. Open at Oakland Hills

After shooting 65-69-69, Taiwan's Tze-Chung Chen carried a two-stroke lead into the final round and boosted it to four by the time he reached the par-4 No. 5. After a good drive, he pushed a 4-iron into the trees and then hit his third shot into thick greenside rough. He took a sand wedge for the short chip, but the ball popped straight up and the clubhead somehow hit it again in midair, sending it sideways and costing him a penalty stroke. Unnerved by the double hit, he chipped onto the green and then two-putted for a quadruple-bogey 8. He bogied the next three holes, losing the title to Andy North by a single stroke and earning the ignominious nickname "Two Chips" Chen.

Hale Irwin, 1983 British Open at Royal Birkdale

On Saturday, in contention for the lead during the third round, Irwin whiffed a 2-inch tap-in on the par-3 14th. On Sunday, he lost the championship to Tom Watson by one stroke. "I guess I lifted my head," he said afterward, "because my club just bounced over the ball."

Jerry Pate, 1982 World Series of Golf at Firestone

The 1976 U.S. Open champion reached the fringe of the par-5 2nd hole in two and had a 50-footer for eagle. His approach putt rolled 5 feet past the hole, and his comebacker for birdie was also too strong, ending up 3 feet away. Annoyed at himself, Pate carelessly hit the short par putt, and it lipped out. Fuming, he then made a careless backhand stab at the bogey tap-in. Not only did the ball miss the cup, but it also hit his foot for a two-stroke penalty. Now lying 8, he managed to hole out for a quadruple-bogey 9. "That was the stupidest hole I ever played," he said afterward. "It just goes to show you that in golf, it's never over until the ball is in the hole."

Tommy Nakajima, 1978 Masters

The Japanese professional tried to cut the dogleg of the par-5 No. 13 at Augusta National, but his drive caught a tree and his ball ended up in Rae's Creek. He took a penalty drop and played a 5-iron down the fairway, leaving himself 100 yards to the green. When his wedge found the creek in front of the green, he tried to hit it out rather than take a drop, but the ball popped straight up and landed on his foot for a two-stroke penalty. Then when he handed the muddy club to his caddie, it slipped from his grasp and fell into the water for another two-stroke penalty for "grounding" a club in a hazard. Lying 9, he hit his next shot over the green and then chipped back on and two-putted for a 13, tying the record for the highest one-hole score in the history of the Masters.

Asked about it later, Nakajima replied, "I don't like to recall unpleasant occurrences."

Billy Casper, 1968 Bob Hope Desert Classic

Casper was two shots off the lead in the final round when he came to the par-3 4th hole. Just as he reached the top of his backswing, a spectator slipped on the rocky hill above him, causing a landslide that startled Casper into a cold shank. The resulting double-bogey 5 dashed his chance to win the tournament.

Roberto DeVicenzo, 1968 Masters

Widely regarded as one of the nicest guys in professional golf, the 45-year-old Argentinean began the final round two shots behind the leader and shot a sizzling 65. His playing partner and marker, Tommy Aaron (in pro events your playing partner keeps your score and you keep his), mistakenly gave him a par 4 on the 17th rather than a birdie 3, and DeVicenzo hastily signed the incorrect card and submitted it to the official scorer. Because the Rules of Golf state that a score card may not be changed after it has been turned in, the 4 counted. Bob Goalby finished tied with DeVicenzo's actual score, but because of the error, Goalby won the Masters by one shot.

This incident, a "rules disaster," was perhaps even more tragic than a standard on-course collapse — claiming not one but three victims: DeVicenzo; Aaron, who would donate a vital organ if it could undo his blunder; and Goalby, whose victory is forever tarnished as resting on a technicality. For his part, DeVicenzo accepted his fate with good humor. At the awards ceremony, he said, "What a stupid I am!"

Marty Fleckman, 1967 U.S. Open at Baltusrol

Twenty-three-year-old Marty Fleckman shot 67-73-69 in a bid to become the first amateur to win the U.S. Open since Johnny Goodman (in 1933), but he ballooned to an 80 in the final round and finished 18th. Asked by reporters what happened, Fleckman replied, "I finally got back on my game."

Arnold Palmer, 1966 U.S. Open at the Olympic Club

With a seven-stroke lead over Billy Casper and only nine holes left to play, Palmer, in typical style, went for the U.S. Open record instead of playing it safe. But he scored five over par on holes 10 through 17 and barely managed to par the 18th hole to tie Casper, who shot 32 on the back nine. Palmer lost the Monday playoff with a 73 to Casper's 69. He never won another major.

After the obligatory post-tournament press conference, an official asked Palmer if he wanted to leave by a back door to avoid the crowd waiting outside. He declined. "The way I played," he said, "I deserve whatever they do to me." He was pleasantly surprised to find that his fans — "Arnie's Army" — were even more adoring than they would have been had he won.

Arnold Palmer, 1961 Los Angeles Open at Rancho Park

Palmer needed a par 5 on the 18th for a 69 in the second round. After a good drive, instead of laying up with an iron for the tight second shot, he went for a birdie and pushed a 3-wood out-of-bounds onto the adjacent driving range. He paused briefly to regroup and then hit another 3-wood. O.B. right again. He gathered himself again and hit *another* 3-wood. This time, he hooked it onto Patricia Avenue. Stubborn if not downright foolhardy, Palmer hit the 3-wood yet again, and again hooked it out-of-bounds. On the fifth try, after four straight penalties, he finally put his 3-wood on the green and went on to make a 12. A long, sad story. Arnie's description was more succinct. Asked by a reporter how he managed to make a 12, he replied, "I missed my putt for an 11."

Billy Joe Patton, 1954 Masters

The affable young amateur from South Carolina found himself in the lead on Sunday after a 32 on the front nine, which included a hole-in-one on the 6th. When he reached the par-5 No. 13, he was told that his closest competitor, Ben Hogan, had just made a double bogey on 11. All Patton had to do was play it safe to become the first amateur to win the Masters. But no. Instead of laying up to avoid Rae's Creek, he went for the green, and his ball found the water. He removed his shoes and socks and waded into the stream but reconsidered and decided to take a drop for a one-stroke penalty. Still barefoot, he pitched onto the green and two-putted for a bogey 6. Patton then parred in for a 290, one shot behind Hogan and Sam Snead (who defeated Hogan in a playoff).

In retrospect, Patton claimed that he wouldn't have played it any differently. "I was elated to play as well as I did," he said. "I'm almost delighted I lost, in fact. Otherwise, I might have turned pro."

Byron Nelson, 1946 U.S. Open at Canterbury

After his caddie accidentally kicked his ball, costing him a penalty stroke, Nelson ended up tied with Lloyd Mangrum and Vic Ghezzi. He then lost to Mangrum in a 36-hole playoff.

Sam Snead, 1939 U.S. Open at Spring Mill

Snead, who has won more PGA events than anyone else in history, is undoubtedly the best player never to win a U.S. Open. He came close several times: He lost by one stroke in 1937; he lost in a playoff in 1947; and at the Spring Mill course at Philadelphia Country Club in 1939, before the advent of electronic leader boards, he mistakenly thought he needed a birdie on the par-5 final hole to win and went for the green in two. He hit his second shot into a bunker and eventually made a triple-bogey 8 to lose by two strokes, when a par would have won.

Ray Ainsley, 1938 U.S. Open at Cherry Hills

Ainsley, a club pro from Ojai, California, hit his approach on the par-4 16th into a stream fronting the green. Rather than take a penalty, he decided to play the ball from the water. As the ball drifted with the current, he slashed at it repeatedly, stubbornly refusing to take a drop. He finally carded a 19, which is still the U.S. Open record for the highest score on a single hole.

From the self-inflicted department

Bobby Cruickshank, 1934 U.S. Open at Merion: On the 11th hole during the final round, Cruickshank's second shot over a stream skipped off the water and ran onto the green. Jubilant, he threw his club in the air in celebration. He was knocked unconscious when it came down on his head.

Al Capone, 1928: The Chicago gangster loved to play golf, although he never shot under 100. But one day in 1928, at the Burnham Woods course near Chicago, he managed to shoot himself — when the loaded revolver he kept in his bag went off and wounded him in the foot.

Mary, Queen of Scots, 1587: The most irrevocable golf disaster in history involved Mary, Queen of Scots, who angered Parliament by playing golf a few days after her husband's death. Her apparent lack of wifely grief was used against her at her trial for plotting the murder of Queen Elizabeth I, and Mary was beheaded.

Roland Hancock, 1928 U.S. Open at Olympia Fields

Hancock, an unknown 21-year-old club pro from Wilmington, North Carolina, reached the final two holes with a seemingly insurmountable lead. As he approached the 17th tee, one of the spectators shouted, “Make way for the next U.S. Open champion!” Hancock promptly double-bogied the 17th and 18th, missing a playoff by a single stroke.

Part VII
Appendixes

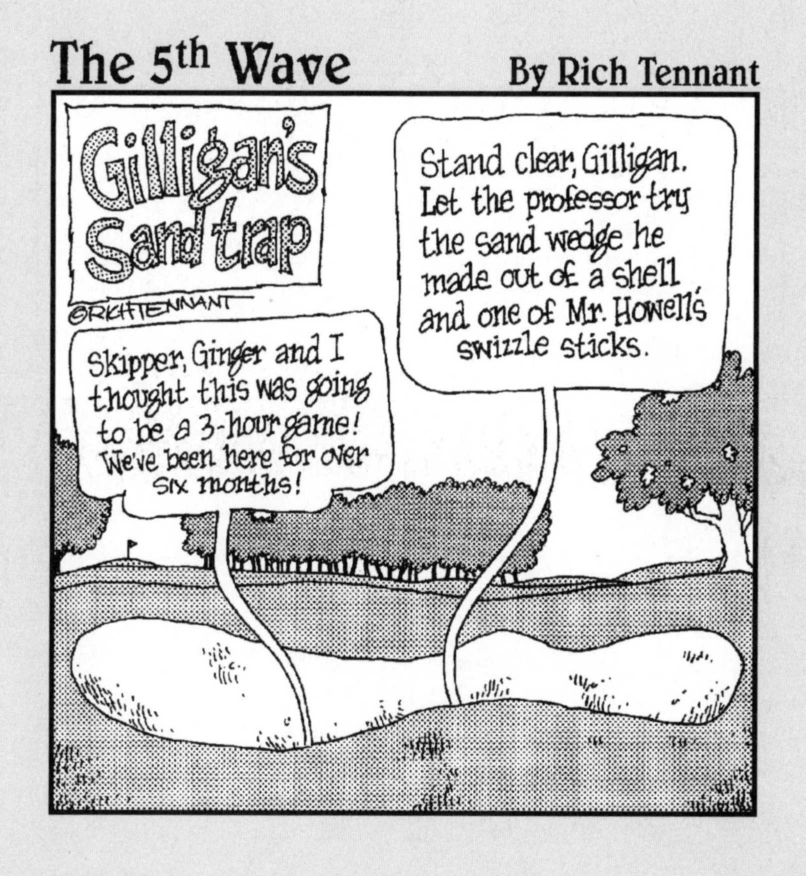

In this part . . .

Golfers have a language all their own. Appendix A lists phrases, terms, and slang you need to add to your vocabulary. Appendix B lists some of the most popular golf organizations, as well as selected golf schools and other resources.

Appendix A

Golf Speak

Five minutes of listening to the conversation in any clubhouse in the world will be enough for you to figure out that golf has a language all its own. Here are the phrases, terms, and slang of that language. Hey, if you're going to be a real golfer, you need to sound like one.

These terms are written with right-handed golfers in mind. Lefties will have to think in reverse!

A

ace: A hole-in-one. Buy a round of drinks for the house.

address: The positioning of your body in relation to the ball just before starting your swing. And your last conscious thought before the chaos begins.

airball: Your swing missed the ball! Blame it on an alien's spacecraft radar.

albatross: British term for *double eagle,* or three under par on one hole. I've only had one.

amateur: Someone who plays for fun, not money. Playing golf for fun?

angle of approach: The degree at which the clubhead moves either downward or upward into the ball. A severe test of agility.

approach: Your shot to the green made from anywhere except the tee. Sounds dangerous; really isn't.

apron: The grass around the edge of a green, longer than the grass on the green but shorter than the grass on the fairway. Or what I wear to barbecue in.

attend: To hold and remove the flagstick as another player putts, usually from some distance.

away: Term used to describe the ball farthest from the hole and, thus, next to be played.

B

back door: The rear of the hole.

back lip: The edge of a bunker that's farthest from the green.

back nine: The second half of your round of golf; the first half is the front nine holes.

backspin: When the ball hits the green and spins back toward the player. Galleries love backspins.

backswing: The part of the swing from the point where the clubhead moves away from the ball to the point where it starts back down again. I hope that your backswing is smooth and in balance.

baffy: Old name for a lofted wood; short for "baffing spoon."

bail out (hang 'em high): You hit the shot, for example, well to the right to avoid trouble on the left.

balata: Sap from a tropical tree; most popular cover for balls until urethane came along

ball at rest: The ball isn't moving. A study in still life.

ball marker: Small, round object, such as a coin, used to indicate the ball's position on the green.

ball retriever: Long pole with a scoop on the end used to collect balls from water hazards and other undesirable spots. If the grip on your ball retriever is worn out, get some lessons immediately.

ball washer: Found on many tees; a device for cleaning balls.

banana ball: Shot that curves hugely from left to right. *See* slice.

bandit: *See* hustler. Avoid bandits at all costs.

barkie: Bet won by a player making par or better on a hole after hitting a tree.

baseball grip: To hold the club with all ten fingers on the grip.

best ball: A game in which two or more players form a team; the best net score for each team is recorded on the score card.

birdie: Score of one under par on a hole.

bisque: Handicap stroke given by one player to another. Receiver may choose which hole it is applied to.

bite (vampire, bicuspid, overbite): A spin that makes the ball tend to stop rather than roll when it lands.

blade: Not pretty. The leading edge of the club, rather than the clubface, strikes the ball, resulting in a low shot that tends to travel way too far. Also a kind of putter or iron. *See* thin *or* skull.

blast: Aggressive shot from a bunker that displaces a lot of sand.

blind shot: You can't see the spot where you want the ball to land.

block (H&R Block, Dan Blocker): Shot that flies straight but to the right of the target. *See* push.

bogey: Score of one stroke over par on a hole.

borrow: The amount of curve you must allow for a putt on a sloping green. Or what you need to do if you play a hustler.

bounce: The bottom part of a sand wedge, designed to slide through sand; also what a ball does when it hits the ground — usually in the wrong direction.

boundary: Edge, of course; it confines the space/time continuum. Usually marked by white stakes.

brassie: Old name for a 2-wood.

break: *See* borrow.

British Open: National championship run by Royal and Ancient Golf Club of St. Andrews — known in Britain as "the Open" because it was the first one.

bulge: The curve across the face of a driver or fairway wood (or fairway metal).

bump and run: *See* run-up.

bunker: Hazard filled with sand; can be referred to as a *sand trap.*

buried ball/lie: Part of the ball below the surface of the sand in a bunker.

C

caddie: The person carrying your clubs during your round of golf. The person you fire when you play badly.

caddie master: Person in charge of caddies.

Calamity Jane: The great Bobby Jones's putter.

carry: The distance between a ball's take-off and landing.

cart: Motorized vehicle used to transport lazy golfers around the course.

casual water: Water other than a water hazard on the course from which you can lift your ball without penalty.

center-shafted: Putter in which the shaft is joined to the center of the head.

character builder: Short, meaningful putt; can't possibly build character.

charting the course: To pace each hole so that you always know how far you are from the hole.

chili-dip (Hormel, lay the sod over it, pooper scooper): A mishit chip shot, the clubhead hitting the ground well before it hits the ball.

chip: Very short, low-flying shot to the green.

chip-in: A holed chip.

choke: To play poorly because of self-imposed pressure.

choke down: To hold the club lower on the grip.

chunk: *See* chili-dip.

cleat: Spike on the sole of a golf shoe.

claw: An innovative grip that takes wrist action out of the putting stroke.

cleek: Old term for a variety of iron clubs.

closed face: Clubface pointed to the left of your ultimate target at address or impact. Or clubface pointed skyward at the top of the backswing. Can lead to a shot that goes to the left of the target.

closed stance: Player sets up with the right foot pulled back, away from the ball.

clubhouse: Main building at a golf club.

club length: Distance from the end of the grip to the bottom of the clubhead.

collar: *See* apron.

come-backer: The putt after the preceding effort finished beyond the hole. Usually gets harder to make the older you get.

compression: The flattening of the ball against the clubface. The faster you swing and the more precisely you hit the ball in the middle of the clubface, the more fun you have.

concede: To give an opponent a putt, hole, or match.

core: The center of a golf ball.

course rating: The difficulty of a course, measured with some silly formula by the USGA.

cross-handed: Grip with the left hand below the right.

crosswind: Breeze blowing from right to left or from left to right.

cup: Container in the hole that holds the flagstick in place.

cuppy lie: When the ball is in a cuplike depression.

cut: Score that eliminates a percentage of the field (or players) from a tournament. Usually made after 36 holes of a 72-hole event. I've missed a few in my time.

cut shot: Shot that curves from left to right.

D

dance floor: Slang for *green.*

dawn patrol: The players who tee off early in the day.

dead (body bags, cadaver, on the slab, perdition, jail, tag on his toe, wearing stripes, no pulse — you get the idea): No possible way to pull off the shot!

deep: High clubface from top to bottom.

deuce: A score of 2 on a given hole.

dimple: Depression on the cover of a golf ball.

divot: Turf displaced by the clubhead during a swing.

dogleg: Hole on which the fairway curves one way or the other.

dormant: Grass on the course is alive but not actively growing. Also my hair.

dormie: The player who's winning the match in match play — for example, five up with only five holes left, or four up with four left.

double bogey: Score of two over par on a hole.

double eagle: Score of three under par on a hole. Forget it, you'll probably never get one. *See also* albatross.

down: Losing.

downhill lie: When your right foot is higher than your left when you address the ball (for right-handed players).

downswing: The part of the swing where the clubhead is moving down, toward the ball.

DQ'd: Disqualified.

drain: To sink a putt.

draw: Shot that curves from right to left.

drive: Shot from teeing ground other than par-3 holes.

drive for show, putt for dough: Old saying implying that putting is more important than driving.

driving range: Place where you can go to hit practice balls.

drive the green: When your drive finishes on the putting surface. Can happen on a short par-4, or when the brakes go out on your cart.

drop: Procedure by which you put a ball back into play after it's been lifted and/or replaced in accordance with a rule.

dub: Bad shot or player.

duck hook (shrimp, mallard, quacker): Shot curving severely from right to left.

duffer: Bad player.

dying putt: A putt that barely reaches the hole.

E

eagle: Score of two under par for a hole.

embedded ball: Portion of the ball is below ground.

erosion: Loss of land through water and wind damage — most common on the coasts.

etiquette: Code of conduct.

explode: To play a ball from a bunker moving a large amount of sand. Or what you do if the ball doesn't get out of the bunker.

extra holes: Played when a match finishes even (is tied).

F

face: The front of a club or bunker.

fade: Shot that curves gently from left to right.

fairway: The closely-mowed turf running from tee to green.

fairway wood: Any wooden club that's not your driver. Nowadays, you say *fairway metal* because you don't see many wooden clubs anymore.

fat: To strike the ground before the ball.

feather: To put a delicate fade on a shot — don't try it yet!

first cut: Strip of rough at the edge of a fairway.

first off: Golfers beginning their round before everyone else.

flag: Piece of cloth attached to the top of a flagstick.

flagstick: The stick with the flag on top, which indicates the location of the cup.

flange: Projecting piece of clubhead behind the sole.

flat: Swing that is less upright than normal, and more around the body than up and down.

flatstick: Slang for a putter.

flub: To hit the ball only a few feet.

flex: The amount of bend in a shaft.

flier: Shot, usually hit from the rough, that travels way too far past the target.

fly the green: To hit a shot that lands beyond the putting surface.

follow-through: The part of the swing after the ball has been struck.

foozle: To make a complete mess of a shot.

fore: What to shout when your ball is headed toward another player.

forged irons: Clubs made one by one, without molds.

forward press: Targetward shift of the hands, and perhaps a right knee, just prior to takeaway.

foursome: Depends where you are. In the United States, a group of four playing together. In Britain, a match between two teams of two, each hitting one ball alternately.

free drop: Drop for which no penalty stroke is incurred, generally within one club length of where the ball was.

fried egg: When your ball is partially buried in the sand.

fringe: *See* apron.

frog hair: Slang for *apron, fringe,* or *collar.*

front nine: The first half of your round of golf; the second half is the back nine.

full swing: Longest swing you make.

G

gallery: Spectators at a tournament.

gimme: A short putt that your opponent doesn't ask you to hit, assuming that you can't possibly miss the shot.

G.I.R: Slang for *greens in regulation* (greens hit in regulation number of strokes).

glove: Usually worn on the left hand by right-handed players. Helps maintain grip.

Golden Bear: Jack Nicklaus.

golf widow(er): Your significant other after you get addicted to the game!

go to school: Watching your partner's putt and learning from it the line and pace that your putt should have.

good-good: Reciprocal concession of short putts. *See* gimme.

grain: Tendency of grass to lie horizontally toward the sun.

Grand Slam: The four major championships: Masters, U.S. Open, British Open, and PGA Championship.

graphite: Lightweight material used to make shafts and clubheads.

Great White Shark: Greg Norman.

green: The shortest-cut grass, where you do your putting.

greenies: Bet won by player whose first shot finishes closest to the hole on a par-3.

green jacket: Prize awarded to the winner of the Masters Tournament in Augusta, Georgia.

greens fee: The cost to play a round of golf.

greenside: Close to the green.

greensome: Game in which both players on a team drive off. The better of the two is chosen; then they alternate shots from there.

grip: Piece of rubber/leather on the end of a club. Or your hold on the club.

grooves: *Scoring* (the set of shallow notches) on the clubface.

gross score: Actual score shot before a handicap is deducted.

ground the club: The process of placing the clubhead behind the ball at address, generally touching the bottom of the grass.

ground under repair: Area on the course being worked on by the groundskeeper, generally marked by white lines, from which you may drop your ball without penalty.

gutta percha: Material used to manufacture golf balls in the 19th century.

H

hacker: Poor player.

half: Tied hole.

half shot: Improvised shot with ordinarily too much club for the distance.

halve: To tie a hole.

ham and egging: When you and your partner play well on alternate holes, forming an effective team.

handicap: Number of strokes over par a golfer is expected to score for 18 holes. For example, a player whose handicap is 16 is expected to shoot 88 on a par 72 course, or 16 strokes over par.

hanging lie: Your ball is on a slope, lying either above or below your feet.

hardpan: Very firm turf.

hazard: Can be either sand or water. Don't ground your club in hazards — it's against the rules!

head cover: Protection for the clubhead, usually used on woods.

heel: End of the clubhead closest to the shaft.

hickory: Wood from which shafts used to be made.

high side: Area above the hole on a sloping green.

hole: Your ultimate 4¼-inch-wide target.

hole-high: Level with the hole.

hole-in-one: *See* ace.

hole out: Complete play on hole.

home green: The green on the 18th hole.

honor: When you score lowest on a given hole, thus earning the right to tee up first on the next tee.

hood: Tilting the toe end of the club toward the hole. To hood a club lessens the loft, and generally produces a right-to-left shot.

hook: Shot that curves severely from right to left.

horseshoe: When the ball goes around the edge of the cup and comes back toward you. Painful!

hosel: Curved area where the clubhead connects with the shaft.

hustler: A golfer who plays for a living. Plays better than he claims to be. Usually leaves your wallet lighter.

hybrid: A club similar to a fairway metal, designed to get the ball airborne quickly; many players prefer hybrids to 2-, 3- and 4-irons.

I

impact: Moment when the club strikes the ball.

impediment: Loose debris that you can remove from around your ball as long as the ball doesn't move.

Impregnable Quadrilateral: The Grand Slam.

improve your lie: To move the ball to make a shot easier. Illegal unless local rules dictate otherwise.

in play: Within the confines of the course (not out-of-bounds).

in your pocket: After you've picked up the ball! (Generally after you finish a hole without holing out.)

insert: Plate in the face of a club, generally a driver, fairway wood or putter.

inside out: Clubhead moves through the impact area on a line to the right of the target. Most tour players do this. *See also* outside in.

inside: Area on your side of a line drawn from the ball to the target.

intended line: The path on which you imagine the ball flying from club to target.

interlocking: Type of grip where the little finger of the right hand is entwined with the index finger of the left.

investment cast: Clubs made from a mold.

J

jail: Slang for when you and your ball are in very deep trouble.

jigger: Old term for a 4-iron. Also a great little pub to the right of the 17th fairway at St. Andrews.

jungle: Slang for heavy *rough,* or an unprepared area of long grass.

junk: Enjoyable golf wagers on such things as hitting the green in one shot, getting up and down from a bunker, or making par after hitting a tree.

K

kick: Another term for *bounce.*

kill: To hit a long shot.

L

ladies' day: Time when a course is reserved for those of the female persuasion.

lag: A long putt hit with the intent of leaving the ball close to the cup.

laid off: When the club points to the left of the target at the top of the backswing.

lateral hazard: Water hazard marked by red stakes and usually parallel to the fairway.

lay-up: Conservatively played shot to avoid possible trouble.

leader board: Place where the lowest scores in a tournament are posted. I don't stay on the leader board too long. In fact, when the scorers are putting up the *d* in *McCord,* they're usually taking down the *M.* Sometimes I wish my name were Calcavecchia.

leak: Ball drifting to the right during flight.

lie: Where your ball is on the ground. Also, the angle at which the club shaft extends from the head.

lift: What you do before you drop.

line: The path of a shot to the hole.

line up: To stand behind a shot to take aim.

links: A seaside course. Don't expect trees.

lip: Edge of a cup or bunker.

lip-out (cellophane bridge): When the ball touches the edge of the cup but doesn't drop in.

local knowledge: What the members know and you don't.

local rules: Set of rules determined by the members, rules committee, or course professional.

loft: The degree at which a clubface is angled upward.

long game: Shots hit with long irons and woods. Also could be John Daly's game.

loop: Slang for *to caddy.* Or a round of golf. Or a change in the path of the clubhead during the swing.

low handicapper: Good player.

low side: Area below the hole on a sloping green.

LPGA: Ladies Professional Golf Association.

M

make: Hole a shot.

makeable: Shot with a good chance of being holed.

mallet: Putter with a wide head.

mark: To indicate the position of the ball with a small, round, flat object, such as a coin, usually on the green.

marker: Small, round object, such as a coin, placed behind the ball to indicate its position when you lift it. Or the person keeping score.

marshal: Person controlling the crowd at a tournament.

mashie: Old term for a 5-iron.

mashie-niblick: Old term for a 7-iron.

Masters: First major tournament of each calendar year. Always played at Augusta National Golf Club in Georgia. The one tournament I can't go to.

match of cards: Comparing your score card to your opponent's to see who won.

match play: Game played between two sides. The side that wins the most holes wins the match.

matched set: Clubs designed to look and feel the same.

medal play: Game played between any number of players. The player with the lowest score wins (also called *stroke play*).

metal wood: Driver or fairway "wood" made of metal.

miniature course: Putting course.

misclub: To use the wrong club for the distance.

misread: To take the wrong line on a putt.

miss the cut: To take too many strokes for the first 36 holes of a 72-hole event and be eliminated. I did this once or twice.

mixed foursome: Two men, two women.

model swing: Perfect motion.

MOI: Abbreviation for *moment of inertia;* in putters, it means resistance to twisting at impact.

mulligan: Second attempt at a shot, usually played on the first tee. This is illegal.

municipal course: A course owned by the local government and, thus, open to the public. Also known as *munis,* municipal courses generally have lower greens fees than privately owned public courses.

N

nassau: Bet in which a round of 18 holes is divided into three — front nine, back nine, and full 18.

net score: Score for a hole or round after handicap strokes are deducted.

never up, never in: Annoying saying coined for a putt that finishes short of the hole.

niblick: Old term for a 9-iron.

nine: Half of a course.

19th hole: The clubhouse bar.

O

O.B. (Oscar Bravo, set it free): Out-of-bounds.

off-center hit: Less than a solid strike.

offset: Club with the head set farther behind the shaft than normal.

one-putt: To take only a single putt on a green.

one up: Being one hole ahead in match play.

open face: Clubface aligned to the right of the target at address, or to the right of its path at impact. Can lead to a shot going to the right of the target.

open stance: Player sets up with the left foot pulled back, away from the ball.

open up the hole: When your tee shot leaves the best possible angle for the next shot to the green.

order of play: Who plays when.

out-of-bounds: Area outside the boundaries of the course, usually marked with white posts. When a ball finishes O.B., the player must return to the original spot and play another ball under penalty of one stroke. He or she thus loses stroke and distance.

outside: Area on the far side of the ball.

outside in: Swing path followed by the clubhead into the ball from outside the ball-target line. *See* inside out.

over the green: Ball hit too far.

overclub: To use a club that will hit the ball too far.

overlapping: A type of grip where the little finger of the right hand lies over the index finger of the left hand.

P

pairings: Groups of two players.

par: The score a good player would expect to make on a hole or round.

partner: A player on your side.

penal: Difficult.

persimmon: A wood from which wooden clubs were made before the age of metal woods.

PGA: Professional Golfers' Association.

Piccolo grip: A very loose hold on the club, especially at the top of the backswing.

pigeon: An opponent you should beat easily.

pin: Another word for *flagstick*.

pin-high: *See* hole high.

pin placement: The location of the hole on the green.

pitch: A short, high approach shot. Doesn't run much on landing.

pitch and putt: A short course. Or getting down in two strokes from off the green.

pitch-and-run: Varies from a pitch in that it flies lower and runs more.

pitching-niblick: Old term for an 8-iron.

pivot: The body turn during the swing.

plane: The arc of the swing.

playoff: Two or more players play extra holes to break a tie.

play through: What you do when the group in front of you invites you to pass.

plugged lie: When the ball finishes half-buried in the turf or a bunker.

plumb-bob: Lining up a putt with one eye closed and the putter held vertically in front of the face.

pop-up: High, short shot.

pot bunker: Small, steeply faced bunker.

practice green: Place for working on your putting.

preferred lies: Temporary rule that allows you to move the ball to a more favorable position because of abnormally wet conditions.

press: You've lost your match, but you want your money back. This new bet takes place over any remaining holes.

private club: A club open to members and their guests only.

pro-am: A competition in which professional partners team with amateurs.

professional: A golfer who plays or teaches for his or her livelihood.

pro shop: A place where you sign up to start play and can buy balls, clubs, and so on.

provisional ball: You think your ball may be lost. To save time, you play another from the same spot before searching for the first ball. If the first ball is lost, the second ball (the provisional ball) is in play.

public course: A golf course open to all.

pull: A straight shot that flies to the left of the target.

punch: A shot hit lower with the ball back in the stance and a shorter-than-normal follow-through.

push: A straight shot that flies to the right of the target.

putter: A straight-faced club generally used on the greens.

Q

quail high (stealth, skull, rat-high): Low.

qualifying school: A place where aspiring professional golfers try to qualify for the PGA and LPGA tours. A punishing week of pressure golf. The ultimate grind.

quitting: Not hitting through a shot with conviction.

R

rabbit: A beginning player.

rake: A device used to smooth the sand after you leave a bunker.

range: Practice area.

range ball: Generally, a low-quality ball used on a driving range.

rap: To hit a putt firmly.

read the green: To assess the path on which a putt must travel to the hole.

regular: A shaft with normal flex.

regulation: The number of strokes needed to reach the green and have two putts left to make par.

release: The point in the downswing where the wrists uncock.

relief: Where you drop a ball that was in a hazard or affected by an obstruction.

reverse overlap: Putting grip in which the index finger of the left hand overlaps the little finger of the right hand.

rhythm: The tempo of your swing.

rifle a shot: To hit the ball hard, straight, and far.

rim the cup: *See* lip out.

ringer score: Your best-ever score at each hole on the course.

Road Hole: The 17th hole at St. Andrews — the hardest hole in the world.

roll: On wooden clubs, the curve on the clubface from the top to the bottom of the face.

rough: Area of long grass on either side of the fairway or around the green.

round: Eighteen holes of golf.

Royal and Ancient Golf Club: The organization that runs the British Open.

rub of the green: Luck.

run: The roll on the ball after landing.

run-up: A type of shot to play when the ground is firm. You bounce the ball onto the green and let it roll to the hole.

S

sandbagger: A golfer who lies about his or her ability/handicap to gain an advantage.

sand trap: A bunker.

sandy: Making par after being in a bunker.

scorecard: Where the length, par, and rating of each hole is recorded. Also, your score.

scoring: The grooves on the clubface.

scramble: To play erratic golf but still score well. Or a game in which several players tee off and then pick the best shot; all then play their balls from that spot; play continues that way until the team holes the ball.

scratch play: No handicaps used in this type of game.

scratch player: A golfer with a 0 handicap.

second cut: Second level of rough, higher than first cut. Some courses have three cuts of rough.

semiprivate: A course with members that is also open to the public.

semirough: Grass in the rough that is not too long, not too short.

setup: *See* address.

shaft: The part of the club that joins the grip to the head.

shag: To retrieve practice balls.

shag bag: To carry practice balls.

shallow: Narrow clubface. Or a flattish angle of attack into the ball.

shank: Shot struck from the club's hosel; flies far to the right of the intended target.

shooting the lights out: To play very well.

short cut: Cut of grass on the fairway or green.

short game: Shots played on and around the green.

shut: Clubface aligned left at address or impact; looking skyward at the top of the backswing. Results in a shot that goes to the left of the target.

sidehill lie: Ball either above or below your feet.

sidesaddle: Putting style where a player faces the hole while making the stroke.

sink: To make a putt.

sit down (full flaps, pull a hamstring, develop a limp): A polite request for the ball to stop.

skins: Betting game where the lowest score on a hole wins the pot. If the hole is tied, the money carries over to the next hole.

skull (hit it in the forehead): *See* blade *or* thin.

sky: Ball flies off the top of the clubface — very high and short.

sleeve of balls: Box of three golf balls.

slice: Shot that curves sharply from left to right.

slope: A measure of the difficulty of a golf course.

smother: To hit the ball with a closed clubface, resulting in a horrible, low, hooky shot.

snake: Long putt.

snap hook: Severe hook.

socket: *See* shank.

sole: Bottom of the clubhead.

sole plate: Piece of metal attached to the bottom of a wooden club.

spade-mashie: Old term for a 6-iron.

spike mark: Mark on the green made by a golf shoe.

spin-out: Legs moving too fast in relation to the upper body on the downswing.

spoon: Old term for a 3-wood.

spot putting: Aiming for a point on the green over which the ball must run if it is to go in the hole.

square: Score of a match is even. Or the clubface and stance are aligned perfectly with the target.

square face: Clubface looking directly at the hole at address/impact.

square grooves: USGA banned them from clubfaces.

St. Andrews: Located in Fife, Scotland; the home of golf.

stableford: Method of scoring by using points rather than strokes.

stance: Position of the feet before the swing.

starter: Person running the order of play from the first tee.

starting time: When you tee off at the first tee.

stick: The pin in the hole.

stiff: A shaft with reduced flex. Or a shot very close to the hole.

stimpmeter: Device used to measure the speed of greens.

stroke: Movement of club with the intent to hit the ball.

stroke hole: Hole at which a player either gives or receives a shot, according to his handicap.

stymie: Ball obstructing your route to the hole — now obsolete.

sudden-death: Form of playoff in which the first player to win a hole wins the match or tournament.

superintendent: Person responsible for the upkeep of the course.

surlyn: Material from which golf-ball covers can be made.

swale: Depression or dip in terrain.

sway: To move excessively to the right on the backswing without turning the body.

sweet spot: Perfect point on the clubface with which to strike the ball.

swing plane: Angle at which the club shaft travels around the body during a swing.

swing weight: Measure of a club's head weight relative to its length.

T

takeaway: Early part of the backswing.

tap-in: Very short putt.

tee: Wooden peg on which the ball is set for the first shot on a hole. Also, the area from which that initial shot is hit.

tee it up: To start play.

teeing ground: Area in which you must tee your ball, between the tee markers and neither in front of them nor more than two club lengths behind them.

tempo: The rhythm of your swing.

temporary green: Used in winter to save the permanent green.

Texas wedge: Putter when used from off the green.

that'll play: A kind reference to a mediocre shot.

thin: To hit the ball around its equator — don't expect much height.

three-putt: Undesired number of strokes on a green.

through the green: The whole course except hazards, tees, and greens.

Tiger tee: Slang for the back tee.

tight: Narrow fairway.

tight lie: The ball on bare ground or very short grass.

timing: The pace and sequence of movement in your swing.

titanium: Metal used in lightweight shafts, clubheads, and even a few golf balls.

top: Ball is struck on or above the equator. *See* thin.

torque: Twisting of the shaft at impact.

tour: Series of tournaments for professionals.

tradesman's entrance: Ball goes in the hole from the rear of the cup.

trajectory: Flight of the ball.

trap: *See* bunker.

triple bogey: Three over par on one hole. Not good.

turn: To make your way to the back nine holes. Or the rotation of the upper body during the backswing and forward swing.

twitch: *See* yips.

U

uncock: *See* release.

underclub: To take at least one club less than needed for distance.

unplayable lie: You can't hit the ball. A one-stroke penalty is your reward.

up: Ahead in the match. Or the person next to play. Or reaching the hole with a putt.

up and down: To get the ball into the hole in two strokes from somewhere off the green.

upright: To swing with a steep vertical plane.

urethane: Synthetic material used in making golf balls, including covers.

USGA: United States Golf Association. The ruling body for golf in the United States.

U.S. Open: National men's golf championship of America.

U.S. Women's Open: National women's golf championship of America.

V

Vardon grip: *See* overlapping.

W

waggle: Movement of the clubhead prior to the swing.

water hazard: Body of water that costs you a shot to escape.

wedge: Lofted club (iron) used for pitching.

whiff: *See* airball.

whipping: The string that helps fix the head of a wooden club to the shaft.

whippy: A shaft more flexible than normal.

windcheater: Low drive.

winter rules: *See* preferred lies.

wood: Material that long clubs used to be made of.

wormburner: Low mishit.

Y

yips: When a golfer misses short putts because of bad nerves, which reduces the afflicted unfortunate to jerky little snatches at the ball, the putterhead seemingly possessing a mind all its own.

Appendix B

Golf Organizations

This appendix lists selected golf associations, golf schools, and club-component firms. Some states are more golf-oriented than others, but you'll find golf schools all over the country — and all over the world. If you can't find one that suits you here, check under "Golf Instruction" in the Yellow Pages of your local phone book or search the Internet.

Some of the addresses listed are the headquarters for a chain of schools. Many chain golf schools have seasonal instruction in the northern states; call their headquarters to find out which have programs near you.

Associations

American Junior Golf Association
1980 Sports Club Dr.
Braselton, GA 30517
770-868-4200
`www.ajga.org`

American Society of Golf Course Architects
125 N. Executive Dr., Suite 106
Brookfield, WI 53005
262-786-5960
`www.asgca.org`

Ladies Professional Golf Association
100 International Golf Dr.
Daytona Beach, FL 32124
386-274-6200
`www.lpga.com`

Multicultural Golf Association of America
3 Sunset Ave.
Westhampton Beach, NY 11978
631-288-8255
`www.mgaa.com`

National Amputee Golf Association
11 Walnut Hill Rd.
Amherst, NH 03031
603-672-6444
`www.nagagolf.org`

National Association of Left-Handed Golfers
3249 Hazelwood Dr. SW
Atlanta, GA 30311
404-696-1763
`www.nalg.org`

National Golf Foundation
1150 S. U.S. Hwy. 1, Suite 401
Jupiter, FL 33477
888-275-4643 (toll-free) or 561-744-6006
`www.ngf.org`

Professional Clubmakers Society
70 Persimmon Ridge Dr.
Louisville, KY 40245
800-548-6094 (toll-free) or 502-241-2816
www.proclubmakers.org

Professional Golfers' Association (PGA) of America
100 Avenue of the Champions
Palm Beach Gardens, FL 33410
561-624-8400
www.pga.com

Royal Canadian Golf Association
1333 Dorval Dr., Suite 1
Oakville, Ontario L6M 4X7
Canada
905-849-9700
www.rcga.org

United States Golf Association (USGA)
P.O. Box 708
Far Hills, NJ 07931
908-234-2300
www.usga.org

Golf Schools

The Academy of Golf
PGA National Resort and Spa
400 Avenue of the Champions
Palm Beach Gardens, FL 33418
800-633-9150
www.pgagolfacademy.com

Aviara Golf Academy
7447 Batiquitos Dr.
Carlsbad, CA 92009
800-433-7468 (toll-free) or 760-438-4539
www.ezgolfswing.com

Ben Sutton Golf Schools
P.O. Box 9199
Canton, OH 44714
800-225-6923 (toll-free) or 330-499-5235
www.golfschool.com

Bill Skelley School of Golf
514-1 East John Sims Pkwy.
Niceville, FL 32578
800-541-7707 (toll-free) or 850-729-1359

Boyne Super 5 Golf Week
Boyne Mountain Resort
600 Highland Dr.
Harbor Springs, MI 49740
800-462-6963
www.boynemountain.com

Chuck Cook Golf Academy
Barton Creek Resort
8212 Barton Club Dr.
Austin, TX 78735
800-336-6158 (toll-free) or 512-301-1054
www.bartoncreek.com

Dave Pelz Scoring Game School
1310 R.R. 620 South, Suite B-1
Austin, TX 78734
800-833-7370 (toll-free) or 512-263-7668
www.pelzgolf.com

David Leadbetter Golf Academy
1410 Masters Blvd.
Champions Gate, FL 33896
888-633-5323 (toll-free) or 407-787-3330
www.davidleadbetter.com

Doral Golf Learning Center
4440 NW 87th Ave.
Miami, FL 33178
800-723-6725 (toll-free) or 305-591-6409

Floating Green Golf Academy
Coeur d'Alene Resort
115 S. Second St.
Coeur d'Alene, ID 83814
800-688-5253 (toll-free) or 208-765-4000
www.cdaresort.com

Golf Advantage School
Carolina Vista Drive
Village of Pinehurst, NC 28374
866-291-4427
www.pinehurst.com

Golf Digest Schools
6210 E. McKellips Rd.
Mesa, AZ 85215
800-243-6121 (toll-free) or 480-998-7430
www.golfdigestschool.com

Hank Haney Golf Ranch
4101 Custer Rd.
McKinney, TX 75070
972-542-8800

John Jacobs' Golf Schools
6210 E. McKellips Rd.
Mesa, AZ 85215
800-472-5007 (toll-free) or 480-991-8587
www.jacobsgolf.com

Kapalua Golf Academy
1000 Office Rd.
Lahaina, Maui, HI 96761
808-669-6500
www.kapaluamaui.com

The Kingsmill Golf School
The Kingsmill Resort and Spa
1010 Kingsmill Rd.
Williamsburg, VA 23185
800-832-5665 (toll-free) or 757-253-1703
www.kingsmill.com

Kostis/McCord Learning Center
8620 E. Thompson Peak Pkwy.
Scottsdale, AZ 85255
888-506-7786 (toll-free) or 480-502-2656
www.kostismccordlearning.com

Legends Golf Academy
P.O. Box 2038
Myrtle Beach, SC 29578
800-827-2656
www.legendsgolf.com

Nicklaus/Flick Golf School
11780 U.S. Hwy. 1
North Palm Beach, FL 33408
407-626-3900

Phil Ritson–Mel Sole Golf School
P.O. Box 2580
Pawleys Island, SC 29585
800-624-4653 (toll-free) or 843-237-4993
www.ritson-sole.com

Seven Springs Golf Schools
Seven Springs Mountain Resort
777 Waterwheel Dr.
Champion, PA 15622
800-452-2223 (toll-free) or 814-352-7777
www.7springs.com

Stratton Golf School
Stratton Mountain Resort
R.R. 1, Box 145
Stratton Mountain, VT 05155
800-787-2886
www.stratton.com

Sugarloaf Golf Club & School
Sugarloaf USA
5092 Access Rd.
Carrabassett Valley, ME 04947
800-843-5623 (toll-free) or 207-237-2000
www.sugarloaf.com

U.S. Schools of Golf
718½ Promenade
Richmond, IN 47374
800-354-7415
www.ussog.com

Wintergreen Golf Academy
Wintergreen Resort
P.O. Box 706
Wintergreen, VA 22958
434-325-8250
www.wintergreenresort.com

Component Companies

Dynacraft Golf Products, Inc.
P.O. Box 4550
71 Maholm St.
Newark, OH 43058
800-423-2968 (toll-free) or 614-344-1191
www.dynacraftgolf.com

Golfsmith
11000 N. 1H-35
Austin, TX 78753
800-813-6897 (toll-free) or 512-837-4810
www.golfsmith.com

The GolfWorks
P.O. Box 3008
Newark, OH 43023
800-848-8358 (toll-free) or 740-328-4193
www.golfworks.com

Hornung's Pro Golf Sales, Inc.
815 Morris St.
Fond du Lac, WI 54936
920-922-2640
www.hornungs.com

Wittek Golf Supply Co.
3650 N. Avondale.
Chicago, IL 60618
800-869-1800 (toll-free) or 773-463-2636
www.wittekgolf.com

Index

• Numbers •

• A •

• B •

• C •

• D •

• E •

• F •

• G •

• I •

• J •

• K •

• L •

• M •

• N •

• O •

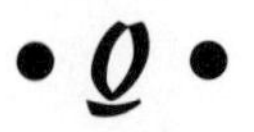

• S •

• T •

• U •

BUSINESS, CAREERS & PERSONAL FINANCE

0-7645-5307-0

0-7645-5331-3 *†

Also available:

- Accounting For Dummies † 0-7645-5314-3
- Business Plans Kit For Dummies † 0-7645-5365-8
- Cover Letters For Dummies 0-7645-5224-4
- Frugal Living For Dummies 0-7645-5403-4
- Leadership For Dummies 0-7645-5176-0
- Managing For Dummies 0-7645-1771-6
- Marketing For Dummies 0-7645-5600-2
- Personal Finance For Dummies * 0-7645-2590-5
- Project Management For Dummies 0-7645-5283-X
- Resumes For Dummies † 0-7645-5471-9
- Selling For Dummies 0-7645-5363-1
- Small Business Kit For Dummies *† 0-7645-5093-4

HOME & BUSINESS COMPUTER BASICS

0-7645-4074-2

0-7645-3758-X

Also available:

- ACT! 6 For Dummies 0-7645-2645-6
- iLife '04 All-in-One Desk Reference For Dummies 0-7645-7347-0
- iPAQ For Dummies 0-7645-6769-1
- Mac OS X Panther Timesaving Techniques For Dummies 0-7645-5812-9
- Macs For Dummies 0-7645-5656-8
- Microsoft Money 2004 For Dummies 0-7645-4195-1
- Office 2003 All-in-One Desk Reference For Dummies 0-7645-3883-7
- Outlook 2003 For Dummies 0-7645-3759-8
- PCs For Dummies 0-7645-4074-2
- TiVo For Dummies 0-7645-6923-6
- Upgrading and Fixing PCs For Dummies 0-7645-1665-5
- Windows XP Timesaving Techniques For Dummies 0-7645-3748-2

FOOD, HOME, GARDEN, HOBBIES, MUSIC & PETS

0-7645-5295-3

0-7645-5232-5

Also available:

- Bass Guitar For Dummies 0-7645-2487-9
- Diabetes Cookbook For Dummies 0-7645-5230-9
- Gardening For Dummies * 0-7645-5130-2
- Guitar For Dummies 0-7645-5106-X
- Holiday Decorating For Dummies 0-7645-2570-0
- Home Improvement All-in-One For Dummies 0-7645-5680-0
- Knitting For Dummies 0-7645-5395-X
- Piano For Dummies 0-7645-5105-1
- Puppies For Dummies 0-7645-5255-4
- Scrapbooking For Dummies 0-7645-7208-3
- Senior Dogs For Dummies 0-7645-5818-8
- Singing For Dummies 0-7645-2475-5
- 30-Minute Meals For Dummies 0-7645-2589-1

INTERNET & DIGITAL MEDIA

0-7645-1664-7

0-7645-6924-4

Also available:

- 2005 Online Shopping Directory For Dummies 0-7645-7495-7
- CD & DVD Recording For Dummies 0-7645-5956-7
- eBay For Dummies 0-7645-5654-1
- Fighting Spam For Dummies 0-7645-5965-6
- Genealogy Online For Dummies 0-7645-5964-8
- Google For Dummies 0-7645-4420-9
- Home Recording For Musicians For Dummies 0-7645-1634-5
- The Internet For Dummies 0-7645-4173-0
- iPod & iTunes For Dummies 0-7645-7772-7
- Preventing Identity Theft For Dummies 0-7645-7336-5
- Pro Tools All-in-One Desk Reference For Dummies 0-7645-5714-9
- Roxio Easy Media Creator For Dummies 0-7645-7131-1

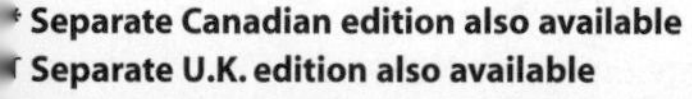
*** Separate Canadian edition also available**
† Separate U.K. edition also available

Available wherever books are sold. For more information or to order direct: U.S. customers visit www.dummies.com or call 1-877-762-2974. U.K. customers visit www.wileyeurope.com or call 0800 243407. Canadian customers visit www.wiley.ca or call 1-800-567-4797.

SPORTS, FITNESS, PARENTING, RELIGION & SPIRITUALITY

0-7645-5146-9

0-7645-5418-2

Also available:

- Adoption For Dummies 0-7645-5488-3
- Basketball For Dummies 0-7645-5248-1
- The Bible For Dummies 0-7645-5296-1
- Buddhism For Dummies 0-7645-5359-3
- Catholicism For Dummies 0-7645-5391-7
- Hockey For Dummies 0-7645-5228-7
- Judaism For Dummies 0-7645-5299-6
- Martial Arts For Dummies 0-7645-5358-5
- Pilates For Dummies 0-7645-5397-6
- Religion For Dummies 0-7645-5264-3
- Teaching Kids to Read For Dummies 0-7645-4043-2
- Weight Training For Dummies 0-7645-5168-X
- Yoga For Dummies 0-7645-5117-5

TRAVEL

0-7645-5438-7

0-7645-5453-0

Also available:

- Alaska For Dummies 0-7645-1761-9
- Arizona For Dummies 0-7645-6938-4
- Cancún and the Yucatán For Dummies 0-7645-2437-2
- Cruise Vacations For Dummies 0-7645-6941-4
- Europe For Dummies 0-7645-5456-5
- Ireland For Dummies 0-7645-5455-7
- Las Vegas For Dummies 0-7645-5448-4
- London For Dummies 0-7645-4277-X
- New York City For Dummies 0-7645-6945-7
- Paris For Dummies 0-7645-5494-8
- RV Vacations For Dummies 0-7645-5443-3
- Walt Disney World & Orlando For Dummies 0-7645-6943-0

GRAPHICS, DESIGN & WEB DEVELOPMENT

0-7645-4345-8

0-7645-5589-8

Also available:

- Adobe Acrobat 6 PDF For Dummies 0-7645-3760-1
- Building a Web Site For Dummies 0-7645-7144-3
- Dreamweaver MX 2004 For Dummies 0-7645-4342-3
- FrontPage 2003 For Dummies 0-7645-3882-9
- HTML 4 For Dummies 0-7645-1995-6
- Illustrator CS For Dummies 0-7645-4084-X
- Macromedia Flash MX 2004 For Dummies 0-7645-4358-X
- Photoshop 7 All-in-One Desk Reference For Dummies 0-7645-1667-1
- Photoshop CS Timesaving Techniques For Dummies 0-7645-6782-9
- PHP 5 For Dummies 0-7645-4166-8
- PowerPoint 2003 For Dummies 0-7645-3908-6
- QuarkXPress 6 For Dummies 0-7645-2593-X

NETWORKING, SECURITY, PROGRAMMING & DATABASES

0-7645-6852-3

0-7645-5784-X

Also available:

- A+ Certification For Dummies 0-7645-4187-0
- Access 2003 All-in-One Desk Reference For Dummies 0-7645-3988-4
- Beginning Programming For Dummies 0-7645-4997-9
- C For Dummies 0-7645-7068-4
- Firewalls For Dummies 0-7645-4048-3
- Home Networking For Dummies 0-7645-42796
- Network Security For Dummies 0-7645-1679-5
- Networking For Dummies 0-7645-1677-9
- TCP/IP For Dummies 0-7645-1760-0
- VBA For Dummies 0-7645-3989-2
- Wireless All In-One Desk Reference For Dummies 0-7645-7496-5
- Wireless Home Networking For Dummies 0-7645-3910-8

HEALTH & SELF-HELP

0-7645-6820-5 *†

0-7645-2566-2

Also available:

- Alzheimer's For Dummies 0-7645-3899-3
- Asthma For Dummies 0-7645-4233-8
- Controlling Cholesterol For Dummies 0-7645-5440-9
- Depression For Dummies 0-7645-3900-0
- Dieting For Dummies 0-7645-4149-8
- Fertility For Dummies 0-7645-2549-2
- Fibromyalgia For Dummies 0-7645-5441-7
- Improving Your Memory For Dummies 0-7645-5435-2
- Pregnancy For Dummies † 0-7645-4483-7
- Quitting Smoking For Dummies 0-7645-2629-4
- Relationships For Dummies 0-7645-5384-4
- Thyroid For Dummies 0-7645-5385-2

EDUCATION, HISTORY, REFERENCE & TEST PREPARATION

0-7645-5194-9

0-7645-4186-2

Also available:

- Algebra For Dummies 0-7645-5325-9
- British History For Dummies 0-7645-7021-8
- Calculus For Dummies 0-7645-2498-4
- English Grammar For Dummies 0-7645-5322-4
- Forensics For Dummies 0-7645-5580-4
- The GMAT For Dummies 0-7645-5251-1
- Inglés Para Dummies 0-7645-5427-1
- Italian For Dummies 0-7645-5196-5
- Latin For Dummies 0-7645-5431-X
- Lewis & Clark For Dummies 0-7645-2545-X
- Research Papers For Dummies 0-7645-5426-3
- The SAT I For Dummies 0-7645-7193-1
- Science Fair Projects For Dummies 0-7645-5460-3
- U.S. History For Dummies 0-7645-5249-X

Get smart @ dummies.com®

- **Find a full list of Dummies titles**
- **Look into loads of FREE on-site articles**
- **Sign up for FREE eTips e-mailed to you weekly**
- **See what other products carry the Dummies name**
- **Shop directly from the Dummies bookstore**
- **Enter to win new prizes every month!**

* **Separate Canadian edition also available**

† **Separate U.K. edition also available**

Available wherever books are sold. For more information or to order direct: U.S. customers visit www.dummies.com or call 1-877-762-2974. U.K. customers visit www.wileyeurope.com or call 0800 243407. Canadian customers visit www.wiley.ca or call 1-800-567-4797.